Social Policies and Decentralization in Cuba: Change in the Context of 21st-Century Latin America

Edited by Jorge I. Domínguez, María del Carmen Zabala Argüelles, Mayra Espina Prieto, and Lorena G. Barberia

Published by Harvard University David Rockefeller Center for Latin American Studies

Distributed by Harvard University Press
Cambridge, Massachusetts
London, England
2017

© 2017 The President and Fellows of Harvard College
All rights reserved
Printed in the United States of America

Publisher's Cataloging-In-Publication Data

Names: Domínguez, Jorge I., 1945– editor. | Prillaman, Soledad Artiz, contributor.
Title: Social policies and decentralization in Cuba : change in the context of
    21st-century Latin America / edited by Jorge I. Domínguez [and 3 others] ;
    [with contributions by] Soledad Artiz Prillaman [and 12 others].
Description: [Cambridge, Massachusetts] : Harvard University, David Rockefel-
    ler Center for Latin American Studies, [2017] | Cambridge, Massachusetts ;
    London, England : Harvard University Press, [2017] | Includes bibliographi-
    cal references.
Identifiers: ISBN 978-0-674-97530-9
Subjects: LCSH: Cuba—Social policy—History—21st century. | Social change—
    Cuba—History—21st century. | Decentralization in government—Cuba—
    History—21st century. | Cuba—Social conditions—1990– | Latin America—
    Social policy—History—21st century.
Classification: LCC HN207 .S63 2017 | DDC 361.61097291—dc23

Contents

List of Figures

List of Tables

List of Contributors

Soledad Artiz Prillaman is a Ph.D. Candidate in the Department of Government at Harvard University. Her research tackles questions in comparative political economy of development about inequities in political participation and representation, and about the subsequent consequences for public policy and economic development. Her research on the distributive impacts of public policies has been published in the *Journal of Politics*.

Lorena G. Barberia is an Associate Professor in the Department of Political Science at the University of São Paulo. Her primary research and teaching interests are political economy, comparative politics, and political methodology. Much of her recent work is aimed at analyzing redistributive politics in Latin America. She is also a research associate at the David Rockefeller Center for Latin American Studies at Harvard University. Her publications include two previous co-edited books published through the Harvard University David Rockefeller Center for Latin American Studies and Harvard University Press, *The Cuban Economy at the Start of the Twenty-First Century*, ed. J. I. Domínguez, O. E. Pérez Villanueva and L. Barberia (2004), and *Cuban Economic and Social Development: Policy Reforms and Challenges in the 21st Century*, ed. J. I. Domínguez, O.E. Pérez Villanueva, M. Espina Prieto and L. Barberia (2012).

Dick Cluster is a writer, translator, and former Associate Director of the University Honors Program at the University of Massachusetts at Boston. He is co-author, with Rafael Hernández, of *History of Havana* (Palgrave-Macmillan, 2006). His translations of Cuban fiction include novels by Mylene Fernández Pintado and Abel Prieto, story collections by Pedro de Jesús and Aida Bahr, and the anthology *CUBANA: Contemporary Fiction by Cuban Women* (with Cindy Schuster). Scholarly and other nonfiction translations include books from Cuba, Mexico, Colombia, and Spain. His new anthology of Latin American baseball fiction, *Kill the Ámpaya*, will be published in spring 2017 by Mandel Vilar Press.

Dayma Echevarría León is a Professor of the Center for Cuban Economic Studies at the University of Havana. Her research focuses on gender and labor issues and their implications for equity and development. On these topics, she has recently co-edited the following books through Editorial Ciencias Sociales: *Cuba: los correlatos socioculturales del cambio económico*, ed. M. Espina and D. Echevarría (2015) and *Retos para la equidad en el* *proceso de actualización del modelo económico*, ed. by M. del C. Zabala, D. Echevarría, M. R. Muñoz and G. Fundora (2015).

Jorge I. Domínguez is the Antonio Madero Professor for the Study of Government and former vice provost for international affairs at Harvard University. He has been president of the Latin American Studies Association. His publications include two previous co-edited books published through the Harvard University David Rockefeller Center for Latin American Studies and Harvard University Press, *The Cuban Economy at the Start of the Twenty-First Century*, ed. J. I. Domínguez, O. E. Pérez Villanueva and L. Barberia (2004), and *Cuban Economic and Social Development: Policy Reforms and Challenges in the 21st Century*, ed. J. I. Domínguez, O.E. Pérez Villanueva, M. Espina Prieto and L. Barberia (2012).

Mayra Espina Prieto is National Program Official at Swiss Agency for Development and Cooperation (SDC) in Havana, where she is coordinator of local development and decentralization projects. She is also an Adjunct Professor at FLACSO-Cuba and a member of the editorial board of *Temas*. Her research focuses on social structure, social mobility inequality and social policy. She is the author of *Políticas de atención a la pobreza y la desigualdad: examinando el rol del estado en la experiencia cubana* (CLACSO-CROP, 2008); *Desarrollo, desigualdad y políticas sociales* (Centro Félix Varela, 2010) and co-editor of *América Latina y el Caribe: La política social en el nuevo contexto* (FLACSO-UNESCO, 2011); *Crisis socioambiental y cambio climático* (CLACSO-CROP, 2013); *Cuba: los correlatos socioculturales del cambio económico* (Ruth Casa Editorial-Ciencias Sociales, 2015); and *Cuban Economic and Social Development: Policy Reforms and Challenges in the 21st Century*, ed. J. I. Domínguez, O. E. Pérez Villanueva, M. Espina Prieto and L. Barberia (David Rockefeller Center for Latin American Studies and Harvard University Press, 2012).

Susset Fuentes Reverón is a Professor in the Cuba Program of the Latin American School of Social Sciences (FLACSO-Cuba), where she also is a member of the Social Inequalities and Equity Policies Group. Her research on social protection, health, social inequalities and development has appeared in *Algunas claves para pensar la pobreza en Cuba desde la mirada de jóvenes investigadores* (FLACSO / Acuario, 2014), ed. M. Zabala Arguelles.

Geydis Elena Fundora Nevot is a Professor in the Cuba Program of the Latin American School of Social Sciences (FLACSO-Cuba). Her research focuses on development strategies, inequality and equity policies in Cuba and Latin America. She is a member of FLACSO-Cuba's organizing committee of the seminar on social policy and Latin America. Her recent publications include journal articles in *Crítica y Emancipación* and *Agenda Latinoamericana Mundial.*

Reynaldo Jiménez Guethón is Director of the Cuba Program of the Latin American School of Social Sciences (FLACSO-Cuba). His research and teaching have focused on public policy, local and community development and participation, rural development and the environment, and agricultural cooperatives and rural communities. His publications include articles in *Caminos: revista cubana de pensamiento socioteológico* and book chapters in *La intercooperación del concepto a la práctica* (IRECUS, 2007) and in *El Gran Caribe en contexto* (Editorial Universidad del Norte, 2014).

Marta Rosa Muñoz Campos is Profesora Titular of the FLACSO-Cuba Program at the Universidad de La Habana. In 2015, she was a visiting scholar in the Cuban Studies Program at the David Rockefeller Center for Latin American Studies at Harvard University. Her research and teaching focus on studies of the environment, sustainable development, environmental education, community environmental management and local development. Her publications include *Retos para la equidad social en el proceso de actualización del modelo económico cubano*, ed. M. C. Zabala; D. Echevarría, M. Muñoz y G. Fundora (Ciencias Sociales, 2015).

Niurka Padrón Sánchez is a Professor in the Cuba Program of the Latin American School of Social Sciences (FLACSO-Cuba). Her research focuses on cooperatives. Together with Reynaldo Jiménez Guethon, she has published articles cooperatives in *Revista Estudios del Desarrollo Social: Cuba y América Latina.*

Mayra Tejuca Martínez is Professor of the Center of Studies for Higher Education at the University of Havana. She studies the educational policy and the access to higher education in Cuba. Her most recent publications include articles in *Revista Cubana de Educación Superior* and with D. Echevarría a chapter in *Cuba: los correlatos socioculturales del cambio económico*, edited by M. Espina Prieto and D. Echevaría (Ruth Casa Editorial-Ciencias Sociales, 2015).

María del Carmen Zabala Argüelles is Profesora Titular at the Universidad de La Habana and a researcher of the Facultad Latinoamericana de Ciencias Sociales (FLACSO). Her recent publications include *Jefatura femenina de hogar, pobreza urbana y exclusión social* (CLACSO, 2009), *Familia y pobreza en Cuba. Estudio de casos* (Acuario, 2010) and the edited volumes: *Pobreza, exclusión social y discriminación étnico-racial en América Latina y el Caribe* (CLACSO, 2008), *Algunas claves para pensar la pobreza en Cuba desde la mirada de jóvenes investigadores* (FLACSO / Acuario, 2014) and with D. Echevarría, M. Muñoz y G. Fundora: *Retos para la equidad social en el proceso de actualización del modelo económico cubano* (Ciencias Sociales, 2015).

1

Social Policy and Economic Change in Cuba

Jorge I. Domínguez

For the first time ever in Cuban history in a revolution built on health care and education, a Communist party leader actually celebrated a reduction in social expenditures. Speaking to the VII Congress of the Cuban Communist Party in April 2016 (Castro 2016, 7), General Raúl Castro declared with evident pride, "The rational use of resources made it possible to cut the health care budget in excess of two billion pesos.")[1] The leader, the Communist Party First Secretary (a post held simultaneously with the presidency of Cuba's Council of State and Council of Ministers), also expressed concomitant praise for cuts also applied to the education sector. President Raúl Castro had inherited a still-ambitious social policy but without the means to pay for it; these decisions sought to address that problem.

In fact, Cuba's published budget statistics imply a different story, namely, the offloading of health and education costs from the central to the local budgets without a net cut to the state budget (compare Tables 6.4 and 6.5, ONEI 2015). Absent numbers from this segment of Raúl Castro's main report, it is difficult to pinpoint the magnitude or impact of the change he reported to the VII Congress. Statistics aside, however, Raúl Castro's celebration of social policy budget cuts is a politically significant novelty.

In many respects, social policy has been and remains a bright jewel of the Cuban experience since the revolution that came to power in 1959. Following the collapse of the Soviet Union, which had provided massive support for the Cuban economy, Cuba made a noteworthy effort to sustain its commitment to implement its social policies. In this century, the economically productive relationship between Venezuela and Cuba continued to fund Cuban social policy. However, during Raúl Castro's presidency, formally begun in February 2008,[2] a significant albeit slow-moving economic policy change (implemented through a limited use of market mechanisms) has had an equally significant impact on a faster-moving change in social outcomes; in particular, a higher poverty rate and wider income inequality.

In his main report to the 2016 VII Party Congress President Castro noted five goals, namely, the achievement of a "sovereign nation that is independent, socialist, prosperous, and sustainable" (Castro 2016, 28). The social policy changes, he emphasized, do not and must never imply a "rupture with the ideals of equality and justice." These changes must also not "break the unity of the majority of the people in support of the Party. Nor will instability or uncertainty be allowed to emerge amidst Cuba's people as a result of these measures." And yet, something is new and different with regard to social policies: their aim is to provide Cuba with "an efficient and sustainable system," not merely to promote justice in our time (Castro 2016, quotations from 5).

The chapters in this book examine these unprecedented Cuban social policy changes, which altered policies that had been unchanged since their first enactment and consolidation during the revolutionary 1960s. The book presents in English the work of Cuban scholars from the University of Havana and other social policy scholars It also sets the Cuban experience within a wider Latin American context. This work is part of a project begun at the start of this century to examine social and economic policies in contemporary Cuba; two previous collaborative books from this project examined a few aspects of Cuban social policy (Domínguez, Pérez Villanueva, and Barberia 2004; Domínguez, Pérez Villanueva, Espina, and Barberia 2012). Draft versions of nearly all chapters were discussed at a workshop held in Havana in November 2015 and hosted by the Facultad Latino Americana de Ciencias Sociales (FLACSO), a part of the University of Havana with which most of these scholars are affiliated. The workshop and this book became possible thanks to generous support from the Ford Foundation and the leadership role of Harvard University's David Rockefeller Center for Latin American Studies. This chapter introduces those that follow and draws from them. The ideas expressed in this chapter owe an immense debt to my colleagues in this book, but all statements, opinions, and errors of fact or interpretation are my sole responsibility.

Cuban academics and public intellectuals have played significant roles in shaping the general contours of social and cultural policies since the 1960s and, at times, have fashioned specific policies in these areas. More particularly, the research undertaken by Cuban academics, and reflected in several of the chapters that follow, cannot yet be carried out in the same way by scholars outside Cuba. Here I will describe the Cuban scholars' various approaches, which range from rational choice perspectives to specific endeavors to connect race, gender, age, and territory.

I begin here by characterizing Cuba's social policy tradition and provide examples of important social policy outcomes. From there I examine what went wrong in Cuban economic and social policies and outcomes and consider what might be future Cuban social policy decisions. I go on to discuss the chapters written by the Cuban scholars. Their thinking leads me to ponder Cuban deliberations and assessments of social policies; the Cuban government's experimentation with state decentralization and semi-private or private cooperatives; and to an analysis of three key issue areas: education, health care, and the environment. I then reflect on the book's last set of chapters to look at the Latin American social policy context as it may bear on Cuba. My last section concludes.

Cuba's Social Policy Tradition

The chapters that follow will delineate the traits that characterize Cuba's social policy tradition from the 1960s through the remainder of the twentieth century and the start of the twenty-first. However, Cuba's capacity to implement this tradition weakened dramatically upon the collapse of the Soviet Union at the start of the 1990s. Given this event, the social policy tradition highlighted below was applied as such principally from the 1960s to the 1980s. The discussion of the significant period break around 1990 will also seek to explain why the policy's sustained implementation may no longer be feasible even though the same tradition continues to govern Cuban social policy.

- Universal rights and universal benefits. All citizens have and should have equal rights to the opportunities and benefits of social policies, and the state should guarantee universal benefits to make those rights effective.
- Comprehensive and undifferentiated rights and practice. Social policy applies throughout the nation without regard to differences in gender, color of skin or any attributes of race, age, territory, or social class. No one is excluded.
- Free of financial cost to the user. Access to health care and to schools is free for all Cuban users; it is paid for from the national budget.
- Non-market compensation for staff. Social service providers are not a privileged caste. Their compensation falls within the wage scale set by Cuba's central government and it applies wherever social service providers may serve in Cuba or abroad. Compensation is non-market in that wages are set in the context of Cuba's wage scale without relying on international market benchmarks to set salaries of physicians or

other professionals. Top-level professional compensation fell already in the 1960s. Doctors retained higher pay than manual laborers but the gap between the top and the bottom salaried workers narrowed very considerably.

- Centralized and unitary. The national government designs social policies and applies them in the same manner throughout the country through national agencies or through subnational agencies under direct central government instruction.
- The state has the right and the obligation to provide for such social policies; it holds a monopoly over social services delivery. It prohibits private fee-paying primary and secondary schools or health care facilities.
- The state owns or co-owns the means of production (until 1990: all manufacturing, construction, transportation, communications and finance, and most agricultural land). It relies mainly on these resources to pay for social policies and for the entities that provide social services. Indirect taxes, nearly all on state enterprises or joint ventures with the state, accounted for about 30 percent of central government budget revenues. In contrast, tax collection directly on individuals has been very limited, in 2015 reaching not quite 4 percent of central government budget revenues (ONEI 2016, 21).
- Social policy seeks to provide for the greatest equality of outcome, subject to differences explained by circumstances independent from policy design; e.g., only women need obstetrics and gynecology services, only the elderly need geriatric care, varying genetic endowments render only some vulnerable to certain diseases, etc. Equity has been a goal.
- Justice in social policy may require and justify special efforts to support those who suffer from a legacy of poverty, from physical or mental handicaps, or from war wounds incurred in service to the nation, thereby allocating disproportionate resources to these persons. Because poverty and inequalities may overlap, the demands of justice may justify the further allocations of resources to break the burdens of a pyramid of injustice. Justice has been a goal.

The results of these objectives have been impressive in the context of Cuban history and by international standards. For example, in his 2016 report to the VII Congress, President Raúl Castro celebrated how low Cuba's infant mortality rate is (Castro 2016, 4). However, there is a debate about how the administration calculates and reports its social policy statistics. A strong scholarly critique indicates that Cuba's method of reporting its infant mortality rate differs from the methods employed by countries to which its infant mortality rate is often compared; in an international comparison, Cuba's rate may be less impressive than general comparative commentary suggests (Gonzalez 2015). Even so, there is no doubt that Cuba's infant mortality rate is low indeed, and much lower than it once was.

In international comparisons employing data from the 1980s, Cuba showed no significant differences in life expectancy or secondary school completion rates between blacks and whites, in both instances vastly outperforming Brazil and the United States with regard to the black-white completion ratio, two countries with which Cuba shares legacies of slavery (de la Fuente 2001, 259–296; Meerman 2001, 1457–1459, 1471–1475). Cuba had enjoyed a period of nearly uninterrupted economic prosperity in the 1970s and first half of the 1980s, which no doubt facilitated this excellent outcome.

An international comparison of one social policy outcome is especially telling. The first international comparative study of educational performance, under UNESCO auspices, was conducted in the late 1990s, near the end of a decade during which Cuba suffered an economic debacle upon the collapse of the Soviet Union and other European communist regimes that had heavily funded Cuba's economy. The study tested third and fourth graders in language and mathematics. Test results were published for twelve participating Latin American countries; Cuba ranked first on each of the four tests. The Latin American standardized regional median was set for all tests at 250. In the language test, Cuban third graders scored 343 and its fourth graders scored 349; in the mathematics test, Cuban third graders scored 351 and its fourth graders scored 353. The second highest-scoring Latin American country on each of the four tests scored 263, 286, 251, and 269, respectively. The median Latin American country scores on each of the four tests were 231, 252, 238, and 252, respectively (*Lagging Behind* 2001, computed from Table A7). The performance of Cuba's students even at a time of national economic distress was impressive.

What Went Wrong in Economic and Social Policies and Outcomes and What Is to Be Done?

Cuba's economy collapsed at the start of the 1990s, following a half-decade of economic stagnation in the late 1980s. Cuban economic policies had rendered the country over-dependent on subsidies from the Soviet Union and European communist regimes; when those regimes collapsed, so too did Cuba's economy and, as a consequence, the funding for Cuban social policies. Cuba's gross domestic product per capita in 1981 constant prices, set equal to 100 in 1985, dropped to 65 in 1993 and was still only 74 in 2000 (Domínguez 2004, 19). This catastrophe had both immediate and longer-term economic and social effects. At the start of the twenty-first century, the caloric intake of Cubans between the ages of 14 and 64 was only 43 percent of the recommended daily allowance (Togores and García 2004, 260.) By 2010, Cuba lagged on important indicators relative to the Latin American benchmark. As a proportion of the gross domestic product for various countries, Cuba's gross capital formation was half of the Latin American average. Cuba's telephone land-lines per hundred inhabitants were half the Latin American average, and its mobile telephones per hundred inhabitants were just about a tenth of the Latin American average (Torres Pérez 2016).

In response to the loss of subsidies,, in the early 1990s President Fidel Castro authorized foreign direct investment in joint ventures with Cuban state enterprises, at first in the tourism and mining sectors but gradually expanding to other economic sectors. Also in the early 1990s, following Raúl Castro's recommendation to his brother Fidel, agricultural markets were established; prices would be set by the interplay of demand and supply. Opportunities for self-employment and, in due course, market-oriented small-business formation also expanded in the early 1990s, and more so upon President Raúl Castro's announcement of the *Lineamientos* in the fall of 2010 as his proposed program of economic policy change. The April 2011 VI Communist Party Congress approved a modified version of the *Lineamientos*. The financing for small-business investment and also for personal consumption came mainly from remittances from the Cuban diaspora, whose funds have been openly welcome also since the early 1990s.

The combination of persisting social hardship and these economic policy changes had predictable results. From the 1980s to the start of the 2000s, the Gini coefficient of income inequality leapt from 0.24 to 0.38, while the poverty rate (officially called the rate for "the population at risk") tripled from 6.6 to 20 percent. In an impressive study of Cuban social mobility patterns from the 1980s to the 2000s, Espina and Togores summarized the impact of the changes during that quarter century on people's mobility experiences: "Men, white people, young people, subjects whose education level is medium or higher, and persons from better-educated families have a higher probability to be in advantageous positions. In addition, those with individual or household resources including skills, relationships, goods that can be put to use to produce saleable services and products, social networks that provide important information to make efficient labor market decisions, and contacts with influence to facilitate access to advantageous posts are also more likely to succeed. In contrast, disadvantaged positions tend to be associated with women, non-whites, low educational levels, and a lack of resources. These factors also combine with cross-generational transmission of disadvantages" (Espina and Togores 2012, 282).

The election of Hugo Chávez as President of Venezuela in 1998 created a brief sub-period in Cuba's social policy trajectory. The Venezuelan and Cuban governments reached an impressive bilateral accord, akin to barter trade, exchanging petroleum for an array of Cuban service exports, significantly in the health care sector (physicians, nurses, technicians) but also in other sectors. Cuba's economy grew between 2003 and 2008 principally thanks to this relationship. In addition, President Fidel Castro had launched the so-called Battle of Ideas following the December 1999 march he led on the U.S. Interests Section in Havana to demand the return of Elián González, the boy whom his mother had taken to the United States by sea. She drowned in the crossing, whereupon the father in Cuba claimed the boy while Miami relatives refused to give him up. The Battle of Ideas soon evolved from that specific goal to secure the boy's return to a wider framework for many Cuban policies. Its main impact on social policy was to re-emphasize the key points of the policy tradition, which Cuba was again able to afford for a few years thanks to the Venezuelan relationship. However, the 2008–2009 financial crisis ended the economic bonanza that stemmed from that relationship. How could President Raúl Castro manage the inherited still-ambitious social policy when he lacked the means to pay for it?

Thereafter, Cuba's social policy tradition has come to suffer serious strains. First, the economic collapse (first the Soviet collapse, then the Venezuelan collapse, all seriously impairing Cuban economic performance) made Cuba's social policy tradition financially unsustainable. President Raúl Castro rightly continues to stress the importance of making social policy financially sustainable. Notwithstanding valiant efforts since the early 1990s to retain the traditional social benefits as much as possible, Cuba's social policies and their outcomes have begun to show adverse outcomes.

Furthermore, the undifferentiated and comprehensive design of Cuba's traditional social policy implied that, under conditions of deeper poverty as well as wider inequality, the pauper and the professional enjoyed the same universal rights and benefits. It was laudable that the pauper would retain access to good schools and adequate health care, but should the state assist only those in need while expecting those with higher incomes and other resources to pay for social services? Should income-tested co-pays govern access to health care? If social rights are to remain universal for all citizens, could social benefits go just to those who need them, thereby saving budget resources and rendering Cuban social policy financially sustainable? Is it better to retain universal price controls on food staples, as Cuba has long done and affirmed with greater vigor in 2016 following the VII Party Congress, or better to provide targeted subsidies to low-income persons while expecting higher-income persons to pay market prices that would also stimulate agricultural production? Alternatively, should all high-salaried persons in both state and non-state sectors be obligated to pay personal income tax? Why should clowns who are self-employed and work at birthday parties but not state-employed Army Corps Generals pay taxes on their earnings or salaries, and why should privately employed street vendors but not state-employed surgeons pay taxes on their respective incomes? (In 2016, the new budget law proposed for the first time to impose direct personal taxes on employees of state enterprises, but not yet on other state administrative employees.)[3] Should social policy benefits and also tax policies be differentiated according to income levels? Is justice served well when the austere state cuts the social policy budget yet at the same time provides the same benefits to the poor and the prosperous?

The economic constraints (lack of sustainability) and the legacy of undifferentiated social policies (lack of targeting) highlight a third problem, that is, centralized and unitary national policies. Cuba applies a homogeneous set of social policy tools across the nation regardless of differences between the recipients, their needs, or their initial conditions in terms of legacies of wealth or poverty. These social policy instruments are, therefore, not as capable at addressing inequality, which is inherently relative and relational and requires policy instrument differentiation.

One general objective of contemporary social policy in many countries is to build up and sustain the capabilities of human beings to take charge of their lives and develop independently and along diverse paths, an idea most associated with Amartya Sen, who explored how to think jointly about justice and freedom. Cuban social policy has long assumed the importance of developing personal capability; that explains in part the leadership's vast investment in education and health care. But such capabilities have always been framed as a collective public good. Should an objective of Cuban social policy be to foster individual capabilities that enable the concrete exercise of free choices in personal lives?

Social policy may also have a set of secondary objectives on which, for the most part, Cuban policy makers have not focused as much. For example, social policy may foster a more efficient allocation of resources by making changes according to circumstances—fewer physicians in pediatrics, more in geriatrics. It may focus on improving the delivery of services, such as public transportation services in metropolitan Havana. Social policy may inculcate a practical, not just an ideological, sense of personal responsibility for collective policies, that is, all citizens bear individual responsibility to pay for the collective cost of "free" social policies, and thus all citizens welcome paying taxes. Social policy could thus foster a culture of genuine collective ownership and responsibility.

Cubans Deliberate and Assess

Not surprisingly, given these experiences and the extraordinary policy changes under way, Cubans talk about the outcomes that have befallen them and the options that they face. The role of the market economy has grown where new taxes apply, the salience of state employment has fallen, and changes are under way in the application of social policies. Geydis Fundora's chapter gives us a sense, vivid at times, of the elements of public discussion. People do not speak with just one voice, as Fundora well demonstrates. She documents broad support for continuing a universal rights social policy that affirms the worth of free public services as well as state responsibility to manage key aspects of Cuba's economic development. At the same time, there is growing acknowledgment of the emergence of a small private sector and the need to pay taxes as well as to undertake compensatory social policies to redistribute resources.

The author notes a general agreement on the value of changing legislation to permit greater economic and political decentralization and to support a culture of participation that engages people from all walks of life and work; these notions softly push back against the long-centralized process of national policy making and implementation. Whereas government officials seem content with the existing means for participation, looking mainly to adjust it for effectiveness, nongovernmental organization members, academics, and others look for new forms of participation. And whereas government officials and small business entrepreneurs accord priority to economic issues, other social actors clamor for greater attention to social policies. Fundora notes that there are also disagreements between government officials at the national and local levels regarding the extent and utility of centralized or decentralized policy making. She adds that small business entrepreneurs are the most heterogeneous group, that is, they differ the most among themselves on such topics as how cooperatives should be regulated, how to interpret the meaning of socialism, how centralized the economic system should be, and what may be proper constraints on their rights as small business entrepreneurs. In this chapter, the nuances of debates and the possibility of choice suggests a reshaped Cuban social policy agenda for the years ahead.

Citizen discussions are also featured in María del Carmen Zabala's chapter. She conductedsystematic community diagnostics in 2013 and 2014, working with several civil society organizations to assess questions of equity and local development in 15 communities spread over 9 provinces, although more are located at sites in eastern Cuba. The discussions uncovered examples of existing inequalities, in particular those related to gender, housing and related territorial issues (pollution, flooding, etc.), and the elderly. Noted but not seen as so important were inequalities about access to economic, cultural, and social resources. Inequalities with regard to participation were not especially outstanding.

Discussions are also a means to "hear silences," that is, the lack of discussion of a topic that a scholarly observer has reason to expect indeed matters. Zabala's chapter alerts us to a lack of discussion about racial inequalities, that is, the cumulative burden of intertwined race and social class inequalities. Notwithstanding ample evidence that such racial inequalities persist in Cuba, this topic surfaced on its own in only four of the fifteen sites; in all four, the nonwhite population was appreciably larger and in three of the four sites the topic was raised precisely to call attention to the lack of attention that it received in the community, including lack of regard for cultural and religious practices valued by the nonwhite population in these communities. Zabala notes the inattention to racial inequalities at multiple sites where it should be pertinent and the absence of discussion of the topic, and therefore the government's lack of engagement of the nonwhite population to address persisting inequalities (see also de la Fuente 2001). Zabala reports that participants found it easier to identify racial inequality in other countries or as a general concern for Cuba as a whole, but not as problem in the communities where they live.

Experimenting with Organizational Designs

In the context of these debates, since 1959 the Cuban government has experimented with various organizational designs. The authors in this book examine two arenas for such experimentation, namely, the role of subnational governments and decentralization as well as the role of semi-private and private cooperatives within and outside the agricultural sector. In each case, experimentation began in the 1960s and never ceased. The chapter on cooperatives describes this long history of organizational design experimentation. The chapter on municipalization focuses on the changes during the second decade of the twenty-first century, but experimentation with regard to local governments has also been ongoing (for examples, see Domínguez 1978, 248–249, and 281–291). These organizational design experiments are not limited to social policy issue areas; they took place as well in subnational economics and politics.

Mayra Espina's chapter identifies five initiatives that seek to decentralize in order to empower provinces or municipalities: each exemplifies experimentation in organizational design at the interterritorial level, that is, between the national government, the provinces, and the municipalities. One is the Ministry of Economy and Planning's fund to stimulate production at the municipal level. Funding has been used for such a purpose in 67 of the 168 municipalities. Municipalities may invest those funds, provided investment allocation is 70 percent to production and 30 percent to social programs. At times, however, these are less "local initiatives" and more initiatives from national entities that channel such funds to support their interests through local partners—an approach that implies less scope for local initiative. Another decentralization effort is the 2012 tax law that requires all production activities in a municipality to pay one percent of earnings to the municipal government, which municipalities may use for their own expenditures. All joint venture enterprises between the state and foreign investors are exempt from this tax while they recover their initial investments, however. One obvious constraint is structural: the tax generates significant funds in wealthy areas but not in poor ones, because the joint ventures are more common in the former than in the latter.

The third decentralization experiment accords somewhat greater autonomy to the newest provinces, Artemisa and Mayabeque, than to the rest; the extent of actual decentralization of authority, capabilities, and resources remains opaque, however. The author goes on to describe another program of the Ministry of Economy and Planning in 29 municipalities that seeks to incorporate local development objectives into the planning and investment work at the national and provincial levels. Municipalities thereby participate in the allocation of financing for national and local projects in their own territory. This program has been difficult to implement. Finally, a fund set up in 2012 serves to support housing construction and repairs at the municipal level to address a long-standing social policy weakness, that is, the quantity and quality of dwelling spaces. Some municipalities publicize this program and provide information to potential users while others do not.

Other local development undertakings have arisen from the interaction between local initiative and international cooperation, in particular training programs for local government officials and other local actors that already operate in 73 municipalities where some 2,300 local officials have been trained. The training focuses on strategic planning to diagnose local problems, identify goals, set priorities, analyze the availability of resources, and design local policies to achieve the objectives. Yet another endeavor has taken place in the old quarter of Havana, featuring participatory budgeting through local decision making with extensive participation from the community that was invited to join in.

The lack of local people prepared for management and effective decision making has been a major obstacle for the consolidation of decentralization initiatives, especially as they bear on social policy at the community level. The principal explanation for such a lack of local capabilities has been the decades-long, nearly-exclusive reliance on the national government. Therefore, an investment in the development of the capabilities of local actors could be a valuable long-term goal for emerging social policies in Cuba and for greater effectiveness in public policy implementation.

Cooperatives have a long and checkered history in Cuba, as Reynaldo Jiménez Guethón and Niurka Padrón Sánchez describe in their chapter. After 1959, the principal organizational design experimentation with cooperatives has taken place in the agricultural sector. In some agricultural cooperatives, farmers kept individual ownership of their land but pooled resources to obtain and operate equipment, services, or credit. In other agricultural cooperatives, farmers have also pooled their land, thereby becoming collective owners of all cooperative resources on their local level. In yet another type of agricultural cooperative, the state owns the land but accords a set of rights and obligations to those who work on it. The key variables that have governed these organizational experiments are the following:

- Who may own property? Is it an individual? Is it the cooperative itself?
- Who decides what cooperatives may do? Do cooperatives only get to decide on how to implement central policies, or may cooperatives of their own volition make nontrivial decisions about their undertakings?
- What is the margin for decision making for a cooperative relative to the powers of national agencies? Must the cooperative follow mandates set and closely monitored by central agencies, even if the cooperative may make some decisions of its own?
- What are the collective obligations of cooperatives to meet objectives set by central agencies, and what are the collective obligations of cooperatives to their members?

- May a cooperative pool the resources of its members, short of pooling individual property, in order to obtain financial loans, purchase equipment to be shared among cooperative members, and market products?

Jiménez and Padrón describe the high hopes over the years regarding various cooperative experiments, but also the many challenges that cooperatives have faced during those same years. As the 1960s advanced, cooperatives increasingly lost their autonomy and margin for decision making and also became marginal actors in generating agricultural output. New experiments with cooperative organization designs in the late 1970s and in the 1980s were also plagued with deficiencies. A seemingly bold experiment in the early 1990s created new production cooperatives (UBPC) out of what had been state farms. Unfortunately, central agencies smothered these new cooperatives with multiple mandates, over-regulation, and insistence that they behave, in effect, as if they were still state farms. Operating mainly in sugar cane production, these cooperatives shared in the debacle in Cuban sugar production at the start of the twenty-first century.

The enactment of the *Lineamientos* program at the VI Party Congress in 2011 gave rise to nonagricultural cooperatives as well. The analytical variables summarized above apply similarly to these new cooperatives. However, a key difference between the long-existing agricultural cooperatives and the new nonagricultural cooperatives is that the former, when best functioning, were created "from below" by the prospective cooperative members, while the nonagricultural cooperatives have sprung "from above." That is, the initiatives to create most cooperatives in nonagricultural sectors stemmed from the state enterprises, which have been shedding certain operations in order to focus on their core competencies. (Some nonagricultural cooperatives operate restaurants, others buy and sell birds to households, etc.) As a result, nonagricultural cooperatives perform all too often as if they still were state enterprises, with limited autonomy at the local level relative to central agencies. The prospects for nonagricultural cooperatives remain unclear also because the process of authorization has been slow, and months go by with no new nonagricultural cooperative being approved.

Cuba now has a rich experience in various experiments in organizational design. The time has come to shift from such experimentation to adopt systematic national-level policies informed by those experiments, and implement them to permit longer-term commitments and provide assurances regarding the future course of policy.

Education, Health Care, and the Environment

The authors in this book focus on education, health care, and environment policy as key issue areas. In higher education, two very different policies have been implemented in this century: the first led to a massive rise in enrollments, and the second to a comparably massive decline. In health care delivery the basic policies have not changed, but the severe constraints on the health care system eroded the effective public provision of services, making room for an informal or *de facto* privatization of forms of access. With regard to the environment, the policy history is more recent, and the challenge has become how to incorporate and combine environmental and development programs under President Raúl Castro, one of whose most prominent goals is sustainability—political, economic, social, and environmental.

In their chapter, Dayma Echevarría León and Mayra Tejuca Martínez analyze the momentous changes that have taken place in Cuba's higher-education policies as the government seeks to prepare students for the world of work (for background on education and the state, Lutjens 1996). They demonstrate that Cuba has followed two quite different higher-education policy trajectories in the twenty-first century, the first one associated with the Battle-of-Ideas array of policies. This one emphasized a substantial expansion of enrollment in higher education, principally through the creation of higher-education institutions in municipalities. The initiative sought to include more women and non-whites in these municipal entities; the number of students enrolled whose parents were not university graduates increased as well. In effect, this policy aimed to realize the social policy commitment to universal rights and benefits, applying those ideas to higher education. Enrollment rose especially in the social sciences and the humanities. Funding came from the short-lasting economic boom that originated in the export of professional services to Venezuela.

The second policy, consistent with others associated with Raúl Castro's presidency, has been budget cost-conscious. Its emphasis is on matching school training to jobs through greater attention to central planning for school and jobs allocation, and its goal is to increase efficiency and productivity. (The economic boom caused by the Venezuela relationship had ended.) The new policy concentrated resources for professional and technical training, reducing enrollment and also the number of centers for instruction. The number of technical graduates fell, but the number of students who graduated as skilled workers rose markedly. A related motivation was to become more selective in higher-education admissions in order to raise academic standards. Starting in the academic year 2010–2011, passing the entrance examinations became required for admission. This was a high bar. In 2014, only 43 percent of those who took these exams passed them; in 2015, the proportion passing was still only 57 percent ("Positivos resultados . . ." 2015). Entry slots were also reduced in the social sciences; indeed, all degree programs except natural science and mathematics experienced enrollment cutbacks. Women's enrollment in the universities dropped more than men's. Thus both policy trajectories featured a tilt in academic disciplines: the first toward the social sciences, the second toward the natural sciences.

Data from the state's statistical office summarize the trends for the second policy trajectory (computed from ONEI 2015, Tables 18.17, 18.19, and 18.20). Between academic years 2009–2010 and 2014–2015, initial enrollment in technical schools fell 56 percent while initial enrollment for training as skilled workers increased 161 percent. Moreover, initial enrollment in universities fell 71 percent (69 percent fewer men and 73 percent fewer women).

To understand the concerns regarding health care delivery, we need to consider the wider policy context. From 2005 to 2014, Cuba's export of services increased 93 percent. This number combines principally tourism with health care exports (computed from ONEI 2012, Table 5.16, and ONEI 2015, Table 5.17). From 2009 to 2014, on the one hand, the number of health care personnel fell 19 percent, presumably as a result of budget cutbacks in the system; President Raúl Castro celebrated these savings at the VII Party Congress. On the other hand, Cuba's health care service exports required mainly sending personnel to work in other countries under a bilateral intergovernmental agreement; the contracting government paid the Cuban government, which in turn paid the Cuban personnel. Cuba's deployment of physicians and other health care workers to foreign countries rescued its balance of payments, but it also strained its own health care delivery system. In 2015, President Raúl Castro proudly reported that 50,000 Cuban health care professionals were deployed in 68 countries. That meant that one out of every five such professionals was working abroad in the service of the intergovernmental agreement (computed from ONEI 2015, Table 19.1). The largest number was in Venezuela, but there were also 11,487 serving in Brazil ("Carta de Raúl . . ." 2015; "Agradece presidenta brasileña . . ." 2015). The health care delivery system for ordinary Cubans may face coordination constraints, and perhaps spot shortages, when so many health care professionals are abroad.

Susset Fuentes Reverón's chapter explores how Cubans coped with the health care system under multiple stresses; in particular, how they made it work with fewer resources and fewer professional staff while also generating significant export revenues. Her focus is on the new difficulties for ordinary Cubans in accessing health care services successfully. She rightly notes that Cuba's health care system emphasizes that health care is a universal right of all its citizens, and that access is free of financial cost to the user because the state monopoly provides the service and pays for it. By mid-decade, however, a range of complaints had arisen, probably as a consequence of the policy changes that had been implemented. In some instances, personnel changes were substantial and disruptive, and queuing to access the service sometimes took a very long time. In other instances, as the Communist Party newspaper *Granma* has reported, recognizing public fury (evident also in the posts on the *Granma* website), patients faced a severe shortage of pharmaceutical products that undermines health and confidence in the health care system ("BioCubaFarma habla . . ." 2015).

Fuentes Reverón follows the experiences of thirty families in their encounters with the health care system. She finds that Cubans indeed value free health care under a universal right of access, which in many instances continues to serve them well. Nevertheless, she also documents in detail that effective access to quality health care is increasingly skewed to best serve those who have connections or who make informal illegal payments to speed up access to health care services. By "effective access" Fuentes Reverón means quality personnel and services, prompt access, and the ease of arranging for follow-up care. Social capital (knowing the right person) or money (direct payment for speedier access or to see the better specialist) became key instruments to ensure the access that the system's universality continues to promise but no longer delivers in the same way. When money and social capital resources are absent or limited, the barriers to access health care services for individuals rise significantly. The policy changes, perhaps inadvertently, also offloaded responsibilities for care onto the shoulders of families and individuals who now had to pay for an array of formal and informal charges to ensure inpatient and outpatient care. Falling sick came to cost money, and people with money were mostly those who received remittances from abroad or who worked in the tourism sector (hotels, restaurants, and other tourist services). Families were also burdened because the official health care system is understaffed to provide convalescent care. The Cuban state, Fuentes Reverón affirms, remains impressively effective in its provision of health care but now less so than its formal standards would imply. Costs in money, time, and family involvement have all risen.

The third salient issue area, environmental policy, has had a somewhat different trajectory from the previous two. Worldwide environmental policy sensibilities developed gradually during the second half of the twentieth century, and Cuba was no exception. Cuba's most significant environmental policy law was approved in 1997, although several environmental measures had been approved in previous years, in particular to protect water resources. Cuba has serious environmental challenges, which Marta Rosa Muñoz Campos' thoughtful chapter examines. For example, 71 percent of agricultural lands are affected to some extent by soil erosion, much of it seriously. Cuba has taken important steps to protect its remaining forests and its animal species, yet its biodiversity has also been adversely affected, as it is in other countries. In recent years, drought conditions and water shortages have been severe. Therefore, Muñoz Campos argues that one of Cuba's challenges is to integrate environmental considerations fully in its development policies.

Muñoz Campos' chapter details the problems to provide for and manage the water supply. Some problems are intrinsic: it is a long island with small rivers and small lakes, with much of the water near the coast line and thus threatened by salinization. In addition, research shows a limited understanding of Cuba's water supply difficulties, and a lack of information, awareness, and means for environmental learning. As a result, Cuba's water potential fell during the second half of the twentieth century, highlighting the need to assess systematically the steps to be taken to prevent the continuation of such adverse trends. A key conclusion is that Cuba's environmental policy has never been fully integrated into either economic policy or social policy, and the task ahead requires its simultaneous incorporation into both. President Raúl Castro's goal of sustainability demands no less and, more importantly, so does the nation's future.

Situating Cuba in the Latin American Social Policy Context

Cuba's social policy has long been dramatically different from that of other Latin American countries. No other Latin American country has had a social policy profile such as that of Cuba's social policy tradition. Yet Cuba does have two things in common with the social policies of Latin American countries: social policy must be paid for, and every country's social policy bears a special ethical responsibility to care for the poorest.

In some countries, the cost of paying for social policy is borne by individuals when the state affords no social protection; in other countries, the cost of paying is shared between state-funded social policies and individuals who pay not only in taxes but also co-pay as users whenever they access a state social policy service. In contrast, individual Cubans do not pay income taxes and make no co-pays for schools, health care access, or attendance at sports events. They do pay when they board a bus, but the amount is insignificant.

Cuba has never avoided the problem of social policy cost, however. It afforded a generous social policy in part through demonetization, that is, by worldwide standards it paid very low salaries to its physicians, nurses, teachers, and athletes. More generally, in order to cover its general costs including those from social policy, the state relied significantly on external sources of funds. Before 1990, the state paid for its social policies thanks to the revenues generated by state enterprises, enriched in part by significant economic support from the Soviet Union. In the twenty-first century, but only briefly, Cuba paid for such costs in part thanks to support from Venezuela. The Soviet Union no longer exists. Venezuela's capacity to fund Cuba fell markedly following the worldwide financial crisis of 2008–2009, and even more in 2013–2016 during the presidency of Nicolás Maduro, when low world petroleum prices and poor government policies injured Venezuela's economic capacities. President Raúl Castro was prescient, therefore, when early in his presidency he focused on the costs and inefficiencies of the Cuban state and promoted policy changes. To this end he made some tough yet necessary decisions.

Beyond belt-tightening, always difficult, never popular, and often at the expense of those who most need the help from social policies, in Lenin's classic question, what is to be done? The chapters by Lorena G. Barberia and Soledad Prillaman think about the Latin American experience as a way to illuminate Cuba's possible options with regard both to costs and to the effectiveness of anti-poverty policies.

Barberia's chapter examines the possible role of migration. Just as the Soviet Union and Venezuela once helped to fund Cuba's social policy outcomes, could Cuba's diaspora now play that role? Barberia examines the research findings regarding monetary remittances to various Latin American countries and the impact of such remittances on poverty and inequality; she then looks at the same question in the context of Cuba. For the comparative Latin American part of her chapter, Barberia finds that the receipt of remittance income substantively and significantly reduces the incidence of poverty. She also concludes, however, that the impact of remittances on inequality is harder to discern. Turning to studies on Cuba, her principal finding is that Cuba lags far behind other Latin American countries in gathering the pertinent data on poverty and inequality, thereby making it more difficult for both scholars and the Cuban government to analyze the facts and design more effective policies. Barberia does find some evidence that monetary remittances may help the Cuban poor but also that such remittances are likely to widen inequalities. Remittances to Cuba may thus co-fund some of Cuba's poverty-reduction efforts, but they are clearly no substitute for well-designed poverty-reducing social policies. And remittances may compound the problem of widening inequalities, which Cuba has confronted since the early 1990s.

Prillaman's chapter builds a different bridge between the Latin American and Cuban social policy experiences. Both in the region as a whole and in Cuba, dramatic changes in economic policies and circumstances, begun in the late twentieth century, have had significant impacts on the welfare of citizens and on social policies. Prillaman notes the decline in agricultural output in the region, which certainly matches the collapse of Cuba's sugar cane sector and other difficulties of Cuban agriculture, as well as Latin America's deindustrialization and its much greater reliance on a service economy, for which there are also Cuban parallels. The drastic change in Latin American economic policies increased employment vulnerability and uncertainty among those who had always benefited from state protection. In Cuba too, there is a sustained decline in state employment and a noteworthy increase in job vulnerability and uncertainty as former bureaucrats try their hand at risk-fraught private entrepreneurship.

Given these shared circumstances, Prillaman finds that deindustrialization and agricultural sector decline in Latin America did not lead to a "race to the bottom" when it came to social policy; instead, new political coalitions emerged that undergirded social policy redesign and provided broader and deeper support for universalizing social protections that expanded benefits beyond the formal labor force. Cuba had already implemented universal social protections; the current concern is whether there is sufficient support for the poor in an economy where some hardship is already a general trait of quotidian life. Could Cuba prevent its own "race to the bottom" and instead create a new consensus to focus social policy to assist the poorest fifth of the population? Or will the newly job-vulnerable former state employees lobby the state for greater public protection now, soaking up the resources that might otherwise have been targeted to help the poor?

Moreover, Latin America paid for its social policy expansion in part from the commodity boom of the first decade of the twenty-first century. How will Cuba now pay for its existing social policy without external transfers of funds? Will cash-strapped Cuba learn from Latin America by enacting social policies that will require citizens to co-pay, and thus bear privately a share of the cost to pay for collective goods? Pension policies in various Latin American countries have been tweaked to focus more resources on the poor, expecting those who are wealthier to be able to cover more of their costs. Similarly, the widespread adoption of conditional cash transfer programs as one means to support the poor, a type of program that Cuba has never had, raises the question whether Cuba might consider adapting and adopting some such policies. Could such a combination of changes make Cuba's social policies more affordable for the state, at the same time that they help those who are disproportionately poor?

Conclusions

The promise of the VII Communist Party Congress (2016) is that the state will abandon no one. Yet it is not clear how this promise can translate into actual outcomes. For the poor, whose numbers have grown since 1990, the urgency of social policy change is acute. Every parent who hoped the kids would have easy access to higher education sees how the bar has risen considerably, in the name of academic standards but also for the purpose of cutting costs. Every child caring for an elderly parent who needs immediate access to health care gets angry at having to make side payments to health care personnel for access that should be free. Every darker-skinned Cuban risks frustration that the cumulative inequalities between race and social class may be ignored by fellow citizens. For a nation on the cusp of more severe water shortages, the relative inattention to this crisis, long foretold by Cuban scientists and scholars, places everyone at risk. And local government and community decision makers, as well as members of agricultural and nonagricultural cooperatives, suffer the heavy hand of central bureaucracies that prevents them from carrying out the tasks that government and Communist Party national pronouncements urge them to undertake. Cubans debate the shape of the future but feel pain and anxiety about its slow arrival.

Cubans have much to be proud about the many accomplishments of over a half century of social policies that have educated the young, healed the sick, protected the elderly, and constructed a deep and wide sense of social solidarity across the nation. But it has become more difficult to pay for continuing those accomplishments, and the task of enacting change to address this new challenge is now at hand.

Notes

1. All translations here and elsewhere in this chapter are mine. I am grateful to the anonymous referees for the publication of this book, and also to Saira Pons Pérez, for their excellent comments on a prior draft. All remaining mistakes are mine alone.
2. Raúl Castro became acting president in August 2006 and president in his own right in February 2008.

3. I am grateful to Saira Pons Pérez for bringing to my attention this change in the budget law and for other very valuable comments on this chapter.

Bibliography

"Agradece presidenta brasileña contribución cubana en la salud." 2015. *Granma*, 8 July, http://www.granma.cu/mundo/2015–08–07/agradece-presidenta-brasilena-contribucion-cubana-en-la-salud, accessed 8 July, 2015.

"BioCubaFarma habla sobre abastecimiento de medicamentos en el país." 2015. *Granma*, 1 December, http://www.granma.cu/cuba/2015-12-01/biocubafarma-habla-sobre-abastecimiento-de-medicamentos-en-el-pais, accessed 2 December 2015.

"Carta de Raúl a los médicos que combatieron el ébola en África." 2015. *Granma*, 9 July, http://www.granma.cu/cuba/2015–07–09/carta-de-raul-a-los-medicos-que-combatieron-el-ebola-en-africa, accessed 10 July 2015.

Castro Ruz, Raúl. 2016. "Informe Central al 7mo. Congreso del Partido Comunista de Cuba," Havana, 16 April, http://www.pcc.cu/pdf/congresos_asambleas/vii_congreso/informe_central_vii_congreso_pcc.pdf, accessed 16 May 2016.

De la Fuente, Alejandro. 2001. *A Nation for All: Race, Inequality, and Politics in Twentieth Century Cuba*. Chapel Hill, NC: University of North Carolina Press.

Domínguez, Jorge I. 1978. *Cuba: Order and Revolution*. Harvard University Press.

———. 2004. "The Cuban Economy at the Start of the Twenty-First Century," in *The Cuban Economy at the Start of the Twenty-First Century*, 1–14.

Domínguez, Jorge I., Omar Everleny Pérez Villanueva, and Lorena G. Barberia, eds. 2004. *The Cuban Economy at the Start of the Twenty-First Century*. Cambridge, MA: Harvard University David Rockefeller Center for Latin American Studies and Harvard University Press.

Domínguez, Jorge I., Omar Everleny Pérez Villanueva, Mayra Espina Prieto, and Lorena G. Barberia, eds. 2012. *Cuban Economic and Social Development: Policy Reforms and Challenges in the 21st Century*. Cambridge, MA: Harvard University David Rockefeller Center for Latin American Studies and Harvard University Press.

Espina Prieto, Mayra, and Viviana Togores González. 2012. "Structural Change and Routes of Social Mobility in Today's Cuba: Patterns, Profiles, and Subjectivities," in *Cuban Economic and Social Development*, 261–289.

Gonzalez, Roberto M. 2015. "Infant Mortality in Cuba: Myth and Reality," *Cuban Studies* 43: 19–39.

Lagging Behind: A Report Card on Education in Latin America. 2001. Washington, DC: Partnership for Educational Revitalization in the Americas.

Lutjens, Sheryl. 1996. *The State, Bureaucracy, and the Cuban Schools: Power and Participation*. Boulder, CO: Westview Press.

Meerman, Jacob. 2001. "Poverty and Mobility in Low-status Minorities: The Cuban Case in International Perspective," *World Development* 29:9: 1457–1481.

ONEI (Oficina Nacional de Estadística e Información, República de Cuba). 2012. *Anuario estadístico de Cuba 2011*. Havana, http://www.onei.cu/aec2011/esp/05_tabla_cuadro.htm, accessed 17 May 2016.

———. 2015. *Anuario estadístico de Cuba 2014*. Havana, http://www.onei.cu/aec2014/06%20Finanzas.pdf, accessed 17 May 2016.

———. 2016. *Panorama económico y social. Cuba 2015*, http://onei/cu, accessed 9 August 2016.

"Positivos resultados en exámenes de ingreso a la educación superior." 2015. *Granma*, 11 July, http://www.granma.cu/cuba/2015–07–11/positivos-resultados-en-examenes-de-ingreso-a-la-educacion-superior, accessed 13 July 2015.

Togores, Viviana, and Anicia García. 2004. "Consumption, Markets, and Monetary Duality in Cuba," in *The Cuban Economy at the Start of the Twenty-First Century*, 245–295.

Torres Pérez, Ricardo. 2016. "Inversión y asignación de recursos: Una discusión del caso cubano." *Cuban Studies* 44: 43–65.

PART

I

Deliberating over Social Policy

2

Alternative Development and Alternatives to Development: The Decentralization Process in Contemporary Cuba

Geydis Elena Fundora Nevot

Introduction

Since its beginnings in 1959, the Cuban Revolution has been committed to building a system that would be an alternative to the underdeveloped third-world capitalism that prevailed in the Republic prior to 1959. This commitment took shape in, among other elements, the socialization of property, more equitable distribution of wealth and services through policies of universal scope, and the construction of a strong state for the transition to communism.

However, the disappearance of the socialist bloc and the rise of neoliberalism (divergent from the Cuban socialist model), as well as accumulated domestic demands,[1] have challenged the revolutionary project to reexamine its current conditions of development. This has led to reforms such as the current process, formally initiated in 2011, of updating the economic and social model.

That new approach has been officially launched in the all-encompassing concept of "prosperous and sustainable socialism"[2] and would specify the continuities and revisions of the historical model. But such concepts acquire their meanings through the experiences and cosmovisions of every social actor. The heterogeneity of such individuals and groups therefore shapes the many notions of development that make up the context of Cuba's updating process, and these notions, in turn, shape the ways in which those manifold subjects behave to achieve their benchmarks of development.

Thus we find many citizens and groups who, all in the name of "prosperous and sustainable development," devise and promote scenarios emphasizing self-management, socialization of power, preservation of social achievements, diversification of social property forms, encouragement of diversity, and the recovery of socialist values—and also scenarios emphasizing increase of private property, more foreign investment as the engine of development, greater market liberalization, recognition and acceptance of social inequalities ("winners and losers in the reform process," "the new rich"), etc.

In most cases, these are not either/or disagreements. The interpretations that a given social actor accepts or rejects within the general concept of prosperous and sustainable development are elements that in other historical periods would have been seen as inconsistent, contradictory, or incompatible. This is a *sui generis* situation, however.

Thus, any discussion of economic and social policies must be accompanied by a discussion of paradigms and models of development, because these provide the framework for an integral and strategic vision of the efforts carried out by all the diverse actors. A key piece of that discussion should be the collection of diverse points of view adapted from the epistemological principles of the "sociology of emergences" as put forward by Boaventura de Sousa Santos[3]:

> The sociology of emergences . . . consists of undertaking a symbolic enlargement of knowledge, practices and agents in order to identify the tendencies of the future (the Not Yet) around which it is possible to intervene so as to maximize the probability of hope vis-à-vis the probability of frustration.[4]

The objective of this chapter—written by one individual but incorporating many voices—is to discuss the development paradigms of a variety of social actors in Cuba with respect to a key element for the sustainability of the revised model: decentralization in access to, use of, and control of economic, social, and political resources.

The first part of this chapter contextualizes the discussion historically, epistemologically, and methodologically. This will be followed by presentation of the various social actors' perspectives on decentralization as a general process and of their views on specific resources including property, production of goods and services, finance, social services (education, health care, social assistance), legislation, institutions, the process of constructing visions and agendas of development, and spaces of participation. This material is a point of departure for an evaluative analysis of some elements (which actors, playing what roles, with what priorities, etc.) of the sorts of development that each actor defends, and of their underlying referents.

What Have the New Times Brought?

Although the updating of the Cuban model was recognized officially with the 2011 approval of the Guidelines for Economic and Social Policy of the Cuban Communist Party and the Revolution, significant changes in forms of property and economic management began to occur in 2008. These transformations came in response to such problems as inefficiency and low productivity in some branches of the state economic sector; availability of idle agricultural land; dependence on the international food market; and unsustainability of social program spending, among others.

These changes included usufruct grants of state land not under productive use (Decree-Laws 259/2008, 282/2008, and 300/2012); the expansion of self-employment (Decree-Laws 274, 275, 277, and 278 of October, 2010, and Resolutions 32/2010, 305/2010, 399/2010, 750/2010, 33/2011, 21/2013, 41/2013, and 42/2013); the approval of non-farm cooperatives (Decree-Laws 305 and 306 of 2012, Decree 390 of 2012, and Resolution 427/2012); and a new law governing direct foreign investment (Law 118 and 2014). Other measures were allowing a person to hold more than one job; work permits for students (Decree-Law 268 of 2009 modifying the Labor Law); and beginning workplace reorganization to reduce inflated payrolls in the state sector as part of the effort to strengthen the system of state enterprise management (Decree-Laws 274/2010 and 286/2010 and Resolutions 35/2010, 36/2010, 285/2010, and 98/2010). This step eliminated 280,000 state jobs between 2011 and 2012.[5] Changes also took place in the tax system (Resolutions 286/2010, 287/2010, and 289/2010 and Law 113 of 2012), and the social security system, which was extended to cover employees outside the state sector (Decree-Law 278 of 2010).

Some of these reforms reconfigured property relations (not in name only but in the real use and management of property), relations of production, the distribution of goods and services, the structure of employment and income, and the labor market. Further affecting the sphere of employment was a new Labor Code (Law 116 of 2013) regulating relations between workers and employers in the new forms of economic management; authorizing greater variation in the length of the work day, types of hiring and contracts, and vacation and leave policies; and decentralizing certain powers to the directors of state sector entities.

In the sphere of social policy, a reorganization, streamlining, and regionalization of health services[6] and a restructuring of education[7] were two of the processes that followed a new criterion of efficiency in resource use. Other new measures (Decree-Law 322 of 2014, modifying General Housing Law 65) offered subsidies and credits toward the purchase of building materials for doing construction on one's own.

Changes in the area of individual rights came in emigration policy (Decree-Law 302), authorization of legal buying and selling of homes and automobiles (Decree-Law 200 of 2011 and Decree 292 of 2011), and increased use of information technology among the general public through new Ministry of Communications policies expanding access to mobile phones, email, and internet service (of which some examples are Resolutions 179/2008, 22/2010, 24/2010, 197/2013, 593/2014, 64/2015, and 280/2015).

This series of transformations, with controversial results ranging from increased rights and opportunities to wider gaps in equality and increased relations of exploitation,[8] depend on factors that overwhelm any theory of development. The process will be successful to the extent that the protagonists of these changes coherently address points of view, systems of values, and ideological positions in keeping with people's interests, aspirations, dreams, and life projects. Thus, decentralization must be a major axis of the process.

Premises for a Discussion: Some Theoretical-Epistemological Reflections

The concept of development is historically determined and so, too, is the questioning of the concept and the design of strategies for its pursuit. The concept has heavy ideological content influenced by material and spiritual conditions of existence and by interaction within other hegemonic discourses, whether scientific, political, mass-media, or those of international actors—the International Monetary Fund (IMF), the World Bank, the United Nations Economic Commission for Latin America and the Caribbean (ECLAC), the United Nations Development Program (UNDP), etc.—and also by leaders of revolutionary processes in various parts of the world. The term's hegemony and level of legitimacy have led to different concepts of "development" in different historical periods and spheres of influence.

The sheer number of ideas complicates any approach to the subject. One must confront multiple conceptions of development—which may, at times, to be mutually exclusive—as well as discrepancies between realities and ideas, and ideological perspectives behind which lie differing political and economic interests.

In the second half of the twentieth century, with the rise of Latin American structuralist thought, centralization became part of the development paradigm. Its theorists assumed the need for a strong, protective, and nationalist state to confront the tendencies toward underdevelopment that derived from the region's place in the international economy and geopolitics. In that period, for ECLAC and for the precursors of the theory of dependence, this view constituted the alternative.[9]

Then, in the 1990s, decentralization became the new alternative discourse. Such proposals were, however, put forward by actors with divergent interests and visions:

- to decentralize the political power of a state that could be an obstacle to the interests of actors with economic power, and that constituted a costly bureaucracy at odds with free development of the market;
- to decentralize the political power of a state that had historically defended the interests of actors with economic power and that watched over the reproduction of empowerment of the bureaucratic class itself.

Therefore, in debates over models of development, decentralization has always been a controversial issue. With the emergence of development paradigms regarded as alternatives (eco-development, local development, sustainable human development, and endogenous development) has come a recovery of the idea of individual and group power of participation as a key condition for development. The re-conceptualization of economics, politics, the state, civil society, community, the social subject, knowledge, etc., has destabilized established configurations of power.[10]

These ideas, promoted by various leftist movements, nongovernmental organizations (NGOs), cooperation agencies, universities, and other actors, have now come to share the stage with other discourses of similar actors that deny the concept of development itself, regardless of the adjectives that might modify it. They consider the term a semantic trap, derived from an etymology rooted in colonization, its meanings historically weighted by the socialization processes that reproduce a system of structural inequalities of power. These actors argue for the recognition of other cosmographies and forms of production and reproduction of life.

For advocates of such positions, decentralization that is functional for capitalist forms of production, for the tendencies of the world market, bourgeois democracy, etc., does not constitute a truly transformational alternative. Decentralization of power must first recognize and make decisions on the basis of the diversity of ways of feeling/thinking/

imagining/constructing other futures without hierarchies that privilege distinct subjects:

> The diversity of the world is infinite. There are distinctive ways of thinking, feeling, and acting; different relations among human beings, different forms of relationships between humans and non-humans, with nature or what we refer to as nature, different concepts of time, different ways of seeing past, present, and future; different ways of organizing collective life and the provision of goods and resources from an economic point of view.[11]

Decentralization must adopt a criterion of social efficiency to replace the mercantile concept of profitability and productivity in the capitalist sense; associative, cooperative production organized by the producers replaces competitiveness; individual and collective well-being replaces social antagonisms (of class, race, and so forth); and a broader reproduction of lifere-places expanded reproduction of capital, needs, and consumption.[12]

In the 2000s, new discourses have emerged—such as communitarian socialism, twenty-first century socialism, the Citizens' Revolution, Socialism of Good Living,[13] and neo-developmentalism or post-neoliberalism[14]—that have combined alternative development goals with those of alternatives *to* development. Decentralization is a key element, but without renouncing the need for a strong transitional state to promote social and economic policies that regulate internal disequilibria such as structural inequality, and to negotiate in the international arena among its powerful economic and political actors (whether national, international, or transnational).

Those who advocate one of these alternatives have found allies and co-participants among some precursors of such approaches who opt for gradual reform processes that can enable more structural transformation. However, they are opposed by two tendencies: those who continue to pursue more radical and immediate systemic transformations and view these agendas as supportive of the hegemonic system;[15] and conversely, the supporters of a minimal state that enables the capitalist market.[16]

In Cuba, such explicit debate about development paradigms and models has been limited to academic circles for a long time, while other spheres continued to operate with concepts that seemed resistant to any process of reinterpretation until 2016, when the theoretical conceptualization of the Cuban model began to be publicly discussed with the involvement of more sectors. Hence the motivation, in this chapter, is to probe between the lines of the discourses of other actors and to identify their perspectives for a meaningful conversation constructed from experiences that considers the interests of all.

Methodological Elements

My principal method is to analyze the discourses of five types of social actors. This approach is inspired by Sousa's exhortation to "reassess the concrete interventions in society and in nature that different kinds of knowledge can offer"[17] by paying attention to the important transformations through which Cuba is living and the contributions that different voices can offer. As Sousa argues:

> We cannot expand the horizon of possibilities without also expanding the horizon of intelligibility. In order to expand the horizon of possibilities, we have to understand more and better; that way, there can be symmetry between the horizon of possibilities and that of intelligibility.[18]

Sousa poses several challenges for this methodological approach in the face of complex political context:

> From what perspective can different kinds of knowledge be identified? How can scientific knowledge be distinguished from non-scientific knowledge? . . . What types of relationships are possible between the different kinds of knowledge? How can we distinguish among incommensurability, incompatibility, contradiction, and complementarity?[19]

These difficulties are compounded by the need to determine to what extent the actors are speaking in their own voices, voicing their own interests and identities, and to what extent they are mediated by voices imposed by hegemonic systems.

Given their leading roles in public discussion, among the actors selected are national government officials (represented in this chapter by the President of the Council of State and Council of Ministers, chosen every five years by the National Assembly of People's Power) and academics generally recognized as expert voices (in discussions of development, socialism, the state, social policies, and the political and economic systems) from varying epistemological positions.

Other voices with less prominent roles on the public stage include those of local government officials; they are key to the process of geographical decentralization that is an important pillar of the renewal of the model. To these must be added the voices of Cuban NGOs that have worked on processes of local and community empowerment and development since the early 1990s, when (until 1996) the Law of Associations (Law 54) allowed the formation of new NGOs during a period of the historical debate (both inside and outside Cuba) over Cuban civil society, a debate among the positions of liberalism, "suspicious Marxism," and "critical Marxism."[20]

Another type of voice selected for inclusion belongs to the members of the self-employed sector (*cuentapropistas*, the small-scale private sector that ranges from the literally self-employed to proprietors of small businesses). In the context of socialist Cuba, this sector has been controversial because it represents private property and thus contradicts the bases of the theoretical concept of socialism. The *cuentapropista* sector went through a period of shrinkage and hyper-regulation from the 1960s through the 1980s. With the advent of the economic crisis of the 1990s, the growth of the sector was encouraged, although with the stigma of being a "necessary evil," until the decade of the 2000s, when a policy of restricting its growth resumed. Since 2010, however, as part of updating the economic model, a variety of new regulations for controlled stimulus of the *cuentapropista* sector have been adopted,[21] with the result that its share of total employment has grown, placing this actor in a more important spot within the debate over the direction of the Cuban socialist process.

My evidence in these pages consists of unpublished field work resulting from three research projects undertaken between 2011 and 2015 (within the framework of the first stage of the process of updating the Cuban model), in which the methods employed were: analysis of content, semi-structured interviews and interviews of experts, and participatory techniques.

- Project 1: "*Cuentapropismo* in the Cuban socialist project: Merely an issue of economic development?" Master's thesis, 2012.
- Project 2: "The process of updating the Cuban economic and social model: in dialogue with new and old paradigms of development." Research as part of the VII Escuela CLACSO-CODESRIA-IDEAS (2014).
- Project 3: Results of group work with Cuban NGOs in the workshop called "Concepciones del desarrollo," within the course entitled "Desarrollo Social y Equidad" (2015).

Given the proposed objectives and the methodology designed for field work, the three research projects investigated a great variety of topics. Given the space limitations for this chapter and its main topic of discussion (policy and local development), and for the sake of greater analytical

Table 2.1: Methods, Techniques, and Sources

Method or technique	Source of information
Development from the government perspective	
Content analysis (2011–2015)	Guidelines for Economic and Social Policy (2011)
	Official gazettes containing the legislative changes embodying the updating process
	Nine speeches by President Raúl Castro to the National Assembly of People's Power and the Sixth Congress of the CCP
Semi-structured interviews (2011)	Officials of the Department of Labor of Havana province and six of its municipalities.
Development from the perspective of academic communities	
Expert interviews (2011 and 2014)	Specialists in Sociology and Political Science: Dr. Mayra Espina, Dr. José Bell, Dr. Juan Valdés Paz, Dr. Dayma Echevarría, Dr. Juan Luis Martín, Dr. Aurelio Alonso
	Specialist in History and Political Science: Dr. Ariel Dacal
	Specialist in Human Geography: Dr. Luisa Íñiguez
	Specialists in Economics: Dr. Omar Everleny Pérez, Dr. Delia Luisa, Dr. Juan Triana, Dr. Julio Díaz, M. Sc. Leonardo Arredondo
	Specialist in Law: M.Sc. Julio César Guanche
	Specialists in Philosophy: Dr. Humberto Miranda, Dr. Gilberto García
	Source: Master's thesis and Research Essay for the VII Escuela Sur-Sur (CLACSO-CODESRIA-IDEAs)
Development from the perspective of community actors	
Participatory techniques (2015)	Group work with 30 persons. Specialists from NGOs and members of groups developing community projects.
	(Workshop: Concepciones del desarrollo. Curso Desarrollo Social y Equidad)
Expert interviews (2015)	Laritza Achón (OAR), Hilda Juliá (Centro de Intercambio y Referencia de Iniciativa Comunitaria), Ileana Núñez (FNG) and Maritza Moleón, María de los Ángeles Vilaboy, Liana Vidart, Ana Margarita de la Torre, Clotilde Proveyer and Mirlena Rojas (CFV)
Development from the perspective of the self-employed	
Semi-structured interviews (2011)	52 self-employed workers (Havana)

Source: Interviews and sources consulted by the author

depth, the data used comes from discourses related to decentralization of property and management of economic and social resources, as well as those related to processes of empowerment.

Decentralization: Between Lived Experience and Projected Change

Discussions of Cuban society feature diverse themes. Different actors express points of view derived from the meanings they assign to daily-life events. However, the three field research projects underlying this chapter reveal a recurrent theme: decentralization, in all its degrees and dimensions, as described by Mayra Espina in her article "Municipalización y oportunidades para las políticas sociales en Cuba."[22] In the present study, this concept extends beyond the relations among governmental actors to include new socioeconomic actors working in the small-scale private sector and the cooperative one. If one element in the desired model of decentralization stands out as a point where diverse discourses converge, it is the need to socialize power through more active, responsible, and real participation by all actors.

National Government (NG): *The excessively centralized model characterizing our economy at the moment shall move in an orderly fashion, with discipline and the participation of all workers, toward a decentralized system. (Castro, 2011)*

Local Government (LG): *We cannot continue with the mentality that the state must continue subsidizing everything. We are in the twenty-first century and we have to seek alternatives so as to build our system the way we want. (MDL, Havana municipality of Playa, 2011)*

Academic Community (AC): *The keys to that change would lie, above all, in what we in the CIPS (Center for Psychological and Sociological Research) working group at one time called multi-actor socialism. The leading role of the state would shift to shared leadership including a variety of other actors." (Espina, 2014)*

Non-governmental Organization (NGO): *The new organizational management forms also favor the possibility of designs that incorporate other elements, because they are more flexible from the institutional point of view. (Juliá, 2015)*

Self-Employed Worker (SEW): *The state wanted to absorb everything; it took the dogmatic position of centralizing everything. (Self-employed worker, 2011)*

Decentralization and the resulting multi-actor perspective on development imply new forms of designing, managing, and financing policies. At this point, two questions emerge: decentralize what, and how?

An indispensable condition for creating true decentralization is the empowerment of the actors who participate in this process. To classify the opinions expressed by those actors, I will make use of the methodological approach called AURA, developed by Information and Knowledge-Management Services in International Cooperation,[23] which disaggregates the concept of empowerment into the verbs *to have* (resources), *to know* (knowledge and abilities), *to be able to* (internal power and that derived from defined roles in the normative framework), and *to want to* (motivation).

"To Have" So as to Participate: Decentralization and Management of Economic Resources

Who has what? How much? How can they use it? Who provides the financing? Who distributes? Decentralization of property and of economic management has become one of the banner calls of the new process of change. It is a response to accumulated popular demands and to recognition by the government itself of its inefficiency in managing some sectors of the economy. However, this is a controversial subject that could define the orientation of the Cuban system. Thus, debates over how property is distributed have shaped discussion of development models. The concentration or socialization of economic power is determined by who owns and manages land, real estate, economic activities, etc.

Thus, the difference in the discourses of the actors reflects their economic and political interests and relates to the types and amount of property to be distributed (see the different positions of the NG, SEW, and AC). Another important element is the role assigned to the state and small private proprietors in economic planning and management. This includes consideration of the practical or strategic contributions they can actually make to promoting processes of development, whether through financing, meeting needs, or other means. On that point, various perceptions of the role of the small private sector see it as facilitator, as contributor, or as sector complementary to the state, which is the primary manager of the sectors that are strategic to development.

NG: *The growth of the non-public sector of the economy . . . is to become an active element facilitating the construction of socialism in Cuba since it will allow the state to focus on raising the efficiency of the basic means of production, which are the property of the entire people, while relieving itself from the management of activities that are not strategic for the country. (Castro, 2011)*

NG: *Slightly more than half a million Cubans are functioning as self-employed workers . . . a figure that will continue to increase in a gradual fashion, as restaurants and services for the population are transferred to this management mode, while preserving state ownership of buildings. (Castro, 2015)*

AC: *No country develops on the basis of small private property, other areas of development must be strengthened . . . I believe it is a contribution to development, but within this larger logic. (Espina, 2011)*

SEW: *Self-employment gives the populace more opportunities; but it doesn't guarantee the country's development—that comes from tourism, the pharmaceutical industry, biotechnology, and export of human capital to provide services abroad. (Self-employed worker, 2011)*

In practice, statistics reveal the process of economic decentralization such as the growth of private sector (from 147,400 SEW in 2010 to 490,000 in 2015) and the cooperative sector[24] (from 217,000 in 2010 to 231,500 in 2014), although the latter shows a growth rate slower than that of the private sector, and in fact a decline of 16,900 workers during 2015.

Cooperative members as a share of total employment varied only between 4.35 percent and 4.66 percent between 2010 and 2014, and then dropped to 4.42 percent in 2015, while the share of self-employed workers grew from 2.96 percent to 10.27 percent between 2010 and 2015. As the non-farm cooperatives have grown slowly and the self-employed workers more rapidly, there has been a drop in the state sector, trade societies, and agricultural cooperatives.[25]

Another discussion of interest—raised by the national government, the academic community, and the NGOs—concerns the redistribution of resources stimulated by the appearance of new actors as a result of economic decentralization. Varying viewpoints on the financing of development can be seen in comments on taxes from an economist and from the government, and social responsibility from an NGO. This discussion clarifies economic relations to the extent that it reveals consciousness of such roles as taxpayer, financier, and collaborator. Total gross revenue from taxes on vehicles, sales, services, profits, and personal income, among others, and from contributions to social security, rose from 39.9 billion pesos in 2011 to 44.3 billion in 2014. The exception is labor-use taxes, which fell by 1.3 billion.[26]

AC: *If some people are getting ahead, good for them. What we need is for many more to get ahead, this is what we need to stimulate. The state, by means of taxes, can make an activity function or not, can stimulate an area or not stimulate it. (Pérez, 2014)*

NG: *We have also considered it necessary to promote among all institutions, enterprises, cooperatives and self-employed workers a culture of civic behavior towards taxation as well as the view that taxes are the main formula to re-distribute national income in the interest of all citizens. (Castro 2014)*

NGO: *In these kinds of experiences in which cooperation agreements provide money for self-employment, we are trying to include a commitment from the* cuentapropistas *in which they have a degree of social responsibility.*

On the basis of experiences from other historical contexts, the government places a warning sign alongside the logic of uncontrolled distribution; it argues for the need to protect the interests of socially disadvantaged sectors to avoid generating greater dynamics of inequality. Weighing the difference between spending and investment is a problematic element in thinking about how to break cycles of poverty, because the government sees equitable distribution only as a result of development, not as a factor that could contribute to it.

NG: *We cannot distribute wealth that we have not been capable of creating . . . Pouring out money into the streets without an equivalent increase in the supply of goods and services will generate inflation, a phenomenon that, among other harmful effects, would reduce the purchasing power of salaries and pensions, which will particularly affect the most humble. (Castro, 2014)*

"To Have" So as to Participate: Decentralization and Management of Social Resources

The topic of decentralization in financing, management, and control of social services deserves separate treatment. Social services have been a major underpinning of the comprehensive policies that have characterized the Cuban system and given it domestic and international legitimacy as well as guarantees of governability. Although some social actors foresee the possibility of a different type of demand emerging from the private sector . . .

AC: *When a stratum of medium- and high-income people arises, they won't care whether education and health care might be privatized, and in fact they might demand private health care as a path to higher quality, not having to stand in line, etc. (Valdés, 2011)*

AC: *Now it remains to be seen what kind of policies are established and what appeal they have to people who know only the discipline of paying taxes, as opposed to people who felt a great debt to free or subsidized public services, which created that sense of dependency among the citizenry. (Guanche, 2011)*

. . . still the universality of services that fulfill the human rights of education, health care, social security, culture, etc.—guaranteed by the state's central management of these services—is an element upon which disparate visions of the future converge. This is corroborated by an increase of 842 million pesos in social security spending between 2009 and 2014, as well as the maintenance of 38 percent of annual state spending for health and education. However, while financing for these types of services continues to come from the central government, there is a tendency to decentralize the management of the outlays. In absolute terms, direct spending by the central government dropped by 1.9 billion pesos for health care and 2.2 billion for education, while at the local level it increased by 1.3 billion and 57 million, respectively.[27] These changes show no obvious effect of the reorganization of the school network or the processes of reorganization, streamlining, and regionalizing health services.

There are still no figures detailing changes in spending related to management changes resulting from decentralizing initiatives such as the Municipal Initiative for Local Development or the Program of Integral Development, created by the Ministry of Economy and Planning and the Physical Planning Institute, under which funds are assigned by central transfer but spent autonomously. Similarly, figures are not yet available to reflect other decentralizing methods such as regional taxes, which depend entirely on local funds.[28]

Various actors agree that management of social services should continue in government hands, although they differ on the geographic level of government that should be involved. Privatization is not seen as a desired option because the public character of education, health care, and other services is recognized as a historic guarantee of welfare and security.

NG: . . . *for the state to continue ensuring health care and education services free of charge and on equal footing to all of the people and their adequate protection through the Social Welfare System; the promotion of physical education and sports; the defense of the national identity; and the preservation of the cultural heritage and the artistic, scientific and historic wealth of the nation. (Castro, 2011)*[29]

SEW: *There can be free enterprise while maintaining the pillars of the revolution, which are the provision of schools, medicine, or nursing homes for old people without charge. Some pillars are inviolable. (Self-employed worker, 2011)*

Despite the principle of guaranteeing services, spending on culture, sports, science, and technological innovation decreased by more than 400 million pesos between 2009 and 2014,[30] as a temporary response to the call for economic efficiency to promote sustainability. However, the Seventh Congress of the CCP concluded that science and technology are a strategic axis of the development plan looking toward the year 2030, which should result in an increase in investment in those areas.

There are also two divergent trends in the discourses about social services:

- a perception of social services as free of charge (see previous extracts from the NG and SEW) versus services as the result of one's own economic contribution joining state guarantee of such rights (note the following perception of one SEW):

With what we're paying for social security, if we have an accident, we'll be protected. They are also now giving maternity leave. I think the state has been concerned about us. (SEW, 2011)

- support for efficiency in supplying the services based on an economic rationale (government actor) and achieved via centralized control, versus a conception of decentralized management (academic community actor) supplying services via approaches of equity and geographic diversity that combine universal coverage with the heterogeneity that characterizes Cuban society and regions.

NG: *In order to guarantee all of these conquests of socialism, without renouncing their quality and scope, the social programs should be characterized by greater rationality so that better and sustainable results can be obtained in the future with lower spending. (Castro, 2011)*

AC: *Mariel is doing fine, but what will happen in Bahía Honda, which is near Cabañas and there's no Free Trade Zone there? I don't see the territorial aspect being taken into account; I don't see that kind of redistribution by the state being very clear. I'm not talking about focused application of universal policies, which is a worn-out formula, but about really trying out localized policies. (Íñiguez, 2014).*

To Be Able to Participate: Proposals toward This Goal

Although control of material resources is a key element of participation in a context of decentralization, empowerment also requires the creation of other conditions if decisions are to be made in a more decentralized way. These include the regulatory environment, openings for creating visions and agendas of development, cultural configurations, new kinds of institutions, and channels of communication and control. Some proposed actions include:

NG: *In order to decentralize and change that mentality, it is indispensable to elaborate a framework of regulations clearly defining the powers of and functions at every level, from the national to the local, invariably accompanied by the corresponding accounting, financial and management oversight. (Castro, 2011)*

NG: *This will advance further with the strengthening of the democratic spirit and collective work of the leading Party, State and Government organs. (Castro, 2011)*

NGO: *We are committed to building citizen participation through horizontal relationships among the government, the project organizing group, and the community. (CFV, 2015)*

AC: *That would be the path, to spark a process of re-politicization . . . in which the people can really say "I prefer this and not that" . . . to socialize the dispute, to sensitize by way of issues, to empower the people to seek criteria and precedents. (Dacal, 2014)*

All the actors identify elements that need to be corrected: concentration of decision-making power, one-directional communication, bureaucracy, and lack of clarity in norms and regulations. The government's analysis centers on political and governmental actors and the legislative framework; the NGOs and the academic community speak rather of opening up the realm of power to the general citizenry. In the formal design of the Cuban political system, the dichotomy between state and civil society has been dissolved given the popular composition of the bodies of government and the Communist Party, the organization charged with representing the interests of various sectors. That is why, for the governmental actor, discussion of democratization focuses mostly on the institutions of representative democracy. But in practice, interests are not always well represented, which accounts for Raúl Castro's repeated calls to "keep our eyes and ears close to the ground" (Castro: 2016: 5). Other actors push the debate about participation beyond formal presence or representation. To enrich the discussion, they propose designing more horizontal ways of participation at different geographic levels and the diversification of subjects and voices that can really make a difference.

There are also some differences of opinion about which actors (local government, political cadres, and heads of enterprises) and which structural elements are responsible for bad practices. All actors agree in identifying specific legal problems such as legislative contradictions or inefficiencies, or lack of knowledge of the law or the custom of complying with it, and they also point to organizational impediments such as bureaucracy, centralized decision-making, and inefficiency in the people's organization for social control. The academic community and the NGOs focus more on structural causes such as institutional design and cultural resistance, while the government focuses on its own deficiencies in applying what has been mandated, especially in terms of decentralization.

Government Level, Macro-Micro
NG: *Our cadres must get used to working with the guiding documents issued by the institutions empowered to do so and abandon the irresponsible habit of putting them on ice. (Castro, 2011)*

AC: *I don't understand why a local development project has to be approved at the highest level. I think there need to be intermediate structures that can give an answer . . . an empowered municipal government. (Pérez, 2014)*

Enterprise Level
AC: *Now the laws governing work and social security simply tie the hands of the workers and give all powers of decision, in the final analysis, to the administrators . . . Sections of the laws offer control of the direct producers to the administrators, who themselves have a free hand. . . . Dacal, 2014)*

Local and Community Level
NG: *The flaws observed a few months back during the implementation of some specific measures . . . due to bureaucratic obstacles and the lack of preparation of the local governments. (Castro, 2011)*

NGO: *There is a contradiction between discourse and practice, with the result that initiatives must navigate a sea of uncertainties. The legal mechanisms . . . are unclear or sometimes unknown. The other problem is cultural resistance among the decision-makers and even among other social actors involved in the project . . . because of lives and histories that are anchored to a restrictive culture. (González, 2015)*

After the April 2016 Party Congress and public demands for partici-pation, a plan for discussion of the Congress documents among various political and social sectors was made public. But these are complex docu-ments in terms of their technocratic language, their length, and the pano-ply of subjects covered, thus a daunting challenge in terms of feasibility of popular participation—in voice and in effect—given the different degrees of mastery of knowledge about economics, law, sociology and of ability to participate in critical and constructive analysis. Such a situation occurred during discussion of the Guidelines for Economic and Social Policy. Thus, empowerment also requires *knowing how* to participate, another key ele-ment in achieving effective decentralization.

To Know How to Participate: Proposals toward This Goal

Strengthening capacities is indispensable to a process of decentralization that would really lead to a more just and balanced distribution of power. Academic actors and NGOs focus more on strengthening the social, cul-tural, political, and ethical dimensions of development, directed toward all sectors of society; government focuses more on the political leaders and, in the rest of the society, the stimulation of a new civic culture with respect to taxation.

NGO: *We propose to contribute toward the beneficial development of Cuban socialist society from a perspective of equity—shaping men and women with critical consciousness and social activism. Promoting equitable relations of gender, inclusive ones . . .with a spirituality committed to solidarity, plural-ism, and participation. (OAR, 2015)*

NG: *We will require a reasonable time to prepare and train, as we have been doing, our cadres at every level; modify the old-fashioned mentality and get rid of old habits; and work out and implement the legal framework and spe-cific procedures that would enable all of us to see to it that the decisions are adequately implemented. (Castro, 2014)*

Decentralization, Empowerment, and Development: Normalization or Alternative?

The government, the academic community, the NGOs, and the self-employed express differing points of view about what ought to be decentralized and how to carry out that process—a process that includes strengthening the material, juridical, and intellectual capacities of the actors who must be part and parcel of this change in the structure of the social system.

One issue to examine is the dichotomy between normalization versus creation of an alternative, which is also part of the political discourse about Cuba as carried out by Cuban residents on the island and abroad and by outsiders who legally and culturally do not identify as such.

In the construction of a truly alternative system, which actors would share the stage where decisions about socioeconomic policies and strategies are made? Why does there need to be a new distribution of power? Are we talking about an alternative more in tune with the conditions of the current world system and its hegemonic actors, or one in tune with critiques that take a more radical approach to human emancipation? Should Cubans continue to be "different" or opt for being "more normal"—with all the gains and losses that such a choice implies?

In the discourses of the various actors, even when they include conceptual distortions, we find elements that suggest a commitment to an alternative. Among these are:

- the way toward decentralization of economic power is not necessarily through privatization of the economy, but rather diversification of economic actors beyond the sphere of the central government;
- the need to opt for an economy that includes various non-hegemonic economic actors . . .
- who may operate in other forms of production, and for whom the economy is not a goal in itself but a means toward social ends.

NG: *There has also been open encouragement from abroad to speed up privatization, even of the main production and service sectors, which would be equal to laying down the flags of socialism in Cuba. (Castro, 2014)*

SEW: *Self-employment has nothing to do with capitalism because social property, which is the most important, is in the hands of the state and the workers. Capitalism is when there are big companies, monopolies, transnationals, and here there's nothing like that. Here what we've got are small and medium-sized businesses that are meeting needs of the population that the state can't cover. (Self-employed worker, 2011)*

SEW: *The way I see it, I like the idea of cooperatives, to create a kind of brotherhood, a confederation, a commune, but with empathy. (Self-employed worker, 2011)*

SEW: *[Cooperativism] I think is good because it involves mutual aid—I've got something he doesn't have, and he has something that I need. (Self-employed worker, 2011)*

At the same time, others reject alternative constructions of development on economic grounds. Also, some fear the risk of a kind of decentralization based on purely productive results which is not necessarily biocentric.[31]

NG: *Cubans are faced with a huge challenge: we must put the economy on a par with the political prestige that this small Caribbean Island has earned thanks to the Revolution, the heroism and the resilience of our people. The economy remains the most important unresolved matter and it is our duty to place it, once and for all, down the right path towards the sustainable and irreversible development of socialism in Cuba. (Castro, 2014)*

LG: *It may be that in a given moment a state entity feels overshadowed by the* cuentapropista *next door who is doing better quality work . . . Competition is what is going to allow restaurants, services, or childcare facilities to re-activate, because if they don't, this affects the people. (MDL, Havana municipality of Plaza, 2011)*

NGO: *Local governments did not include the [community development] project in the municipal development strategies because it is not a productive community. This is how gaps and misunderstandings arise between the residents and the economistic and vertical mindsets. (FNG, 2015)*

AC: *Cubans' common sense makes them inclined to try out a capitalist pattern that exploits them but pays them a little more, that subsidizes the American Dream in contrast to a cumbersome bureaucratic pattern that discourages them, exploits them, and pays them little. (Dacal, 2014)*

AC: *The economistic vision simplifies the management of social systems. It assumes that improving the economy will improve everything else, which is not always true. (Espina, 2011)*

Another issue around which there is both agreement and disagreement is related to how to place multiple actors in these dynamics of decentralization and management of goods and services. In the recent Latin American context, in countries with governments considered alternative, the idea emerged of achieving new forms of direct daily participation of all subjects in collective life.[32] This logic of true democracy, in which "the other" is recognized as a subject with power, confronted a logic of homogenization and unequal participation in decision making.

Thus, the form in which official political power and Cuban society itself have viewed the plurality of economic actors and their roles in economic management (even with more encouragement of private and cooperative actors) has been an object of debate with respect to the continuities and ruptures of the essence of the Cuban revolution. Decentralizing economic power is a means, but how does it serve the end, which is a more just and equitable system?

AC: *[Self-employment] technically favors an individual solution to a social problem, individualizes the economic problem . . . Therefore potentially, given its design, social function, and objective, which is to increase earnings from production of goods and services, it does not generate a mentality or structure of a socialist nature. (Dacal, 2011)*

AC: *Contradictions will emerge between the owners and their paid workers. Also, the private pattern is the other extreme: on one hand, you have a lax state pattern that doesn't demand anything of you, and on the other hand, a pattern with more capitalist behavior, that pays you a salary and you have to produce because you need to deliver the surplus value that justifies your hiring. (Valdés, 2011)*

AC: *In the crisis of the 1990s, self-employment gained strength, as did joint ventures and small businesses, and all this is what caught the imagination of the people. There was no alternative plan involving reorganization of state enterprises, involving cooperatives. Today, in the common wisdom, there is still a conscious or unconscious propensity to think of capitalist forms of production. (Dacal, 2011)*

SEW: *About cooperatives, I don't know. I've always worked individually, I don't know whether cooperatives function very well, because at least in my work experience, this is capitalism—if you produce, you earn money; if you don't produce, you don't. (Self-employed worker, 2011)*

Returning to the previous question, there is a need for reflection about the kind of development that is truly desired. On that basis, it would be possible to assess how strategic the ongoing decentralization really is. Lack of clarity about definitions leads to the contradictory notions of development expressed by the interviewees in the private sector.

In characterizing the non-state sector of the economy and its function in any sort of system, the people interviewed cite models as varied as the United States, China, the USSR, and Argentina. Their themes range from individualism, competition, de-politicized professionalism, and economic growth to—in a single case—assigning the sector a key role in distribution.

SEW: *This is pure capitalism; this is how they live in the States . . . people need room to go after what they need. (Self-employed worker, 2011)*

SEW: *There are plenty of socialist countries whose systems include self-employment, like the USSR. This type of occupation has nothing to do with politics. (Self-employed worker, 2011)*

SEW: *After its economic crisis, Argentina completely cooperativized, and it has grown and emerged from the crisis. I think that would be an intelligent option. (Self-employed worker, 2011)*

SEW: *We have to adapt the economy to the modern world. If we have small and medium-sized businesses, then the state can live off both taxes and the large enterprises. That's in any kind of economy, whether capitalist or socialist. What better example than the Chinese? (Self-employed worker, 2011)*

At the same time, some interlocutors speak of the need to interact with models in which the economy and its participating actors are viewed in a different way:

AC: *I don't know whether those who are deciding and designing the political economy have ever participated in, for ex7ample, a meeting at a busy factory, or whether they are considering the Venezuelan communal model or the alternative of* Buen Vivir. *There are some areas of silence. (Dacal, 2014)*

An alternative vision of decentralization must do more than make room for new economic actors; it must make room for their role in economic decision-making. The historical debate about the state-vs.-market binomial is also reflected in the various actors' agendas. The space occupied by state and market in the functioning of the system is a key contributor to the correlation of forces among the participating actors. With the gradual fading of prejudices in the theoretical and empirical history of strictly anti-capitalist alternatives, there is greater recognition of a role for markets. At the same time, the academic actors and the self-employed express differing positions about forms of control of that market (both ideal forms and the ones that currently exist).

NG: *[We are moving] toward a decentralized system where planning will prevail, as a socialist feature of management, albeit without ignoring the current market trends. (Castro, 2011)*

AC: *The earnings and impact of the cuentapropistas are bolstered by a market controlled by supply. The state is slowly withdrawing from those spaces, and we are moving from state domination to domination by the self-employed. (Valdés, 2011)*

SEW: *For me, socialism and capitalism are the same thing; the only difference is who is in charge. In socialism, capital flows into the coffers of the state, and in capitalism it flows into the coffers of both the state and some entities called consortiums, industries, private businesses. (Self-employed worker, 2011)*

From 2011 to 2014, household consumption spending in the state market declined by 9.3 billion pesos, while in the market of the self-employed it grew by 3.0 billion.[33]

Another controversial issue is what role the state should play in a system committed to decentralization. Representatives of local government and some academic sectors continue to favor a strong state role as the guarantor of a way of life alternative to capitalism, because it can put the brakes on purely economic criteria. What is missing is any consideration of capitalist systems that also have strong, centralized states that support them. However, some representatives of civil society (academics, NGOs, and their social networks) argue for the development of other forms of collective control that supersede the role assigned to the state in the Cuban political worldview.[34]

LG: *Cuba is far from being capitalist because the state controls everything. (MDL of Guanabacoa municipality of Havana, 2011)*

AC: *What we call self-employment is one element within a very statist economy . . . but at the same time there has to be a strong state economy, with a strong state that can look out for the common good and halt the logic of profit when that threatens the future of the system. (Alonso, 2011)*

AC: *Today no one is talking about workers' councils that would administer factories. Today there's no worker-control alternative that allows for really strengthening other collective forms, associative forms, so as to develop a model of economic relations tending toward socialism. (Dacal, 2011)*

In the ongoing discussion of decentralization, another controversial topic relates to how to guarantee economic, social, and cultural rights. As noted above, the government explicitly assumes that this role will continue to belong to the state. That model is categorized as an alternative to the global trend toward privatization of the services that guarantee those rights, which leads to exclusion of the economically disadvantaged sectors.

Nonetheless, new vulnerabilities have appeared as responsibility for some of these rights has been decentralized under new state laws governing social security and a new labor code. Despite these changes, the continued illegal status[35] of some forms of employment and the labor market growth primarily in the private sector have led many workers to accept working conditions that violate these rights.[36]

AC: *In the* cuentapropista *sector, insecurity is the norm because they can fire you whenever they want. (Valdés, 2011)*

SEW: *You don't have any backup if you get sick or anything. If you have an accident, as a self-employed person, that's your problem, the state doesn't pay you. (Self-employed worker, 2011)*

AC: *The Cuban experience has tried to escape those logics of development. Maybe there are specific things, certain rights like health and education that have been de-mercantilized, and that's a very important achievement. But at the same time, today economistic notions are making themselves felt and moving, with worrisome force, toward the mercantilization of life and social relations. (Dacal, 2014)*

At the same time, some actors note aspects of responsibility in the private sector:

LG: *Our formation, the way we are shaped, is different. When people come in here and talk, you realize that Cubans have no capitalist mentality at all . . . [Small business] proprietors come and want to pay everything for their employees, even their social security contributions. What kind of capitalist mentality is that? (MDL of Guanabacoa, 2011)*

How much of an alternative such employer benefits represent is subject to debate. Operative, practical needs are met, but attention is diverted from other forms of exploitation. The unequal distribution of power is not changed, and when the employer is seen as benefactor providing assistance rather than as an equal, the result is a distortion in the relations of domination. That's why one researcher posed this challenge:

AC: *Cuba faces the challenge of constructing a notion of collective development, of socialism as socialization, not statism. But I feel that right now . . . the correlation of forces is that the groups trying to rethink development in a more integral manner are a minority. (Dacal, 2014)*

Conclusions

It is difficult to draw conclusions from this diversity of perspectives in the process of constructing a development model. The choice for the many-voiced conversation was a methodological choice inspired by Boaventura de Sousa Santos's precept about the ecology of knowledge—a corrective to the oversimplified domestic and international images of Cuba as a monolithic and static unity. The perceptions shared in this chapter reflect the areas of consensus and division today; they also give us clues as to how these will evolve.

For both government and non-government actors, the historical consensus on some issues survives, such as the continuation of a comprehensive, universal social policy based on free public services, and the state's responsibility to manage strategic sectors of economic development. Also, consensus appears on some new points, such as recognition of non-state actors within the national economic system, though only as complements to the state sector. The main actors seem to accept the idea of creating new mechanisms for financing development, such as taxes and actions of social responsibility, to create just and equitable redistribution. Two other important areas of agreement are the need to reform the legal framework that slows down economic and political decentralization, as well as to reform the culture of participation of different actors.

With respect to participation, however, perceptions diverge, sometimes in complementary fashion and sometime incongruently. For the government actor, the existing design for participation remains appropriate. What needs to be changed is how it is practiced, particularly by the government and the Party. NGOs and academic actors, by contrast, see a need to think about new forms of direct participation that, alongside some existing ones, would contribute to stimulate a deeper participatory culture.

Another area of disagreement has to do with the preponderance accorded to the economy in the development model. The governments, the SEWs, and the economists tend to agree on putting the economy first, while other actors in the academic community and the NGOS argue for a more balanced way of looking at the dimensions of development and a need to rethink the criteria of economic efficiency and rationality. Still, one must recognize an evolution in the national government's approach to the economy, as reflected in this passage of the Main Report to the Seventh Congress of the CCP:

> Decisions made with regard to the Cuban economy will never, under any circumstance, mean a break with the ideals of equality and social justice of the Revolution and much less rupture the strong union between the majority of the people and the Party. Neither will we allow such measures to generate instability or uncertainty within the population. This is why I insist on the need for much sensitivity and clear political vision in order to move forward in the process of implementing the Guidelines. (Castro, 2016: 5)

Furthermore, there are also diverse perspectives within the categories of actors constructed for this study. Among government actors we find differences between the national and local officials in their concepts of centralization and their assessment of its current reach; there are also differences in the complexity of their critical examination of current problems. Local government is criticized by many actors, especially with regard to levels of preparation, a finding that matches Ada Guzón's research as cited by Espina.[37] Proper preparation and training is an indispensable condition for effective governmental decentralization.

In general, the NGO viewpoints share a more community-oriented approach that recognizes the diversity of interests in such spaces and makes a strong argument for a kind of participation that will restore the notion of citizenship. Academic communities have a more critical and integrated vision of reality, in which the prevailing ideas involve a structural analysis of property, the design of the system of participation, the normative framework, and associative forms of management, all within the framework of the capitalism-socialism dichotomy. There are also areas of disagreement, such as the conception and financing of social policy, the degree of statism the model should have, and perceptions about the self-employed.

The self-employed, for their part, are the sector expressing the most varied opinions. Although they agree in some areas, differences stand out in their assessments of cooperativism, socialism, the economic system, the use of social services, and the perceptions about labor rights guarantees. Both their personal experiences and the international points of reference that inspire them appear to be determinant.

From the most common-sense ideas to critical sociology; from perspectives on the national scale to local or individual ones; from an overemphasis on the economic or social sphere to a de-centered integral perspective; from a cathartic approach to a prescriptive one; from a focus on effects to one on structural causes—in all these and other ways diverse actors are judging the Cuba of today and imagining the Cuba of tomorrow.

The need to decentralize some areas of development while retaining universal social policies is a point of significant agreement among the various actors. However, this effort too requires the creation of conditions for applying such a combination in an equitable way. Those conditions include better distribution of resources, knowledge, and roles so as to empower diverse social sectors.

With the emergence of alternative paradigms of development and of alternatives to development, the recognition of multiple epistemologies[38] has been an important premise for encouraging more participatory and balanced processes of social transformation. The Cuban revolutionary process, which preceded many of those currents, concentrated on bringing attention to the most invisible and marginal sectors and in giving voice to the subaltern. This allowed Cuba to achieve levels of empowerment that made it a model of social change for the Latin American region and beyond.

Today, however, Cuba's statist tendencies in some periods toward homogenization and centralization, which limited the sort of citizen participation based on specific identities that transcended the political and nationalist dimension, are being called into question by actors as diverse as the national government, the academic community, the private sector, and others. Among the historical tendencies criticized today are the simplified concept of forms of property in a socialist system, centralized economic management, vertical decision-making, and participation defined only as information and consultation, or as being involved through the mere presence of a representative of one's group. Such methods eventually got in the way of the system's own goal: a highly socialized society with relations freed from the forms of domination of some subjects by others.

Therefore, today, a balance between centralization and decentralization, based on recognition of the diversity of actors in decision-making and in the design, management and collective control of the social system, has become an indispensable condition for the alternative construction of a legitimately alternative form of development.

Notes

1. See Castro, 2007, pp. 5–9.
2. See Castro, 2013, p. 1.
3. "We are more and more conscious that our horizons of possibilities are more limited . . . When we ask these difficult questions about the future, when we wonder whether this world can go on the way it is now . . . what answer can we give? Is this a just world? The answers we have today are weak ones, that do not convince us we can adequately respond." Sousa, 2011, p. 14.
4. Sousa, 2011a, p. 34.
5. See Mercader, *Las últimas reformas laborales,* pp. 3–4.
6. MINSAP, 2010.
7. See Quintana, *Los cambios en la Educación Superior.*
8. See Espina, 2014; Zabala, 2013; Íñiguez, 2013; Pañellas et al., 2014; and Fundora, 2015.
9. See Bell, 2009.
10. See Espina, 2005.
11. Sousa, 2011, pp. 16–17.
12. See Gudynas, 2011. See also Sousa, 2010; and Acosta, 2010.

13. ["*del buen vivir*," which is in turn a translation of the Quechua *sumak kawsay—tr.*]

14. Among the factors identified in neo-developmentalist agendas are: "Economic strategy centered around diversification of product lines . . . revitalization of the state apparatus as the principal agent of development . . . social policies of protection and inclusion that posit reduction of inequality as a force around which to structure the dynamic of development . . . mechanisms of public micro-policy oriented toward localities as arenas for design and implementation of policies and links among economic, social, and administrative actors, in spaces of different scales, so as to increase their influence on the generation of social agendas . . . deepening democracy." Espina, 2012.

15. "For a long time, critical theory employed words that were used only by the critical theorists, the thinkers about alternatives. We mean words like socialism, communism, class struggle, reification, commodity fetishism, alienation . . . Critical theory has been losing all these nouns to the point of being left only with adjectives. That is, if conventional theory speaks of democracy, we speak of democratic development, or radical, or deliberative; if conventional theory speaks of human rights, we speak of collective human rights, or intercultural, or radical . . . Clearly, nouns are not the property of bourgeois or conventional knowledge and thought . . . The problem is that we have to know their limits . . . because nouns do determine the terrain of the debate." Sousa, 2011.

16. See Fundora, 2015.

17. Sousa, 2006, pp. 59–60.

18. Sousa 2011, pp. 17–18.

19. Sousa 2006, p. 65.

20. See Recio, et al.

21. See Fundora, 2012, p. 28; ONEI 2013, "Sección empleo y salarios;" ONEI 2015, p. 172; ONEI 2016, p. 11.

22. See Espina, 2016, pp. 4–7.

23. See Auto-Refuerzo Acompañado AURA, 2013.

24. This decentralization should be viewed differently depending on the type of cooperative. The UBPC (Basic Units of Cooperative Production, former state farms) and the induced urban cooperatives such as those in the area of transport and some food services (former state enterprises that make usufruct use of state property) in general have a higher level of dependence on centralized decisions. A more problematizing look at economic decentralization, one that goes beyond the macro perspective of distribution by sectors, would require future field studies within these forms of property, where asymmetric power relationships can exist between owners and employees, or between the president of a cooperative and other members.

25. See ONEI, 2015, p. 171; ONEI, 2016, p. 11; ONEI, 2013, "Sección empleo y salarios."

26. See ONEI, 2015, p. 161.
27. See ONEI, 2015, pp. 162–63.
28. See Espina, 2016, pp. 21–24.
29. The state's guarantee of covering services that insure social rights, as a part of the continuity of the Cuban Revolution, is a point repeated in every speech given by the President of the Councils of State and Ministers to the National Assembly of People's Power.
30. See ONEI, 2015, p. 161.
31. "Biocentrism is . . . an anthropic construction, although not anthropocentric; it visualizes man as de-centered, as one more piece of the delicate weave of the biosphere on which he depends . . . a vision of the world in which humanity and nature are inseparable. The human species does not have a privileged position in the cosmos; every person is as worthy as every other being, since all are modifications of the unique divine substance. In concordance with this, deep ecology stresses the biospheric egalitarianism of all beings." Bugallo, 2005. See also Gudynas, 2009.
32. See Moldiz, 2009; Houtart, n.d.; Borón, 2008; Lebowitz, 2009.
33. See ONEI, 2014, p. 152.
34. For more information on the conformation of the Cuban sociopolitical worldview, see Fernández & Guanche, 2008, p. 127. See also Espina, 2008, pp. 137–39.
35. See Castro, 2016, p. 10.
36. See Fundora, 2012, pp. 47–48 and 123–25.
37. See Espina, 2016, p. 14.
38. ". . . recognition of the plural nature of heterogeneous knowledges (one of which is modern science) and the continuous and dynamic interconnections between them, without compromising their autonomy. The ecology of knowing is based on the idea that all knowledge is inter-knowledge." Sousa, 2006, p. 53.

Bibliography

Acosta, Alberto. 2010. "El Buen Vivir: una filosofía por (re) construir." In: *CIP-Ecosocial. Boletín Ecos.* Volume 11:1–19.

Auto-Refuerzo Acompañado AURA. 2002. *Guía Metodológica.* Leuven: ATOL.

Bell, José. 2009. *Introducción a las teorías y los problemas sobre el desarrollo.* Havana: FLACSO-Programa Cuba, Universidad de La Habana.

Borón, Atilio. 2008. *Socialismo del siglo XXI.* Buenos Aires: Ediciones Luxemburg.

Bugallo, Alicia. 2005. "Ecología profunda y biocentrismo, ante el advenimiento de la era pos-natural." In *Cuadernos Sur.* Volume 34. Consulted 10 August 2016 at http://bibliotecadigital.uns.edu.ar/scielo.php?script=sci_arttext&pid =S1668–74342005001100008.

Castro, Raúl. 2007. *Discurso pronunciado en el acto central con motivo del aniversario 54 del asalto a los cuarteles Moncada y Carlos Manuel de Céspedes.* Camagüey.

———. 2011. *Informe Central al VI Congreso del Partido Comunista de Cuba.*

———. 2013. *Intervención en la Primera Sesión Ordinaria de la VIII Legislatura de la Asamblea Nacional del Poder Popular.* Havana.

———. 2014. *Discurso en la clausura del III Período Ordinario de sesiones de la VIII Legislatura de la Asamblea Nacional del Poder Popular.*

———. 2014. *Discurso en la clausura del IV Período Ordinario de sesiones de la VIII Legislatura de la Asamblea Nacional del Poder Popular.*

———. 2015. *Discurso en la clausura del V Período Ordinario de sesiones de la VIII Legislatura de la Asamblea Nacional del Poder Popular.*

———. 2016. *Informe Central al VII Congreso del Partido Comunista de Cuba.*

Espina, Mayra. 2005. "Re-emergencia crítica del concepto de desarrollo." In Carmen N. Hernández, Ed., *Trabajo Comunitario*, pp. 311–321. Havana: Editorial Caminos.

———. 2008. "Mirar a Cuba hoy. Cuatro supuestos para la observación y seis problemas nudos." In *Revista Temas.* Number 56:132–141.

———. 2012. "Retos y cambios en la política social." In Omar E. Pérez and Ricardo Torres, *Miradas a la Economía Cubana. El proceso de actualización.* Havana: Editorial Caminos.

———. 2014. "Políticas de equidad." Presentation at Seminario Científico por el XXX aniversario de FLACSO.

———. 2016. *Municipalización y oportunidades para las políticas sociales en Cuba.*

Fernández, José. A., and Julio C. Guanche. 2008. "Se acata . . . pero se cumple. Constitución, República y socialismo en Cuba." In *Revista Temas.* Number 55:125–137.

Fundora, Geydis. 2012. *El cuentapropismo en el proyecto socialista cubano. ¿Solo cuestión de desarrollo económico?* Master's Thesis, FLACSO-Cuba.

———. 2015. "El proceso de actualización del modelo económico y social cubano. En diálogo con nuevos y viejos paradigmas de desarrollo." In *Crítica y Emancipación*, Volume 13:85–110.

———. 2015. *Relatoría del Curso Desarrollo Social y equidad.* Havana: unpublished.

———. 2016. *Repensar nuestras prácticas: el enfoque de equidad.* Master's Thesis, IDEIH, Geneva.

Gudynas, Eduardo. 2009. "La dimensión ecológica del buen vivir: entre el fantasma de la modernidad y el desafío biocéntrico." In *Revista Obets.* Volume 4:49–53.

———. 2011. "Germinando alternativas al desarrollo." In *ALAI.* Number 462:1–20.

Houtart, Francoise. n.d. *Un socialismo para el siglo XXI. Cuadro sintético de reflexión.* N.p.

Íñiguez, Luisa. 2013. "Desigualdades territoriales y ajustes económicos en Cuba." In Omar E. Pérez and Ricardo Torres, Eds., *Miradas a la economía cubana. Entre la eficiencia económica y la equidad social*, pp. 101–116. Havana: Editorial Caminos.

Lebowitz, Michael. 2009. *El socialismo no cae del cielo. Un nuevo comienzo.* Havana: Editorial Ciencias Sociales.

Lineamientos de la Política Económica y Social del Partido y la Revolución. 2011.

Mercader, Jesús R. n.d. *Las últimas reformas laborales en Cuba (2009–2014).* Madrid: Universidad Carlos III.

MINSAP. 2010. *Transformaciones necesarias en el Sistema de Salud Pública.* Havana: MINSAP.

Moldiz, Hugo. 2009 ¿Reforma o revolución en América Latina? El proceso boliviano. México: Editorial Ocean Sur.

ONEI. 2013. *Anuario estadístico de Cuba del 2012.*

———. 2015. *Anuario estadístico de Cuba del 2014.*

———. 2016. *Anuario estadístico de Cuba del 2015.*

Pañellas, Daybel, Dayma Echevarría and Teresa Lara. 2014. *Cuba: los impactos sociales de las transformaciones económicas.* (forthcoming)

Quintana, Danay. *Los cambios en la Educación Superior cubana o la "invisibilidad" de lo público. Apuntes para un debate.* Consulted 8 August 2016 at: http://cubaposible.net/articulos/los-cambios-en-la-educacion-superior-cubana-o-la-invisibilidad-de-lo-publico-apuntes-para-un-debate-2-aa6-4-aa-3-4.

Recio, Mirlena, Jorge L. Acanda, Miguel Limia, Armando Hart, Rafael Hernández et al. 1999. "Sociedad civil en los 90. El debate cubano." In *Revista Temas.* Number 16–17:4–15.

Sousa, Boaventura. 2006. *Más allá del pensamiento abismal: de las líneas globales a una ecología de saberes.* Presentation at Fernand Braudel Center, SUNY Binghampton.

———. 2010 "Hablamos de socialismo del Buen Vivir." In *ALAI.* Number 452:4–7.

———. 2011 *Una epistemología del Sur. Introducción.* Presentation at Davos Forum. Buenos Aires: CLACSO.

———. 2011a "Epistemologías del Sur." In *Utopía y Praxis Latinoamericana.* Volume 54:17–39.

Zabala, María. 2013. "Retos de la equidad social en el actual proceso de cambios económicos. In Omar E. Pérez and Ricardo Torres, Eds., *Miradas a la economía cubana. Entre la eficiencia económica y la equidad social,* pp. 161–174. Havana: Editorial Caminos.

3

Social Inequalities: Sites of Transformation for Community Actors and Social Policy

María del Carmen Zabala Argüelles

Equity and social justice have been essential pillars of the Cuban social model, as underlined in the 2011 Guidelines of Economic and Social Policy of the Party and the Revolution, which affirm "equality of rights and opportunities for all citizens." The April 2016 Seventh Congress of the Cuban Communist Party[1] has reaffirmed the continuity of these ideals and placed equity and justice among the strategic axes of the country's development. At the same time, the Guidelines stress the importance of local solutions for a variety of problems, ratifying the need to strengthen participatory local management throughout the country. For these two priorities—equity and local participatory management—to develop in harmony, the agents of local development will need to understand local issues and make use of existing potentials, carry out dialogue with various social groups, form local links among them, and include their interests in local development capacities.

This is the context in which the program called "Education and Training in Participation, Equity, and Local Development" has taken shape. Its goal is to train agents to implement local development while fostering both participation and contribute to strengthening the processes of participation and the inclusion of an equity approach in decentralized development strategies. through a process of educating and training agents of local development. This essay will present a panorama of existing social inequalities in the communities where the program is active, from the perspective of social actors linked to social transformation activities there. That perspective will be placed in dialogue with the most recent research results on this subject and with the theoretical bases of that work—i.e., social equity and social policy.

Theoretical Axes

Social inequality should be understood as resulting from social reproduction that is associated with the transmission of social inequality from
one generation to the next, and that understanding should be associated
with "the distribution of compensations, both material and symbolic, for
inequality in access to well-being and power" (Espina, 2006:4). This is a key
ingredient for envisioning social development and designing social policy.

The analysis of social inequality also implies analysis of its opposite,
equality, which along with social justice[2] is one of two basic concepts of
equity that are part of the legitimate aspiration for human betterment.
Equity is defined as equality of opportunities and assumes equality of
rights, not only in a formal sense but in such a way as to guarantee real
equality in the distribution of power, opportunities, options, and outcomes. The equity approach stresses that inequality in any of these dimensions is based on unjust or exclusionary treatment (D'Elia and Maingon,
2004). However, in analyzing inequality, the use of economic indicators—
distribution of riches and resources such as income, credit, and land—
has predominated, with the result that studies of such topics appear most
closely related to distribution of wealth,[3] and less so to access to human
opportunities.

In keeping with an emphasis on equality and social justice, the many
existing inequalities (rights, opportunities, access, achievement), and the
recognition of such gaps and disparities that derive from social injustice,
discrimination, or exclusionary treatment, a definition of equity developed
by a team of Cuban researchers is worthy of note. This group understands
equity as "impartial treatment of all people, independent of social position
or origin, in relation to their opportunities for access to well-being and to
distribution of the costs and benefits of development, on the basis of the
establishment of rules that assure such impartiality . . ." (Espina, Núñez,
Martin, et al., 2010:4). Further, to accomplish equity, equality needs to be
linked with diversity. The former signifies equality of access or (amounting to the same thing) an absence of discrimination or exclusion, which
in turn requires universalist and inclusive policies. These may be complemented, as needed, by differentiated policies to close unjust gaps. The
perspective of diversity supposes equality of opportunity in basic human
areas, along with a diversity of options for their fulfillment in accordance
with the differences, needs, and aspirations among individuals; this perspective recognizes the possibility of unequal treatment as well as of forms
of positive discrimination to counter existing disadvantages (D'Elia and
Maingon, 2004).

A cardinal element in the understanding of inequalities and inequities is their multi-dimensional and plural character: the interconnected economic, social, political, and cultural elements that reproduce these phenomena and shape the various types of inequalities, of which the most important are class, gender, and ethno-racial ones. The analysis of Carlos Reygadas extends to the levels and factors involved. With respect to levels, it stresses the individual, relational, and structural aspects, and thus establishes the limitations of individualist, interactionist, and holistic approaches to inequality, which have examined each of these dimensions separately. With respects to factors, it identifies the dissimilar elements through which inequalities are manifested: " . . . differences in resources that allow agents to take possession of goods (inequality of assets), inequity in procedures for distributing those goods (inequality of opportunities), or asymmetry in the final distribution of the goods (inequality of results)" (Reygadas, 2004:14).

Acceptance of a multi-dimensional approach to inequality allows for consideration of its multiple dimensions, the different types of existing inequalities, and the synergies and intersections of these dimensions. In practical terms, it allows for mounting actions on diverse scales: at the individual level, through capacity-building in the most disadvantaged sectors; at the institutional level, taking action to affect existing discriminatory mechanisms; and at the macrosocial level, transforming the structures that promote inequality while adopting policies that encourage equity. All told, the approach allows for interrelating the economic, political, and social aspects that shape equity and the gaps associated with specific groups and areas. The most significant inequalities are those categorized by class, gender, race or ethnicity, age cohorts or generations, and geography. The particular areas in which these inequalities are expressed include the economy (work/income/consumption), citizen participation, housing and habitat, and access to social services, other protections, and culture.

With a view toward reconstructing "social inequalities" as an object of knowledge, Espina (2010) summarizes several aspects, of which those most pertinent to the present analysis are the externality-internality connection and the spatial-territorial perspective. These issues, still insufficiently studied in the Cuban context, can lead to the social perceptions and daily practices of local actors, manifestations of inequality in particular spaces, and mobilization of strategies by different actors.

Among the goals of social policy, the highest priority is reducing social inequality (and poverty as one of its manifestations), assuring social rights, improving the quality of life and well-being, and providing social services and social protection for the entire population in various diverse environments.[4] In general, achievement of these goals requires strategies, programs, standards, guidelines, and other intervention mechanisms, with action by the state, government, and public administration. Yet participation by the population and local communities in the design, organization, implementation, and evaluation of policies is usually not viewed as essential, although some policies are oriented to favor local development. That is, in itself, a contradiction, because social policies, as an expression of public policies, imply an interaction between deciders and social actors. This interaction, in turn, constructs and legitimates processes that are affected by factors such as communitarian identity and local participation.

A focus on local actors would offer insight into social subjectivity joined to daily practices, underlining the transformative and protagonistic nature of individuals, groups, and institutions, with their agency, capacity for self-management, and diversity. Such issues have been synthesized in the category "Integrative Autonomy," which includes social integration, self-determination and empowerment. The latter describes actions to be taken to incorporate social actors into leading roles, which in turn requires sensitization to problems associated with social participation, building capacity to carry out social dialogue, and building capacity to carry out actions and projects of community transformation, with the actors' needs and interests as a starting point (D'Angelo, 2010).

All these issues lead to analysis of the connection between externality and internality, and point to the importance of social subjectivity—social perceptions and representations, identities, life projects, and strategies—as it is associated with those categories. That analysis leads to examining the role of context, micro-practices, and various perceptions of inequality, its causes, and thus to take relevant action. The influence of those perceptions on the setting in which they arise must also be considered. In effect, the subjective and symbolic dimensions of inequality have the capacity to reproduce and reinforce themselves.

Methodology

The methodological underpinnings of this essay are: a qualitative and participatory perspective[5] (especially as the latter refers to respecting and valuing subjects' knowledge, reflection, and social transformation); recognition of the situated, non-neutral nature of knowledge; and, particularly, the use of intersectionality in analyzing inequities.

The nucleus of information underlying the analysis consists of diagnostic studies of inequity in different territories[6] of the country where Cuban civil society organizations are carrying out socio-communitarian programs for the benefits of the population, with emphasis on the most disfavored social groups and areas. These diagnostics share characteristics that have already been identified in similar efforts in the Cuban context: a participatory character (individual, group, and community), where members of the communities and organizations are all subjects of the research process and collectively construct knowledge about the equity situation in their areas; a predominantly qualitative approach to the systematic analysis of social reality; and the educative character of these processes, in which knowledge is shared, learning takes place collectively, and capacities for critical analysis and commitment are developed (Romero and Hernández, 2005). Analysis of equity gaps identified in the diagnostics is complemented by discussion of the effects of the community projects on those gaps, toward the end of assessing their contribution to reducing inequities that exist.

Because not all the subjects carrying out these diagnostics have academic backgrounds, nor have all been observing the traditional canons of scientific rigor, the results could be seen as open to question. Hence the importance of an epistemology that questions the exclusive confidence in scientific knowledge, values diverse kinds of knowledge (including those produced by historically excluded groups), and examines its non-neutral and commitment-laden character (Sousa, 2011). Along the same line, the perspective of complexity and trans-disciplinarity legitimates dialogue among different kinds of knowledge, including those that have been disqualified or stigmatized, which are generally tied to perceptions, practices, and interrelations that take place in daily life (Sotolongo and Delgado, 2006).

Another relevant perspective is that of situated knowledge, which recognizes the legitimacy of scientific knowledge offered by the researchers ofthat comes from those implicated in the issues under study, and also the legitimacy of balancing rigor with commitment and responsibility. This implies a critique of traditional scientific objectivity, recognition of the reflexive nature of subjects/researchers and the commitments underlying their participation, consideration of one's own experiences and perceptions as being equal to those of others, and taking responsibility for the effects of the process of construction of knowledge (García Dauder, 2003).

Diverse social actors[7] have participated in the process of creating and collecting the diagnostics and other information that form the basis of this essay and its analysis, and their complete legitimacy has been recognized; all of them, in spite of playing different roles, share the commitment to improve living conditions in the implicated communities.

This essay does not attempt to carry out a comparison of the equity situations, and their causes, in the various geographic areas. It does, however, seek to analyze and systematize the multiple social inequities identified, as well as their synergies. Therefore it adopts intersectionality[8] as a complex, critical understanding of social inequalities. Intersectionality has been defined as "the complex, irreducible, varied, and variable effects which ensue when multiple axes of differentiation—economic, political, cultural, psychic, subjective and experiential—intersect in historically specific contexts" (Brah, 2012:14).[9] As a research methodology, intersectionality departs from additive models and adopts an interdisciplinary perspective (Brah, 2012). However, Yuval-Davis (2012) judges that inter-categorical approaches (focusing on the intersection of differing social categories) do not escape from the additive approach, and therefore should be complemented by intra-categorical ones that deepen the meanings of the categories themselves.

Ferree (2009) identifies two models of intersectionality: that of localization and that of systems. The former emphasizes specific locations and needs of people and groups, their intersections, and how this manifests in axes of oppression; according to that author, however, it does not reveal the systems or processes that produce oppression. The systems model focuses precisely on the interaction of the processes that produce oppression, inequities, disadvantage, and exclusion. The present work will use both models in combined form, although insufficient information prevents me to go deeply into the processes that generate inequity.[10]

The Cuban Context

The Cuban model of social development has been based on an integral conception promoting economic growth along with more equal distribution of wealth, universal access to basic social services, and attention to existing social problems. The state has been the primary manager of implementation through integrated, consistent, and systematic social policies. Among these policies, those related to health, education, and employment have been fundamental.

As previously noted, equity and social justice have been the basic pillars of Cuban social policy. According to Cuban researchers, the distributive and redistributive objectives have included: ending inequality associated with relations of exploitation; ending poverty; guaranteeing spaces of equality; awareness of the existence of inequalities associated with work, social disadvantage, and the manifestation of differences among groups and individuals; using affirmative action to respond to historical disadvantage; the right and duty to contribute individually to the common good; progressive reduction of the relative importance of sources of upward economic mobility other than work; and organizing redistribution through processes of democratic participation and self-management (Espina, Núñez, Martin, et al., 2010). However, the realization of these objectives has varied at historical moments.

The economic crisis and reforms of the 1990s marked an evident watershed. Although equity remained the guiding principle of social policy, undesired social effects emerged: a marked deterioration in the population's quality of life, growing socioeconomic differentiation, growing poverty and vulnerability, and the production or reproduction of equity gaps. The gaps occur among specific territories and human groups and they appear in diverse spheres such as access to comfortable housing and habitat, public services and protections, employment, income, consumption, and citizen participation. In terms specifically of income distribution, there was a moderate increase in the Gini coefficient over those of previous decades.[11] Still, in a Cuban study making use of a PNUD Human Development and Equity Index (HDEI), the country was number two among all the countries of Latin America and the Caribbean. Comparing HDEI ranks to those of the United Nations Development Program's Human Development Index (HDI), Cuba's HDEI exceeded its HDI by more than that of any other country (CIEM/PNUD, 2000). This is very significant considering the declines in social indicators during the crisis of the '90s, which had resulted in Cuba's drop in rank in the HDI, a decline that was reversed from 1998 on. Throughout the period, the country remained within the category of countries with moderate human development.[12]

Under the inertial effects of the economic crisis and reforms, the implementation of new economic measures within the framework of the "updating process," begun in 2011,[13] has marked another key moment for what was happening to equity in Cuban society. The programmatic documents of this initiative ratify the principles of the social project—equity and social justice, protection of socially disadvantaged sectors and assurance of basic social services—though this affirmation is accompanied by reductions in state social spending and in the potential beneficiaries of some programs, elimination of subsidies, more measures particularly targeted to vulnerable groups, a more efficient utilization of available resources (including human ones) in consonance with economic possibilities, and recognition of a greater role for individual and family resources. The economic measures also include promotion of non-state forms of management (self-employment, usufruct land grants, and cooperatives) whose possible benefits are distributed unequally, depending on available resources, geographic location, and access to social networks and information.

Some of these measures imply taking into account existing inequalities, especially the growing differentiations in incomes and the growth of poverty and vulnerability. Thus, for example, there has been greater use of targeted benefits in the form of subsidies for the needy, such as funds for low-income households to build or repair their dwellings[14] and the sale of some basic goods at lower prices to families who qualify for social assistance. At the same time, unregulated markets for individual buying and selling of homes and used cars have been legalized, as has access to tourist facilities for the sector of the population with the greatest economic resources. In this new environment, some inequalities have come to seem natural, and traditional equity gaps have returned, reinforced both subjectively and symbolically.

Nonetheless, discussions in the recently concluded Seventh Congress of the Cuban Communist Party (2016) confirm the central position of equity as the guiding principle of development. The document entitled "Conceptualization of the Cuban Economic and Social Model of Socialist Development" links the country's sustainable development to distributive justice and improved quality of life; similarly, the strategic axes defined in the National Plan for Economic and Social Development through 2030 include human development, equity, and justice.[15] These, together with the universality of social policy and the confrontation of every form of discrimination, constitute essential continuities of the model, as modernized via policies targeted to groups with special needs, including subsidies to people in situations of risk or vulnerability. Such propositions are not without tensions and challenges, but they surely have programmatic value.

On a different scale, Cuba's territories and communities constitute appropriate spaces for analysis of existing inequalities and especially of social transformation, because they have been accumulating social and economic problems and territorial differentials in a marked tendency toward inequality. Since the 1990s, community organizations have emerged that represent a significant force, an "emerging model of small-scale, place-based, participatory planning and monitoring of services, which could greatly complement the reach and effectiveness of current models of service delivery."[16] Later, the 2011 approval of the Guidelines of Economic and Social Policy of the Party and the Revolution highlighted the need to strengthen local administrations as a means toward the solution of multiple problems. This directive has taken shape in greater activity by municipal governments and the development of local projects under the principle of financial self-sustainability (Municipal Initiatives for Local Development).

The main challenges for social policy in this context are, first of all, to maintain the link between social policy and economic policy, so that the goals of social development (including equity and social justice) are not postponed in the pursuit of economic efficiency and sustainability. As part of this effort, it is necessary to precisely identify the disadvantaged individuals and groups so as to be able to offer them differentiated treatment in various spheres, both those related to basic needs and those involving capacity-building, and to implement affirmative actions that compensate for historical disadvantages. Second, the existence of geographical disparities testifies to the importance of deploying selective and differentiated strategies in pursuit of inclusive territorial development.

Equity Diagnostics

The following discussion analyzes the community diagnostics carried out between 2013 and 2014 by five Cuban civil society organizations involved in the project entitled "Education and Training in Participation, Equity, and Local Development"—Centro Félix Varela (CFV), Centro Oscar Arnulfo Romero (OAR), Centro Memorial Martin Luther King Jr. (CMMLK), Centro de Iniciativas y Referencias Comunitarias (CIERIC), and Fundación Nicolás Guillén (FNG). All are characterized by diversity in relation to their missions and their autonomy in institutional, economic, and resource management.

These organizations' cooperation in this project is based on their experiences in the development of community programs intended to strengthen equity in particular dimensions: OAR in gender inequalities as linked to other inequities, and in the prevention of gender-based violence; CFV in sustainable strategies for environmental rehabilitation, in mediation training, and in promotion of a humanist ethic; CMLK in building capacity for local participation and decision-making; CIERIC in participation in management of local cultural patrimony; and FNG in understanding and valuing equity to address racial and gender gaps through recourse to culture and traditions. In all cases, their actions are directed toward local governments in order to promote participation and equity in the implementation of municipal development strategies, and toward vulnerable groups in order to strengthen their ability to participate in local economic and social development.

The communities are located in fifteen municipalities[17] within nine of the country's provinces, especially in the eastern region and with a preponderance moderate of levels of urbanization. Diverse social actors participate in all the programs. Among the most important are: local governments and their Local Development Groups; program organizers; universities and municipal university centers[18]; social and community groups; municipal departments of education, culture, agriculture, social security, and science; institutions in the cultural system (including the Casas de Cultura); NGOs; research centers; and community leaders. Their work is reinforced by the actions of social networks coordinated by three of the cited organizations: Mapa Verde (CFV), Red de Educadoras y Educadores Populares (CMMLK), Red de Casas de Cultura (CIERIC).

The role of the Cuba Program of FLACSO (Facultad Latinoamericana de Ciencias Sociales) has been one of linking and advising, coordinating education and training processes (workshops, lectures, courses, diploma programs, discussions, regional conferences) related to the subjects of social development, equity, and participation, and designing methods for evaluation and monitoring of project impacts. Among the achieved results are sensitization and capacity-building of diverse actors; carrying out diagnostics of the equity situation in each community; discussion in academic and political spaces at various levels, with concrete recommendations for shaping development strategies with an equity approach; and linking diverse actors to these activities.

The methodology underlying the project's activity is essentially participatory, as noted above,[19] involving both participation and commitment by the social actors. Specifically, that means using the Participatory Action Research and Popular Education approaches, privileging dialogue among kinds of knowledge, and collectively constructing knowledge in the phases of diagnosis, training, and systematization and sharing of results. In each locality, the groups organizing the project carry out the diagnostic procedures in permanent consultation with local governments and diverse social actors, discussions with civil society organizations, and deepened understanding that grows out of the ongoing training and education processes. Building capacity has been viewed as a continuous process of training trainers and educating educators, so the number of trained agents is multiplied and guarantees the sustainability and expansion of these activities. The stage of sharing results has allowed the communities to deepen, complement, and correct the information produced, as well as make use of it.

The analysis will be presented in two stages. The first stage examines the gaps found according to gender, age, skin color, geography, economics, sociocultural factors, and participation, as well as the multidimensional synergies and intersections among them. The second stage analyzes the gaps by type and identifies the trends and variations among localities, organizations, and other factors. In both stages, analysis of the diagnostic will be complemented by knowledge developed in the projects' education and training formation (which incorporate subjective and experiential dimensions and include diverse social actors as well as the coordinating researchers), to deepen the understanding of the intersections of equity gaps. This analysis matches, to a degree, the gaps that other social research over the past two decades has identified as the most important ones in Cuba: gender, territory, skin color, economic, and age gaps. These are, moreover, connected to the dimensions identified in the initial stage of the project: access to economic resources, access to the resources of power and decision-making, and access to social and cultural resources.

Gender-related inequities are found in employment, income, access to social and cultural resources, and power and decision-making. The employment gap stems in part from the lack of options available in these localities, and as a result, fewer women in economic activity (most markedly in the non-state sector, which has greater economic benefits) and their higher unemployment rates as compared to men. On the national level, the tendency toward feminization of the technical-professional job sector has been seen as an advance (occurring predominantly in services and in higher education, especially in the social sciences, as reported by Echevarría and Tejuca, 2015). It may be that the localities under study do not have enough employment opportunities that match women's qualifications in this sector. Women's employment situation appears to be worse in rural areas; their presence in farming or as cooperative members is limited, as is their access to active resource assets, property or usufruct titles and their participation in management roles. There women work in typically female jobs (taking care of smaller animals, seedbeds, subsistence gardens, etc.) as either family workers or wage-earners, outside direct management of productive units. These results have been confirmed in research about the Cuban rural areas (Leyva and Arias, 2015).

These inequities are expressed in differentiated access to economic resources, given that part of the female population does not have any personal income (because these women are involved exclusively in domestic or reproductive work) and many more women are found in sectors without the greatest economic benefits. In the rural areas, much of women's work activity is not usually recognized as such in workforce, legal, and income terms (again, because it is intra-family aid). No important gaps related to knowledge and abilities appear in access to social and cultural resources, but there is an overburden of domestic functions including caretaking, given that many women are heads of one-parent families[20] (some in conditions of vulnerability), and both sexist stereotypes and gender-based violence persist. As for access to resources of power and decision-making, what stands out in the diagnostics is that men are overrepresented in decision-making bodies (within enterprises, people's councils, and municipal assembly districts), while women achieve greater leadership roles in the domestic sphere. Although gender inequities are the most deeply studied, the prevailing approach considers them in homogeneous way, ignoring their differentiation according to factors such as age, occupational status, and economic conditions. Nonetheless, this analysis intersects with economic dimensions—employment, income—as well as sociocultural and access-to-power ones, although it is detailed only for the particular situations of rural women, housewives, and heads of single-parent families.

Territorial gaps are associated with several conditions. One is residency in improvised, unhealthy or substandard settlements; this phenomenon is connected to migration from countryside to city and changes the functions of settlements, such as temporary communities of people in transit that later become permanent residences. Other conditions are housing deterioration and economic disadvantage, especially in the urban peripheries. The rural status of some localities implies breaches in access to economic, social, and cultural resources in comparison to urban spaces. This is accentuated in the most outlying settlements, where the rural population's access to employment and services in the larger towns is hindered by problems of transportation, isolation, and distance: low quality of infrastructure and technical services, limited supply of cultural and recreational options, and distance from education, health care, and commercial institutions.[21] In general, a relationship appears between the type of territory (urban, rural, semi-rural, central, or peripheral) and the quality of access to services. In addition, some settlements display situations of environmental vulnerability and risks associated with climate change, including flooding in coastal locations, pollution, deforestation, soil compaction, and water salinization. To a lesser degree there are gaps relative to the community identity and position of social groups with diverse orientations or behavior. Analysis of such territorial gaps shows intersections with economic, social, cultural, and environmental dimensions, which combine to shape the disadvantage faced by some localities.

The age gaps identified in the diagnostics concern access to: employment and income, social and cultural resources, and power and decision-making. In general, the more vulnerable groups are youth and older adults, intersecting with gender and geography, respectively.

In the case of the young population, in addition to gender gaps in employment or income, insufficient employment options also particularly affect young women. Young people encounter gaps in access to recreation and have less presence in managerial posts. In the most rural and isolated areas, opportunities for high school and university studies are far away; those for employment are insufficient, are mostly in farming jobs, and do not always match the education that female youth have attained; cultural and recreation options are limited and not very attractive. These situations may cause migration to cities and diverse social problems. Those who have children find there is limited child care, a situation that affects mothers' employment opportunities. This age group also experiences limitations in cultural consumption, which depends on family resources and interests.

With respect to the elderly, the diagnostics find deficits in services of attention and care and of spaces for socializing and recreation; some conditions of vulnerability related to absence of family or institutional support and to economic disadvantage; and additional risks in the most isolated localities in the case of any health crisis. The general context of this situation is a demographic panorama characterized by the notable aging of the population. The proportion of the Cuban population who are sixty or older has been growing continuously; in 2012 it reached 18.3 percent. This process has occurred simultaneously with a drop in the proportion of people under fifteen and the growth in life expectancy at birth (78.45 years). According to demographic predictions, this trend is irreversible: by 2025 one of every four Cubans will be sixty or older, and by 2030 this segment will constitute 30 percent of the population (Albizu-Campos and Rodríguez, 2015). All of this presents important challenges for attending to the material, health, and sociocultural needs of that population segment.

For both youth and older adults, the analysis of existing gaps reveals the importance of the economic dimension—employment options and economic disadvantages, respectively—and intersections with gender, especially in youth, and of territory insofar as access to social and cultural resources is concerned. The political dimension (i.e. participation) was important for youth.

Racial inequities have been identified in studies carried out in recent decades, which have recognized various situations of economic disadvantage—in the labor structure, income, housing, habitat—for the black and mixed-race population, as well as persistence of stereotypes and prejudices and subtle forms of racial discrimination. However, this is the equity gap with the least presence in the diagnostics, identifiable only in four municipalities, which are precisely those with a greater percentage of population with black or mixed skin color; in the rest of the areas, the absence of such problems, it was suggested, could result from the low proportion of that population.

This gap of discussion could be caused by various factors: lack of available information or of methodological tools to analyze these inequities; absence of education about this topic; or the projects themselves failing to emphasize the lack of discussion about race as a dimension of equity analysis due to resistance in analyzing it, both in the society in general and among specific agents and groups. Nevertheless, the political discourse has moved somewhat away from the position that the racial problem had been definitively solved with the revolutionary transformations begun in 1959, and toward greater consciousness of this problem in the context of the socioeconomic differentiation that took place during the crisis and economic reform of the 1990s.[22] More recently, the base document for the National Conference of the Cuban Community Party (2012) recognized a number of social disadvantages present in Cuban society, including racial ones. The academy has contributed important findings on this subject that have been published over the past two decades.[23] Discussions among writers and artists have also underlined diverse problems with implications for education and culture; mass media too have contributed to critical analysis of this issue. However, the subject of racial gaps remains controversial as far as recognition, analysis of causes, and the actions needed to solve the problem. Hence this topic needs more critical analysis in public and educational spaces. Such analysis involves, first, recognizing that racial inequalities pose a problem and questioning the "natural" character of such phenomena; and, second, revealing the contradictions and interests inherent in these inequalities (Montero, 2004).

For these reasons, it was deemed necessary to design a workshop that would delve more deeply into this topic,[24] with the following goals: acquainting participants with the main concepts and methodologies associated with racial equity or inequity; identifying gaps in racial equity in the Cuban context; identifying (with attention to territorial particularities) weaknesses, strengths, opportunities, and threats present in development projects when they include a racial equity approach; and identifying needs for education to incorporate that approach. Workshop participants included diverse social actors from the localities under study, who were selected according to certain criteria:sensitivity to the topic, potential multiplier effects, and the amount of information they had about their localities as well as their ability to share it, which would allow for later design of training and education initiatives on the subject.

The reflections that emerged in these workshop sessions—by way of presentations, discussions, and analysis of both documents and personal experience—revealed the persistence of racial prejudices in the society and sometimes of disguised racial discrimination. Among the gaps facing the black and mixed-race population are economic, cultural, and habitat ones, as well as the existence of a variety of social problems such as violence, unemployment, crime, and addiction. The personal experiences revealed discrimination in workplaces, schools, families, and social activism. The perceptions of social actors identified areas of the country with greatest presence of the black population as those facing deteriorating living conditions, poverty, social disadvantage, or risks of sociocultural discrimination; such perceptions as: " . . . you go to a marginal community, a poor neighborhood, or whatever you want to call it, and there's more color, you see a difference on this scale . . ."[25] However, some aspects of these areas were seen as favorable, including the cultural identity of the community, the presence of community projects, and values of solidarity and participation. By contrast, for the areas with high presence of the white population, perceptions of economic advantages stood out: more personal possessions, prosperous private businesses, high incomes, workplaces with better conditions and higher pay, healthier habitat, and more central and well-connected location.

Local community projects did not spontaneously emerge as possible sites for modifying the existing gaps in racial equity, because the emphasis was placed on economic and social policy, in particular the idea of more targeted (as opposed to universal) policies; only in five of the projects represented (the four above-mentioned and one additional) is direct or indirect work on this gap taking place, all in communities that are within or near areas with large black and mixed-race population, with poor living conditions and sociocultural discrimination. However, the existence of project groups made up of people sensitized to social equity and inclusion was recognized as a strength that could support local work on racial equity. Weaknesses included: the near-total absence of racial issues in education, training activities, and the community projects; insufficient treatment of this dimension in the diagnostics; scarce consciousness about the topic among community actors; and limited incorporation of the black population in activities. A challenge identified in transforming this reality in the local arena was insufficient knowledge among those carrying out the local projects (including their own prejudices), an obstacle that would not be removed by incorporating more black or mixed-race people into the projects, because its removal demands modifying the subjectivity of all those involved in managing the projects and in the social groups within the communities. Participants also noted low sensitivity to the racial equity issue in their daily lives, as compared to its recognition in other spheres; community actors more frequently identify events affecting racial equity in international or national arenas, and less those that occur in local community spaces.[26] This disparity is also connected to self-recognition and self-perception of the people involved, an issue related to racial composition and racial identification in each context.

Among the conclusions growing out of the workshop discussions are the need to make the racial dimension of equity more visible, to recognize existing racial gaps (including their intersections with the economic, territorial, and sociocultural dimensions), and to make racial equity a central topic in the diagnostics and educational activities of the projects. Analysis of other issues, such as the intersection between gender and skin color, possible effects in terms of socioeconomic disadvantage, and the mechanisms of reproduction of these phenomena in a context where institutionalized racism has been eliminated, is absent from the diagnostics carried out.

Gaps related to economic resources were explicitly identified in eleven communities, associated especially with high levels of unemployment or limited sources of employment (mostly in farm work) in certain areas far from the cities that house the main enterprises and institutions—thus demonstrating the intersection of the economic and territorial dimensions. Other factors are low incomes and buying power, which lead to economic insecurity and deterioration of material conditions for some families. While these criteria are broadly used in scholarly literature and mass media to identify poverty, that term was not explicitly used, but rather vulnerability and disadvantage, the more common phrases used in Cuba.

Gaps in participation were rarely identified and were limited to the issue of representation in the spheres of power and leadership, where they intersect with the gender and age dimensions. In this regard, there was agreement in identifying greater male than female presence in decision-making in enterprises, people's councils, and municipal assembly districts. Similarly, adults are better represented in leadership and administration than are youths. However, a broader analysis still remains to be undertaken to consider how the exercise of citizens' rights, social responsibility, and capacity-building could get people and groups to undertake actions promoting equity. This proposed analysis would need to take into account factors such as the degree of growth in the intensity of popular participation—especially within the organizing groups and their collaborators—though this has primarily been visible in terms of information, consultation, and cooperation in the new processes and spaces created, and only to a lesser degree in decision-making. In a workshop carried out with community actors,[27] low participation was traced to some limitations in the implementation of the projects themselves: the instrumental use of participatory tools, limited consciousness among the facilitators about access to power as a dimension of equity, insufficient follow-up and monitoring of the effects of the actions carried out, and limited time devoted to education and training activities; all this within in a general context where citizen participation faces challenges in the political-institutional and cultural order.

Based on the previous analysis, it is possible to identify trends and variations among neighborhoods, organizations, and other important dimensions. A first finding has to do with the wide spectrum of existing inequalities among the communities where the social projects have been carried out,[28] marking important territorial differences inside ten of the fifteen municipalities. Even within a given municipality, the comparative advantages and disadvantages of certain localities can create socioeconomic contrasts. Advantages include proximity to tourist facilities and easier connections to a variety of institutions, transportation options, social networks, and communications; disadvantages include unhealthy neighborhoods, marginalization, deterioration, and environmental vulnerability. As noted above, the more urban and central communities have more advantages, especially in services and connections. This finding confirms the need to carry out multi-scale analyses that focus on communities and municipalities but are complemented by national data.

All told, the most-identified equity gaps in the diagnostics are those of gender, age, and geography, present in all the sites. Next come those associated with access to cultural and social resources (eleven municipalities) and economic resources (ten municipalities). Gaps related to skin color and access to power and decision-making (participation) were more rarely identified, in both cases in only four municipalities.

The variety of situations identified in the diagnostics also reflects the diversity of the localities themselves, as well as the knowledge and subjectivity of the actors. The former has already been discussed within the analysis of territorial gaps; the latter highlights the construction of the diagnostics by different actors whose perceptions are shaped by various factors, especially their roles, interests, and links to the problems under study.[29]

Local governments, for the most part, contributed information related to socioeconomic indicators that generally allow for differentiation by sex and age cohorts, as well as information related to actions they carried out in response to problems identified by the population, many of which derive from policies and programs designed at the national level. Where universities and municipal university centers are part of the actions of transformation, the diagnostics have a more holistic and integral vision of the multiple dimensions. The profiles of the organizations leading the social projects, along with those of the community organizations, have an important effect on the diagnostics because the actions of transformation contribute to sensitization and consciousness with regard to certain dimensions of social inequality, especially gender, age, territory, and socio-cultural and economic aspects.

As we have said, gaps related to skin color were identified in only four localities. Three of them were tied specifically to lack of visibility or under-standing of the contributions, cultural values, and religious practice of the black and mixed-race population, identified through an effort to revalue cultural traditions led by one organization—CIERIC—that carries out community initiatives and organizes sociocultural development projects to strengthen arts, culture, and cooperation with various social actors. In the fourth case, specialists in the organization leading the transformation projects—CFV—coordinated their actions with a neighborhood network of Afro-descendants, an activity that has sensitized them to identify gaps related to skin color and hidden forms of racial discrimination in a pre-dominantly black community that includes migrants living in an illegally constructed neighborhood.

The infrequently identified gaps with regard to participation were diag-nosed by organizations that center their work on community social par-ticipation: CIERIC, which promotes a culture of local participation from a sociocultural perspective, and CMMLK, which trains grassroots educators for community transformation and sharing knowledge through dialogue. In these cases, participation means more than the representation of spe-cific groups in sites of power; analysis extends also to limitations on cit-izens' responsibility and involvement in problem-solving, an attitude of waiting for solutions to come from outside, and demands and expectations with respect to community spaces and dynamics.

Findings from one area in the central region of the country may help present a deeper picture of the inequalities that can exist within a com-munity and the intersections among those identified gaps, according to the perceptions of the local actors as well as the ways in which they try to affect such situations. That territory includes neighborhoods comprising several people's councils, three of them recognized as vulnerable. This territory's population is slightly more urban than rural; demographically it has a high level of aged residents, and some of its neighborhoods are majority black.

This community exhibits all the equity gaps. In terms of gender, few of the female residents are members of cooperatives, and women have limited access to land, usufruct grants, and leadership posts; there is also gender-based violence, especially in one of the neighborhoods recognized as vulnerable. In terms of territory, the difficulties lie in access to basic services, quality of service, and problems of pollution of soil, water, and air. The economic gaps refer to population groups—individuals and households—with low incomes, some of whom receive social assistance. In terms of access to resources of power and decision-making, the issues are a limited culture of citizenship, insufficient training in decision-making, and limited spaces in which to exercise participation. Access to cultural and social resources is seen as being limited by lack of cultural offerings.

The identified intersections underline the association between one neighborhood's classification as socially disadvantaged—a neighborhood characterized by low income, unemployment, violence, and addiction— and its majority black and mixed-race population, as well as the specific needs of groups disadvantaged in terms of income, consumption, and habitat. In addition, some socio-economically disadvantaged groups become marginalized because of their preferences or lifestyles—such as "rockers," homosexuals, and people living with HIV; the intersection between these processes generates further inequities. The synergies that reinforce inequalities incorporate economic variables and sociocultural dimensions; the latter are shaped by the former, and in turn reinforce them.

Based on the gaps identified in this particular territory and the profile of the organization working there—CIERIC—new initiatives are being developed to attend to the vulnerable groups: housewives, victims of gender-based violence, youth unconnected to school or work, and the elderly. The intentions are to enliven the social life in the municipality by promoting community identity and preserving grassroots traditions and local heritage in close harmony with the environment; strengthen local development through culture; generate self-financing sources of employment and income by offering recreational services; support active participation by the community; and contribute to a more integral upbringing and education of new generations. The center of this organization's strategy is sociocultural, but it also includes economic self-management as a potential for improvement. The idea is toprocess constitutes a multi-actor space where diverse actors—local government, Casas de Cultura, the municipal university center, and social organizations—can contribute different visions for the area, different interactive practices, and different experiences. The challenges facing these initiatives concern their integration with other local development actions in the municipality, consolidation of multi-actor integration, and sustaining the project from its own income.

To summarize the set of community diagnostics carried out, the most important social categories to emerge for the understanding of inequalities are gender, territory, and age, as well as the intersection of the various axes of differentiation, especially the economic and sociocultural ones. In spite of the limited identification of gaps related to skin color and participation, the triads territory-economy-color and gender-economy-participation sum up the fundamentally strongest synergies. These allow an understanding of the needs and economic disadvantages present for women, people of color, and certain territories; thus they orient inquiry into the processes that generate such inequities.

Final Comments

The diagnostics analyzed here offer a vision of the ways local social actors perceive social inequalities in their territories, and demonstrate their potential as agents of change. However, the analysis also reveals some theoretical-methodological weaknesses in the process of constructing the diagnostics, including a lack of relevant indicators to identify equity gaps and some imprecisions in the shaping and implementations of the diagnostics (e.g., procedures, instruments, and information sources). The majority of diagnostics reveal a group of problems present in the localities, but do not always allow for a clear vision of equity gaps.

The information included in the diagnostics does not always facilitate an analysis that would offer an intersectional perspective on the identified gaps. It is not always possible to see more deeply into the causes of the gaps, which would require identifying the processes of exclusion, marginalization, vulnerability, and power relations that produce them. This lends additional importance to the information gathered in the multi-actor discussion workshops, which uncovered the participants' perspectives, beliefs, and assessments about the topics discussed—including consciousness-raising on sensitive issues—which had not been discovered during the process of construction of the diagnostics with traditional instruments, procedures, and sources.

In spite of these limitations, the diagnostics contribute to identifying the most important inequalities and their manifestations in population groups and specific territories. Altogether, they confirm the multidimensional nature of the inequalities and supply some useful indicators for understanding them. The dialogue between these results and those of social research on these problems shows general consistency, which suggests the validity, credibility, and transferability of both.

The diagnostics reveal the social actors' sensitization to the problems and inequalities in their local environments and their diverse social perceptions of these. Those perceptions are also shaped by the profiles of the organizations promoting the community transformations, the methodologies used by each, and the goals of their projects. Thus, in some cases the emphasis falls on environmental problems, in others on sociocultural ones, or specifically on gender. At the same time, those perceptions—constructed through dialogue among diverse community actors—also shape the actions and projects undertaken to respond to the diagnosed problems. Thus, the subjective and symbolic dimensions of inequalities—in this case expressed in the social perceptions of the actors and the profiles and identities of the community organizations—have the capacity to reinforce or mitigate them by virtue of the actions taken.

The diagnostics could affect policy by providing inputs that would facilitate the shaping of actions in favor of equity at local levels, especially in terms of the identification of specific conditions and needs of groups in conditions of vulnerability and poverty; such policies should interrelate economic aspects (work/income/consumption), political ones (citizen participation), and social ones (housing and habitat, access to social services and protections, and cultural consumption) to promote equity. Also, the intersectional analyses of inequalities, although limited, in conjunction with the diversity and heterogeneity demonstrated by the situations analyzed, present an alternative approach to the homogeneous vision of population groups that is traditional in Cuban social policy. Thus they could contribute to more diverse forms of action—such as targeted and differentiated policies, programs, and subsidies—that begin to appear in plans for Cuba's development, as well as to strengthening intersectoral or interinstitutional action to solve complex problems.

The incipient processes of municipal decentralization and strengthening of local participatory management could result in targeted policies to reduce territorial disparities and strengthen equity, in accordance with the situations and needs of the communities identified in the diagnostics. However, taking into account the historical and current advantages/disadvantages of the different territories, as well as their own internal diversity, that possibility depends on sustained monitoring of the equity situation to avoid reinforcing the existing gaps through decentralization; it also depends on transparent use of the tax system, the municipal budget, and necessary transfers from the central government to compensate for the existing disadvantages of localities and specific social groups and to favor greater social inclusion.

The recent transformations in Cuba offer opportunities and challenges for strengthening equity in communities. These opportunities involve a continuing government commitment to equity, social justice, non-discrimination, and the universal and inclusive social policies that assure basic social services throughout the country and egalitarian access to opportunities. Local self-management offers a potential, not yet sufficiently realized, to support those goals through participatory management of the budget and territorial control of resources. Among the challenges are adequate responses to the increase in inequities and situations of disadvantage and vulnerability in the society, the insufficient recognition of this phenomenon and its processes of production, as well as the imprecise identification of the individuals and social groups affected; diversifying social policy by means of instruments that combine universal and differentiated application, at different levels, to capture the existing diversity, differentiate the needed actions, and on that basis eliminate unjust gaps; and seeking innovative ways to increase democratic participation and self-management processes so as to strengthen equity.

Notes

1. See: Partido Comunista de Cuba, 2016, "Informe Central."
2. The concept of social justice emphasizes ethical-normative aspects, such as universal basic rights that should guarantee human opportunities, the real exercise of these rights, and impartiality in the treatment of people regardless of their condition or origin.
3. The most utilized metrics are the Gini coefficient (an index of relative income inequality) and measures of poverty according to the income or poverty line method (PL) and the unsatisfied basic needs method (UBN).
4. Among the most important are education, health, housing, food, social security and assistance, employment, environment, culture, information, sports and recreation, transportation, and communications.
5. The qualitative or structural methodological perspective is based on an interpretive approach to social research and a hermeneutic epistemological perspective; it attempts to understand social phenomena from the perspective of the actors involved. Among a great diversity of approaches, the basic shared characteristics include the importance of contacts and interactions with participants and the primacy of subjective aspects (meaning) of human conduct; a naturalistic, contextualized, and field-oriented perspective; a close relationship between researcher and participants; technical flexibility; holistic and interpretive character; and emergent design. There is relative consensus on viewing the participatory methodology as one of its approaches.

6. This usage accepts the definition of space as a complex of historical and current social relationships, and territory as "the delimitation of areas in which politico-administrative or administrative-sectoral power is exercised." Íñiguez, 2006:24.

7. See Mederos, 2012, for a discussion of the identification of local development actors: public, private, or mixed.

8. This term was used by the U.S. black feminist scholar Kimberlé Crenshaw, 1989, to analyze the oppression and exclusion of black women, processes in which the categories of race and gender interact.

9. That author refers here to the concept developed with Ann Phoenix. See Brah and Phoenix, 2004.

10. Alongside general limitations on obtaining information on such topics in Cuba, there are two additional issues: the lack of information about historical and recent trends related to equity at local levels, necessary in the identification of causative processes; and the sectoralization of much of the data available, gathered and structured in response to the needs of specific institutions.

11. By 1986, this indicator had descended to 0.22, reflecting the trend of redistribution of wealth. In 1996 and 2000 it was estimated at 0.38 (Zimbalist, 1989; Baliño, 1991; Ferriol, Therborn and Castiñeiras, 2004; Añé, 2000); these measures do not include transfers in the form of health care, education, and housing.

12. For more information, see the Human Development Reports issued by the UNDP, 1992–2015. In 2003 and subsequent years Cuba advanced to the HDI category of "high human development" except for 2014, when it was classified as "very high."

13. Although 2011 is the official date of the initiation of this process, with the approval of the Guidelines of Economic and Social Policy, the analysis of the country's economic problems and its need for new solutions had been evident since Raúl Castro's first speeches in 2007. Some actions were announced in 2008; popular discussion of the draft Guidelines began in 2010.

14. Between 2011 and 2015, 11,810 individual credits totaling more than 77.4 million pesos (CUP) were issued, intended for purchasing construction material, paying construction workers, and acquiring cooking equipment (*Granma*, 30 March 2016). This policy embodied a targeted approach to two generally related problems: insufficient income and lack or deterioration of housing.

15. See Partido Comunista de Cuba, 2016, Plan Nacional, and 2016, Proyecto de Conceptualización, both at: www.granma.cu/file/pdf/gaceta/Copia%20 para%20el%20Sitio%20Web.pdf.

16. According to Uriarte, the wide variety of actors involved in these processes include: local governments, mass organizations, Cuban NGOs, international development agencies, higher education institutions, and groups of neighbors. Particular institutions stand out for their potential, namely, the Talleres de Transformación Integral de Barrios (neighborhood transformation

workshops, which exist only in the City of Havana) and the Consejos Populares (people's councils, neighborhood bodies made up of the municipal assembly delegates and representatives of local entities and organizations).

17. These are: Viñales, Plaza, Habana del Este, Sagua la Grande, Camajuaní, Quemado de Güines, Cumanayagua, Céspedes, Guáimaro, Jobabo, Holguín, Báguanos, Cueto, Baracoa, and Bayamo.

18. These are community-based centers that are part of the university system. In 2010, the municipal branches of universities belonging to various cabinet departments (the ministries of education, higher education, sports, and public health) were placed under the authority of the Ministry of Higher Education.

19. See previous section on Methodology.

20. In Cuba there is a marked trend toward feminization of the head-of-household position. The proportion of female-headed households, which was 40.6 percent in 2002, rose to 44.9 percent in 2012; single-parent households were 21.9 percent of all households in 2002, and of those, 83.7 percent were made up of mothers and children; there are no more recent data on this point (ONE, 2002; ONEI, 2012).

21. Some characteristics coincide with the classification "Rural areas in decline" (Leyva and Arias, 2015), which includes economic decline, inefficient land use, scarcity of infrastructure and services, low standard of living, few emerging activities and sectors, exodus, and aging population.

22. See Castro, 2000 and 2003.

23. See articles and essays included in *Temas* 7 (July–September 1996); *Revista Cubana de Antropología* 4:6 (July–December 2002); *Caminos. Revista Cubana de Pensamiento Socioteológico* 24–25 (2002)2002; and *La Gaceta de Cuba* 1 (2005). Later came books: Esteban Morales, *Desafíos de la problemática racial en Cuba* (Havana: La Fuente Viva, 2007); Instituto de Antropología, ed., *Las relaciones raciales en Cuba. Estudios contemporáneos* (Havana: La Fuente Viva, 2010); and Zuleica Romay, *Elogio de la altea o las paradojas de la racialidad* (Havana: Casa de las Américas, 2012).

24. The "Taller enfoque de equidad social en los proyectos de desarrollo: la dimensión racial" consisted of five work sessions involving people from fifteen municipalities, 29–30 September 2015.

25. A member of the management group of one of the organizations, who is a specialist in a research center.

26. Among the community activities promoting racial equity are the community and sociocultural projects, the electoral processes for delegates to the Municipal Assemblies of People's Power, and interest circles for children. Among the few situations cited by actors in the workshops were discussion of religious practices, representations of people of color in public spaces, and cultural products.

27. Taller de Intercambio de Experiencias, 8 December 2015, presentation by Jethro Pettit, project consultant with International Development Studies (IDS).

28. Sometimes this designation matches that of the Consejo Popular, while at other times it corresponds to neighborhoods, settlements, or communities within these demarcations.
29. Such diversity was confirmed in Mederos 2012.

Bibliography

Albizu-Campos, J. C., and G. Rodríguez. 2015. A propósito de la dinámica demográfica cubana actual. In Zabala, Echevarría, Muñoz and Fundora, Eds., *Retos para la equidad social en el proceso de actualización del modelo económico cubano*, pp. 37–48. Havana: Editorial de Ciencias Sociales.

Añé, Lía. 2000. La reforma económica y la economía familiar en Cuba. In *Reforma económica y social en América Latina y el Caribe. Cuatro casos de estudio: Colombia, Costa Rica, Cuba, México.* Bogotá: Ediciones Tercer Mundo.

Brah, Avtar. 2012. Pensando en y a través de la interseccionalidad. In Martha Zapata, S. García, and J. Chan, Eds., *La interseccionalidad en debate: Actas del Congreso Internacional "Indicadores Interseccionales y Medidas de Inclusión Social en Instituciones de Educación Superior" (Berlín, 23–27 Noviembre 2012.)* Berlin: Instituto de Estudios Latinoamericanos de la Freie Universität.

Brah, Avtar, and Ann Phoenix. 2004. "ain't I a woman? revisiting intersectionality." *In Journal of International Women's Studies.* Volume 5:75–86.

Baliño, Gerardo. 1991. *La distribución de los ingresos en Cuba.* Havana: INSIE.

Castro, Fidel. 2000. Discurso pronunciado en el acto de solidaridad con Cuba. Riverside Church, New York, 8 September 2000.

———. 2003. Discurso pronunciado en la clausura del Congreso Pedagogía 2003. Teatro Carlos Marx, Havana, 7 February 2003.

CIEM / PNUD. 2000. *Investigación sobre desarrollo humano y equidad en Cuba 1999.* Havana: Caguayo S. A.

Crenshaw, Kimberlé. 1989. "Demarginalizing the Intersection of Race and Sex: A Black Feminist Critique of Antidiscrimination Doctrine, Feminist Theory and Antiracist Politics." In *The University of Chicago Legal Forum.* Volume 140:139–67.

D´Angelo, Ovidio, et al. 2010. *Desarrollo de subjetividades y espacios de participación comunitaria para la transformación social.* Research report. Havana: Fondos del CIPS.

D'Elia, Yolanda, and T. Maingon. 2004. *La equidad en el desarrollo humano. Estudio conceptual desde el enfoque de igualdad y diversidad.* Caracas: UNDP/ Editorial Torino.

Echevarría, Dayma, and M. Tejuca. 2015. Educación y empleo en Cuba, 2000–2014: entre ajustes y desajustes. In Mayra Espina and D. Echevarría, Eds., *Cuba: los correlatos socioculturales del cambio económico*, pp. 50–78. Havana: Editorial de Ciencias Sociales and Ruth Casa Editorial.

Espina, Mayra. 2006. "La comprensión de la desigualdad." In *Temas.* Number 45:4–16.

———. 2010. *Desarrollo, desigualdad y políticas sociales. Acercamientos desde una perspectiva compleja.* Havana: Publicaciones Acuario.

Espina, M., L. Núñez, L. Martin, V. Togores and G. Angel. 2010. *Informe Desigualdad, equidad y política social. Integración de estudios recientes en Cuba.* Havana: Fondos del CIPS.

Ferree, Myra. 2009. "Intersectional Framing: The Implications of American and European Approaches for Feminist Politics." Presented at Celebrating Intersectionality? Debates in a Multifaceted Concept in Gender Studies, Goethe-University, Frankfurt, 22–23 January 2009.

Ferriol, A., G. Therborn, and R. Castiñeiras. 2004. *Política social: el mundo contemporáneo y las experiencias de Cuba y Suecia.* Havana: INIE.

García Dauder, Silvia. 2003. "Fertilizaciones cruzadas entre la psicología social de la ciencia y los estudios feministas de la ciencia." In *Athenea Digital.* Number 4:109–150.

Íñiguez, Luisa. 2006. "Los archipiélagos donde vivimos los cubanos." In *Temas.* Number 45:23–32.

Leyva, Arisbel, and M. Arias. 2015. Reforma, ruralidad y nuevos campesinos/as en Cuba. Desafíos y propuestas para las políticas públicas. In Mayra Espina and D. Echevarría, Eds., *Cuba: los correlatos socioculturales del cambio económico.* Havana: Editorial de Ciencias Sociales and Ruth Casa Editorial.

Mederos, Anagret. 2012. *El tratamiento de las desigualdades sociales en los proyectos de desarrollo local en Villa Clara.* Master's Thesis, FLACSO-Cuba, Havana.

Montero, Maritza. 2004. *Introducción a la psicología comunitaria. Desarrollo, conceptos y procesos.* Buenos Aires: Editorial Paidós.

ONEI. 2002. *Panorama Económico y Social, Cuba 2001.* Havana.

———. 2012. *Panorama Económico y Social, Cuba 2011.* Havana.

Partido Comunista de Cuba. 2011. *Lineamientos de la política económica y social del Partido y la Revolución.* Havana.

———. 2012. "Documento Base de la 1ra. Conferencia Nacional del Partido Comunista de Cuba."

———. 2016. "Informe Central al 7mo. Congreso del Partido Comunista de Cuba." Havana, 16 April 2016. http://www.cubadebate.cu/noticias/2016/04/17/informe-central-al-vii-congreso-del-partido-comunista-cuba/.

———. 2016. "Proyecto de Conceptualización del Modelo Económico y Social Cubano de Desarrollo Socialista." In *Granma.* 19 April 2016.

———. 2016. "Plan Nacional de Desarrollo Económico y Social hasta 2030: propuesta de visión de la nación, ejes y sectores estratégicos." In *Granma.* 19 April 2016.

PNUD. 1992–2015. *Informes sobre Desarrollo Humano.* Bogotá: Tercer Mundo Editores; New York: Oxford University Press; México: Harla S.A. de C.V.; Madrid: Ediciones Mundi-Prensa.

Portocarrero, Ana Victoria. 2012. Retos de la inclusión social en las instituciones de educación superior. In Martha Zapata, S. García, and J. Chan, Eds., *La interseccionalidad en debate.*

Reygadas, Luis. 2004. "Las redes de la desigualdad: Un enfoque multidimensional." In *Política y Cultura*. Number 22:7–25.

Romero, María Isabel, and Carmen N. Hernández. 2005. Diagnóstico: un acercamiento al tema. In Carmen Nora Hernández, Ed., *Trabajo comunitario. Selección de lecturas*, pp. 523–530. Havana: Editorial Caminos.

Rubalcava, Rosa M., and Vania Salles. 2001. Hogares pobres con mujeres trabajadoras y percepciones femeninas. In Alicia Ziccardi, Ed., *Pobreza, desigualdad social y ciudadania: los límites de las políticas sociales en América Latina*. Buenos Aires: CLACSO, pp. 245–270.

Sotolongo, P. L., and C.J. Delgado. 2006. La complejidad y el diálogo transdisciplinario de saberes. In *La revolución contemporánea del saber y la complejidad social*, pp. 65–77. Buenos Aires: CLACSO. Available at http://bibliotecavirtual.clacso.org.ar/ar/libros/campus/soto/Capitulo%20IV.pdf.

Sousa Santos, Boaventura de. 2009. *Una Epistemología del Sur. La reinvención del conocimiento y la emancipación social*. Buenos Aires: Siglo XXI Editores, CLACSO.

Uriarte, Miren. 2002. *Cuba, Social Policy at a Crossroads: Maintaining Priorities, Transforming Practice*. Boston: Oxfam America.

Yuval-Davis, Nira. 2013. Más allá de la dicotomía del reconocimiento y la redistribución. In Martha Zapata, S. García, and J. Chan, Eds., *La interseccionalidad en debate*.

Zimbalist A., and C. Brundenius. 1989. *The Cuban Economy: Measurement and Analysis of Socialist Performance*. Baltimore: Johns Hopkins University Press.

PART

II

Experimenting with Organizational Designs

4

Municipalization and Social Policy in Cuba

Mayra Espina Prieto

What is known as the "process of updating the economic and social model" has been under way in Cuba since about 2008. This reform seeks to manage a domestic crisis characterized by low economic growth, decapitalization of productive resources, low efficiency and productivity, and a growing trend toward social inequality and disadvantage; at the same time, it seeks to make the social project of socialism more sustainable.[1]

Among the many facets of this reform, those that stand out most—both because they are stressed in the political program and because of their potential impact on social equity and inequality—include a reorganization of property tenure to widen options for non-state property (mixed enterprises, foreign capital, cooperatives, and micro-, small-, and medium-sized private businesses) to generate income and create jobs; a reduction in the function of the state as owner, producer, and central administrator in order to strengthen its role as strategic coordinator, planner, and actor on the national, regional, provincial, and municipal levels; a greater role for local government; social policy mechanisms that specifically address vulnerabilities; and construction of a universal tax system to include all economic subjects and social groups generating and earning income.

Among these changes, the most novel are municipalization, geographic decentralization, and promotion of local development. They imply a substantive change in the way development is managed within the country.[2] A long tradition of centralized management of the economy and social policy, administered along economic sector lines, has thus far resisted attempts at geographical decentralization. However, it appears that now (though not without new and old sources of resistance and obstacles) there is a stronger political commitment to decentralization, and more support from many different actors. Two manifestations confirm that commitment.

The first is the repeated reference to the priority of the municipal sphere in the programmatic documents approved in April 2016 by the Seventh

Congress of the Cuban Communist Party. The document, "Conceptual-ization of Cuban Economic and Social Model of Socialist Development" (PCC, 2016), defines the municipality as the fundamental level of govern-ment and emphasizes its "appropriate authority" (point 100, p. 7); it states that centralized directives must be combined with the decentralization of their implementation (point 210, p. 11); it calls for taxes to develop munic-ipalities (point 337, p. 12) , and it indicates that authority over strategic questions and structural changes will be concentrated at the higher levels, while intermediate and base levels of government and of the state enter-prise system should make decisions about implementation and adminis-tration in the areas of their respective competencies (point 255, p. 13).

Second, in a 2010 address to the National Assembly of People's Power, President Raúl Castro declared that "the authority of . . . provincial and municipal governments will increase. They will be further supported and their faculties will be decentralized from above. . . . municipal governments must have faculties and resources" (Castro, 2010).

Alongside these general political declarations and directives, practical experiences of decentralization are now under way. Although most of these efforts are labeled "experiments" for the moment, they display elements of what the authorities consider the most appropriate path to decentral-ization. Probably because this process proceeds at a pace that is steady but slow, and because public information about it remains limited to general political assessments, there is still no definitive research characterizing and evaluating it beyond preliminary impressions. The first steps of a research project now in progress are centered on the ties linking social policy to municipalization-decentralization-development[3] in order to assess to what degree those processes allow for reduction of poverty and inequality and for promotion of equity and social inclusion.

Theoretical and Methodological Keys to Analyzing Municipalization in Cuba

Within the municipalization/local-development/decentralization triad, the third concept serves as the axis turning the others. It is impossible to manage development at a local (municipal) level without at least a mini-mum degree of decentralization; that is, without opportunities for auton-omous political decision-making and economic resource-management by subnational authorities and institutions.

This study begins by formulating an analytical model to locate the Cuban reform within the theory of decentralization and its potential to gener-ate inclusive development, particularly in reference to reciprocal ties and causalities among decentralization, local social policy, poverty reduction, and increased social equity. Theorists who study state organization and social policies hypothesize the historical exhaustion of the unitary, centralist model as a basic principle of administration. This means that nations no longer apply centralist models of management; rather, the observable and documented trend is toward the disappearance of pure unitary states and the expansion of a public sector structured through multiple levels of government, with a greater or lesser degree of decentralization (Casado, 2005).

This finding implies a corollary underlying the hypothesis and a resulting dynamic of change: local, autonomous governments are positioned to make better decisions about endogenous resource use, launch more productive initiatives, find sources to create local income and offer social services attuned to the demands and needs of their residents. However, the scholarly literature does not provide a conclusive assessment of the results of this process, nor does it describe an unequivocal trend toward better functioning of governments and administrations and effective social policy. Research on such topics is currently under way.

Nonetheless, given that Cuba starts decentralizing after the accumulation of vast experience in Latin America and elsewhere, it is worth comparing the Cuban reform with the theory and practical results produced elsewhere in the region. This allows for drawing inferences about what to expect from this type of change, and what are the optimum conditions for its successful implementation. The logic followed in constructing an analytical model for our research has been to identify the most common approaches to decentralization, municipalization, and local development (the definitions, actors, degrees and dimensions of these processes), as well as the potential for change and the conditions and factors of success most recognized by previous studies.

Economic theory defines *decentralization* as a concept of geographic reorganization of the distribution of power that opts for shifting responsibilities for planning, management, assembly, and distribution of resources from the central government and its agencies to subnational geographic-administrative units, distinguishing three *degrees of decentralization:* deconcentration, delegation, and devolution (Rondinelli, 1981):

- *Deconcentration* refers to the redistribution of decision-making and financial and administrative responsibility from the central government to entities spread out throughout the national territory.[4]
- *Delegation* implies the transfer of decision-making and administrative power, including financial aspects, toward semi-autonomous

organizations not completely controlled by the central government, yet ultimately responsible to that level.

- *Devolution* transfers authority, financing, and administration to local governments with a relatively high level of autonomy; autonomy is understood to mean legally recognized authority (with respect to the central government and/or other territorial management levels) over the use of the resources under their responsibility.

According to Rondinelli, autonomy does not mean freedom from responsibility to render account vertically to higher levels of government or horizontally to the local citizenry but, rather, a strengthening of the political aspects of decentralized decision-making including, among others, shaping local development strategies and designing and implementing local social policy. Thus the crux of decentralization lies in the devolution of political authority to local governments. Obviously, though, such autonomy is always relative in the sense that every subnational territory in a decentralized management system retains ties of subordination-cooperation-complementarity with the national unit.

Given that this is a matter of distributing power, an important issue is that of the *actors* in decentralization and their positions with respect to the necessary, possible, or pertinent radicalness[5] of the process. From the perspective of structuration theory (which permeates studies of decentralization and local development), a *social actor* (also called *social agent*) is an individual or collective subject with the capacity or potential (depending on their degree of power over the matter in question) to intervene in a course of action, influence its tendency of change, and modify some aspect of its results; this demonstrates the nexus between agency (transformative capacity) and power (Giddens, 2001).

Thus, the introduction of decentralization and local development policies has followed two paths: an inductive (top-down) variant driven by central governments motivated to lighten state budget responsibilities, alleviate financial crises of their central treasuries, and efficiently mobilize and manage local resources toward national development; and a reactive (bottom-up) variant responding to civil society demands for citizen rights and the demands of local levels of government to increase their resource administration functions.

The inductive approach also comes from international agencies (those that supply financial resources and methodological approaches), seconded by national governments. It had the most strength in Latin America during the 1980s in the political-administrative reforms designed by international finance agencies as part of a crisis-management methodology and as part of the package of neoliberal fiscal adjustment policies. The "bottom-up" path has been supported by civil society organizations, especially since the 1990s as part of the local development approach. It has also been supported by international cooperation agencies (United Nations, governmental international development agencies, and international NGOs), and a decisive role has been played by the academy in providing concepts, approaches, and methodological means of implementation and evaluation, as well as in advisory roles.

Decentralization from above has the advantage of being able to begin with a given technical design that can be implemented through existing public institutions by means of the necessary normative framework. However, various studies show that in the examples of national states in Latin America, the key behind their cession of powers was their pressing need to eliminate services that the national budget could not cover, a cut not necessarily accompanied by a well-designed policy or a coherent change in legal norms. The crisis-management factor has been decisive, more than the possibility of empowering local civil society (Finot, 2001).

The literature identifies five interrelated *dimensions* of the decentralization process (Mejía & Atanasio, 2001):

- *Political-Administrative.* Total or partial transfer of state functions to local governments, provided they have been directly elected and have legislative powers. The nucleus of this dimension consists of an electoral system and a legal-constitutional framework.
- *Spending.* Subnational governments will make spending decisions and provide social services under the principle of *subsidiarity* (each function should be assigned to the lowest level of government that could efficiently perform it). This ranges from complete discretion in assigning resources to a model in which much spending remains centrally determined. Although the underlying assumption is that greater autonomy in spending leads to better adaptation of local policies and services to the needs of the populace, there are also arguments in favor of inflexible spending: national policy, importance of certain public goods, and local institutional incapacity.
- *Taxing Power.* Local government income to be generated through taxes and through total or partial control over local tax policy.
- *System of Territorial Transfer.* Appropriations from the central government to support local budgets, with greater or lesser degrees of centralized decision-making about their uses. These monies

complement local income, compensate for territorial disadvantages, guarantee local implementation of national policies, and reward successful activity.

- *Decisions about Debt.* Autonomy to borrow funds from public or private institutions to support identified local development policies (not current operational spending).

It is not always possible or necessary to implement all five dimensions or to do so to the same degree. The strength of the national and local institutions that guarantee the effective functioning of these mechanisms, and the subnational authorities' capacity to implement and manage them, are critical factors for the radicalness of the process.

All of the above leads to the conclusion that the nature of decentralization is essentially political because it implies increasing the capacities and decision-making powers of local actors. Yet key to this political character is the coordination and reconciliation of administrative and financial decisions with strategic choices about local economic and social development. The political profile is strengthened to the degree that local actors can make more strategic decisions, not only administrative ones.

Drawing on a long legal tradition, municipalities and their place in the territorial organization of a national state have an organic connection with decentralization. The concept of *municipalization* as used in this chapter refers to a reorganization of public administration and finance that prepares the municipal authority to manage its resources autonomously, albeit to varying limits and degrees and in various areas. It also alludes to the emergence and strengthening of local actors (government, civil society, disadvantaged groups) in making policy decisions on a micro-level.

A municipality is a community of persons located within in the same area, working toward the goal of meeting common needs. The municipality becomes a basic local entity of the state's territorial organization, one with full juridical status and the capacity to fulfil its goals (Casado, 2005). The municipality's profile as a small space and entity for managing and meeting popular needs also legitimizes it as a space for implementing social services on a micro-scale.

A central issue in the confluence of decentralization, municipalization, local development, and social policy is that of *local autonomy*, that is, the community's right to participate, through its own organs of government, in the administration and oversight of the issues and areas that concern it. Effective exercise of local autonomy depends on two elements: making sure that local entities are competent to manage sectors of public activity of local interest, and endowing the representative bodies of the community with *powers* to make sovereign decisions about these.

This requires a normative framework that defines, at minimum, the legal status of the municipalities and the principles, regulations, and instruments for coordination between this level of government and other public bodies at other levels; the mechanisms that reconcile local autonomy with overall state action; the form in which local entities participate in making legislative decisions that affect their interests; and adequate financing (Casado, 2005).

Completing our analytic triad by combining a variety of "classical" Latin American definitions, we may define *local development* as a process of growth and structural change that, by activating a given territory's existing potential under local community leadership, generates increased welfare among the population. Development results from concerted action on the part of multiple agents to transform a given territory in a desired direction, with local actors' decisions being preeminent, and depending on the territory itself as the fundamental resource—its physical area and its resources, the organized citizens, local institutions, culture, shared values that generate confidence and solidarity, and its historical patrimony. Local development is based on the capacity of the agents who live in, act in, and share that micro-space to mobilize those potentials on behalf of consensually created progress goals. The working hypothesis is that localities and other territorial units have untapped resources and economies of scale that form the basis of their development potential (Vázquez Barquero, 1988, 2000; Arocena, 1995; Coraggio, 2003; Alburquerque, 2004).

The literature recognizes decentralization, municipalization, and local development as having a variety of *potentials and advantages* for reducing poverty and promoting inclusion and social equity (Jütting, et al., 2005):

- Generating their own budget funds and thus increasing opportunities for progressive growth in local social services and other policies.
- Identifying the needs and demands of the public as a whole and of poor and disadvantaged groups would improve, because the authorities are closer to citizens and can consult citizens directly without large transaction costs.
- Seeing and responding to the heterogeneity of people's preferences and needs would overcome the homogenization involved in national social policies and thus favor social polices of diversity.
- Increasing citizen control over the results of government as carried out by the authorities.

- Reducing the cost of providing services by using local resources and simple solutions with designs adapted to local needs and culture.
- Increasing the efficiency of public services to the degree that public policies come closer to the preferences of voters.
- Contributing to reducing disparities in regional development by generating opportunities for autonomous identification and mobilization of local resources.

The possibilities for positive results from implementing systems of lesser or greater degrees of local autonomy depend on specific circumstances of national and subnational contexts, such as the absolute and relative resources of the subnational governments, the degree of distributive and territorial inequality, the level of fiscal pressure, historical and cultural elements, population density, and others. But despite the influence of such specificities, it is possible to identify *basic conditions* and *success factors* for generating the expected effects (Rondinelli, 1981):

- A policy of decentralization that clarifies goals and reflects a level of consensus among actors at diverse levels of public administration and civil society.
- A normative framework that legitimizes local competencies and establishes relationships among the levels of government.
- Mechanisms of coordination, both horizontal (inter-locality) and vertical (between levels of government).
- Local financial sufficiency.
- Capacities (in terms of knowledge, information, and management tools) of local authorities.
- Decision-making at the local level should be a democratic and participatory process. The citizenry has a real opportunity to participate directly in decision-making about local policy issues and, as voters, it can reward or punish officials for their actions and results. Local democracy is an indispensable prerequisite for public goods being adequately aligned with popular needs.
- The population receiving benefits of public goods must take on (totally or partially) the cost of providing them. The bulk of local resources should come from local taxes or other local sources.
- Subnational governments must not be captured by local interest groups and must avoid the risk of corruption at a local level that would offset the potential benefits of decentralization.
- Desire and commitment from central government to preserve equity and develop greater social cohesion by means of transfers when necessary to assure comparable services in all regions.

- Quality of information systems and knowledge management sufficient for making informed decisions.

Under *measuring results*, four types of indicators are recommended: *administrative process*—real capacity for decision and action by local government working together with central government (important decisions for local development) and in relation to the municipal budget; *effects on the populace's welfare*—performance in areas such as education, health, housing, employment, income, poverty level, social equity, and gender equity; *macroeconomic changes*—increases in per-capita output and productivity, decreases in budget deficits; *regional convergence*—narrowing of output gaps between regions and/or municipalities, and between levels of municipal development.[6]

This analytical framework serves as a methodological guide for a preliminary assessment of the Cuban decentralizing reform, especially as it affects changes in social policy and opportunities to promote equity.

Decentralization and Social Policy in the Cuban Reform: Actors and Proposals

The decentralization efforts in the current Cuban reform are not completely new. Over the past four decades, this project has had various promoters following various approaches, and it has arguably taken root in diverse areas of politics and academia within the country, giving it a certain base and national legitimacy. A survey of that recent history helps to map out four key actors: government (national and local), civil society organizations, international cooperation agencies, and the academy.

The government actor is the central public institutional order—the actor holding the real power to make nationwide decisions. It had initiated at least three experiences of distributing degrees of power to subnational levels. The first was the creation in 1975 of provincial and municipal levels of government whose officials are chosen by citizen vote. The second, during the 1993 reforms, gave some autonomy to localities, such as a wider range of decision-making for provincial and municipal governments about local industries and services and the financing of development projects; central authorities also introduced the approach called *Dirección por Objetivos*, which involved local governments in the definition of objectives for their level in response to the needs and demands of their voters. The third experience, by a law enacted in 2000, has been the creation of People's Councils, a submunicipal structure made up of representatives of local government and local organizations and state enterprises to increase knowledge of, and attention to, the needs and interests of the population.

The government actor has also included a territorial approach within the design of economic and social policies under the principle of socio-economic leveling of the country's regions. The creation of the Physical Planning Institute is the most important reflection of this commitment; the Institute has both provincial and municipal departments, charged with planning at their levels, identification of local resources and potentials, and design of urban planning and provision of services.

However, none of these reforms brought a substantive change in the system of centralized administration. The purpose of the first was to improve the organization of decision-making at the aggregate level, maintaining the supremacy of the national level and the sectoral[7] approach to economic and social management. Still today, municipalities lack clear powers (they have only assigned functions), and the main powers remain with the national structure. The second was limited to immediate crisis management and a certain degree of delegation of functions from the national level to more local ones. The third is a structure of agreement and coordination but without resources or authority to make binding decisions or implement accords.

Their real importance lies in having created an institutional scaffolding in the subnational territories, structured as a replica of the central government to carry out government directives; local resources are devoted primarily to fulfill national interests but with the capacity to take on functions of local interest.

At the same time, the severity of the crisis of the 1990s and the attendant unraveling of the country's productive fabric (and, thus, of the sources of employment and income) and weakening of public services and of the state's ability to meet the population's basic needs, along with a rise in poverty and social inequality, generated a context open to the search for alternative solutions. This offered an entry point for local development and initiatives for change at the micro-level.

Among these initiatives, what stands out in terms of national government action involving both localities and the academy is the 1995 creation of the Ministerial Group for Integrated Community Work and of its Technical Advising Team. This team crafted a diagnostic instrument that revealed the major obstacles generated by centralist and sectoral practices with regard to active mobilization of local resources. These include: direct action by national agencies affecting municipalities; uniformity in policies (which annuls and ignores territorial heterogeneity); fragmentation and verticalism in local institutions' decision-making; insufficient citizen participation; absence of local development strategies; and weakness in

municipal authorities' preparedness for local management and identification of priorities and resources (Guzón, 2006).

The crisis was also the context for the rise of various NGOs as result of
increase in social heterogeneity and international contacts that followed the
disappearance of the European socialist bloc. Many of these NGOs focused
on working directly with communities and activating micro-spaces, which
aligned them with a local development approach that sought a recovery
of values, environmental protection, strengthened identities, access to cultural goods, active citizenship, and attention to vulnerable groups.[8]

In their relations with the national government and academic institutions, international development agencies have also contributed to the visibility of the topics of decentralization and local governability, principally
by way of the emphasis on sustainability and human development.[9]

The academic sector has been very active in working on these issues.
Without any direct power over decisions, but with legitimated knowledge that enables it to generate and propose innovations and to transmit
demands to decision-makers in the course of a dialogue between research
and policy, the Cuban academy has especially promoted the path to
municipalization, local development, and local social policy. The demand
for municipalization has come primarily from the fields of law, constitutional studies, and political science. Its promoters form part of a long
national historical tradition centered on recovery of the municipal sphere
as a means to strengthen popular action in government by virtue of its
built-in opportunities for participation. This current of thought, though
internally heterogeneous, has two points of essential consensus: promoting
the municipal space as a site for access to citizens' rights and platform of
democratization, and urging municipal autonomy and guarantees for its
exercise. These imply, at a minimum, the need for a normative framework
(a law of municipalities, for instance) to institutionalize municipal authority and competencies (including financial ones) and participatory organs
for decision-making (see Pérez and Díaz, 2015).

From the economic side, the local decentralization agenda grows out
of a diagnosis that the lack of efficiency and productivity in state enterprises and of self-sustainable regional or local development in Cuba can be
explained by the indecisive swinging between various degrees of centralization and decentralization in decision-making, and also by regional and
local lack of autonomy. Overcoming these faults requires: 1) a combination
of centralization and decentralization as complementary elements rather
than antagonistic poles; and 2) incorporating subnational territories into
a positive sustainable development dynamics on the basis of municipal

administration that is efficient, effective, and efficacious (See Díaz, 2014; Mulet, 2015).

A current of thought identifying the micro-level as a development arena has been present since the 1990s, born out of the ideas of urban planners and researchers of territorial heterogeneity, inequality, social policy, participation, and the construction of knowledge. A factor favoring localism has been the presence of universities and their branches in every province and municipality of the country, so that the subnational sphere has been an object of immediate and direct investigation and an optimal space to develop knowledge for decision-making and innovation. These thinkers' agenda centers on recognizing the local level (the municipality and its communities) as both legitimate and relevant to any country's development strategy—linked to the national level but important on its own and with its own options for progress in local terms (see, for instance, Dilla et al., 1998; Guzón, 2006; Íñiguez, 2014; Núñez, 2014).

Researchers on poverty and inequality have contributed proposals for municipalization-territorialization of social policy. One thesis contends that the current increase in inequality and disadvantage and the difficulty in eliminating a growing stratum of poverty result from the preeminence of universal, centralized, and sectoral policies, with insufficient implementation of affirmative and targeted actions. This policy model conserves inequality-producing mechanisms because of excessive generalism and insufficient sensitivity to diversity (because it treats the needs of diverse social groups and regions in a homogeneous way). Because of the weight of this system, disadvantaged groups are less able to take advantage of equal opportunities; while in absolute terms they may improve their socioeconomic condition, they do not overcome relative disadvantage and remain in a vulnerable condition with respect to any negative occurrences (see Espina, 2008; Espina and Echevarría, 2015; Zabala, 2013; Zabala, et al., 2015).

Combining the conclusions and recommendations of studies of inequality and social policy carried out in the past decade with additional expert consultation yields the following panorama of the ten most prioritized social problems and proposals for managing them:[10]

A. Prioritized Problems for Social Policy

1. Impoverishment. Presence of a 20 percent stratum of urban poverty that has been difficult to reduce.
2. Inability of income from wages and social security to guarantee access to consumption of basic goods and services.

3. Strengthened awareness of class, race, and gender, and the equity gaps associated with them.
4. Process of concentration of income (growth in the Gini coefficient).
5. Generational reproduction of disadvantage.
6. Overrepresentation of the elderly in the stratum of poverty, insufficient service network to attend to their needs, and difficulties in getting access to the services that exist.
7. Few employment and income options that match the qualifications and expectations of the youth.
8. Strengthened association of territory, inequality and social disadvantage, and spatial concentration of disadvantage and poverty: disadvantaged territories with low Territorial Development Indices (the eastern provinces plus Camagüey and Pinar del Río); critical living conditions in mountain areas; rural areas with lower levels of development and comparative disadvantage with respect to access to social services (education, water, electricity).
9. Exclusion or weak connection to networks of social support and services for people in unhealthy and improvised neighborhoods formed because of domestic migration and insufficient housing supply. Emergence of substandard settlements in urban areas; emergence of slum conditions in urban neighborhoods and re-emergence of "spontaneous" settlements that have revived social and environmental segregation.
10. Inequality of access to comfortable housing and habitat. Spatial disconnection because deficient public transportation and road networks limit exchange and communication among localities.

B. Social Policy Proposals

1. Maintain the existing principle and universal coverage of social policy while introducing elements of targeting, affirmative action, and territorialization that are preferential to disadvantaged groups so that the benefits prove more effective in reducing equity gaps.
2. Create specific social policies for the poor and vulnerable population, combining assistance with investment and social inclusion (providing jobs, access to higher qualification and educational levels, and family services that facilitate work and study).
3. Privilege the local-territorial level in social policies because of its potential to identify diversity of needs and demands, and its potential to create inclusive services using minimal and local resources.
4. Change macroeconomic policies of social spending: strengthen the areas of housing, employment-income, habitat, and community environment.

5. Craft direct affirmative actions (favoring disadvantaged groups' access to advantageous positions) and indirect actions (territorially targeted universal policies) to close off channels that reproduce disadvantage associated with race, gender, territory, and their spatial expressions.

6. Invigorate direct mechanisms of citizen participation (public consultation on policy, participatory planning and budgeting, grassroots audits assessments) in the design of local social policy and monitoring of its results and benefits.

7. Reform municipal administration by means of a bottom-up planning approach. Local government should lead territorial strategic development projects (horizontal synchronization of interests), and should have powers of financial administration and resource management.

8. Expand the role of subnational territories for generating jobs, production, and incomes. There is a need for municipal employment policy based on a real determination of local capacities and potentials and a broad vision of contemporary avenues of job creation.

9. Establish at the municipal level specialized services of information, advising, and training for work and job searches.

10. Reform the current model (centralized and sectoral) of habitat management, converting it to a decentralized model based in municipalities and on economic, social, and environmental viability. Combine public, private, and cooperative subjects in the local production of materials and the construction, repair, and financing of housing. Shape and link assistance and proactive tools.

This panorama of identified social problems and policy proposals may not be complete, but it reveals the potential seen in the territorial-local-municipal level for overcoming poverty and equity gaps, when accompanied by a change in the overall focus of social policy, shifting away from the nearly exclusive use of homogenized/universal policies, centralization, and sectoral organization, toward attention to diversity and disadvantage by means of municipalization, focus on particular groups and territories, and citizen participation. This also implies spending priorities directed toward access to jobs, income, housing, and habitat.

Decentralization in the Current Cuban Reform: Advances and Obstacles

As set forth in the Guidelines and corroborated in the 2016 Seventh Congress of the PCC, social policy will preserve its universalizing style and provision of free and equal services in areas seen as basic (education, health, culture, and sports), but it will accord greater weight to compensate needy individuals, to the tax system as a tool to redistribute income and a key source of financing for social policy, and to municipalization and territorial decentralization so that municipal governments can increase their powers to stimulate local development.[11]

Beyond this general strategic intention, the reform process has so far tried out five mechanisms of decentralized municipal administration to empower local social services with the potential to strengthen equity and reduce poverty. These mechanisms are means for financing local development and social policy, granting a degree of deconcentration and delegation, and decentralizing the political-administrative and public-spending spheres. The general characteristics of these mechanisms are as follows.

Municipal Initiatives for Local Development (Spanish initials IMDL). This is a stimulus fund created within the Ministry of Economy and Planning (MEP) to support productive initiatives identified by municipal governments, approved by Municipal Administrative Councils (CAM), and authorized by Provincial Administrative Councils (CAP). Such funding increases local governments' ability to implement social policy and services because its procedures require that 70 percent of profits from these initiatives must be reinvested in productive projects, and 30 percent in social projects. As of this writing, 67 municipalities (of the total 168 in the country) have been able to finance projects out of this fund; appropriations from the respective CAMs total approximately 670,000 CUC (convertible Cuban pesos).

The main difficulties identified by the MEP lie in the absence of medium-term, municipal-level development plans, which limits the local institutions' ability to identify initiatives and priorities; insufficient number of productive entities to create and implement local projects; lack of wholesale markets; delays in importing resources; and insufficient identification and mobilization of local human, financial, infrastructural, and organizational resources. Some experts note that, besides these obstacles, sectoral interests and national priorities weigh heavily in the IMDL approval process, so the priority on developing a preeminence of local actors and interests is not always fulfilled (Llanes, 2015).

Territorial Taxation. The 2012 tax law[12] says that every productive establishment must pay one percent of its annual profits to the municipal government under whose jurisdiction it falls. The local CAM can freely decide what this local income should be used for, except for using it for investments, which require approval at higher levels. The limitations on this measure's impact are related to the sums that may be available, which depend on each municipality's economic development (sums currently range from 80,000 to 4,000,000 pesos). There are also limitations in the use to which they may be put (since they cannot be used for investments), and by municipalities' lack of experience with this type of autonomous management.

At the same time, the law exempts some entities from paying taxes (including hotels administered by foreign companies, joint ventures, and other mixed-capital firms), and many of these are the entities with the highest earnings. The decision to exempt them from taxation is made at the national level on an annual basis. The main goal is to create incentives for foreign investment, but the exemptions also deprive municipalities of significant income that could be decisive to their opportunities to promote local development. The municipalities also lack decision-making power over tax policy, so they cannot use this element to generate local policy and local services by means of offering tax advantages to the small business sector or the cooperative one.

Marked territorial differences in wealth translate into sizable asymmetries in the collection of taxes and the creation of decentralized municipal budgets. For the moment, central transfers compensate for inequalities and disadvantages,[13] assuring universal offerings of social services (primarily education, health care, and social assistance) throughout the country. However, there is as yet no solidarity fund supported by municipal taxes to reward efficient operations and to assist disadvantaged areas when necessary.

New Experimental Structure of Provincial and Municipal Governments. The provinces of Artemisa and Mayabeque are conducting an experiment in separation of functions of the entities currently involved in the subnational governing structure—the administrative councils (CAP in the provinces, CAM in the municipalities) and the corresponding Assemblies of People's Power.[14] This new division of power concentrates executive functions in the Councils and subordinates them to the Assemblies, whose roles as local representative and legislative bodies are reinforced. The national state institutions acting on the local level (referred to as "delegations") are converted into departments of the municipal and provincial governments themselves, with only a methodological link to the national level. This experiment is still in process. Its preliminary results have just recently been assessed by political authorities, and the extension of this system throughout the country, beginning in 2017, is expected. The 2016 Seventh Congress of the Cuban Communist Party declared in this regard:

. . . also underway is the experimental project in the provinces of Artemisa and Mayabeque, with a view toward their subsequent generalization that, among other aspects, involves separating the functions of the Provincial Assemblies of People's Power leadership and those of the Administration Council, allowing the Assemblies to focus their attention on their work with delegates, people's councils, and the work of commissions responsible for supervision and fiscal control. The application of the new local administrative model has seen a notable reduction in positions within these bodies at a provincial and municipal level, without disrupting their functioning, but rather strengthening their ability to carry out the state role assigned to them (Castro 2016).

One study concluded that the new administration model still supplants local autonomy by a centralizing mechanism because the decree states that the mission of the local administration created by the Assembly of People's Power is to "fulfill functions of state character assigned to the territorial government to carry out." The analyst observes that this is not the same as governing the territory; it is merely being the executor of certain governmental functions assigned by a different entity of public power (Matilla, 2015). This deformation should be corrected in the planned extension of the best practices of this experiment.

Program of Integrated Development (PDI). This is a program created by the MEP and the IPF (Physical Planning Institute), experimentally applied in 29 municipalities. It seeks to create local development programs that integrate nationally planned economic activities with those of the provinces and municipalities. Municipalities are empowered to decide where to place national and local financing. In this experience, too, limited local administrative powers and the still-present and predominant centralization make an integrated vision of local development difficult to fulfill (IPF, 2012). These variants of decentralized administration generate tensions with the official instruments still in use (the *Plan Annual de la Economía* and the *Planificación por Objetivos*, among others) which retain their sectoral and vertical character and are difficult to adapt to the logic of local development.

Subsidies for Housing Construction and Repair. This completely local instrument to identify and assist socially disadvantaged groups has been functioning since 2012. Assignment of the funds is in the hands of the CAM, and the financing source is revenue from sale of construction materials at the municipal level. In 2015, a total 63,000 people in disadvantaged situations received these subsidies, worth 1 billion CUP.

One difficulty of implementation lies in insufficient training of the municipal officials in charge of identifying the groups in need and facilitating their application and award of the subsidy. Some innovative municipalities (Aguada de Pasajeros in the province of Cienfuegos, and Manicaragua in Villa Clara)—having realized that existence of the service is not a sufficient condition to get those who most need it to make use of it—have initiated an outreach service in which specialists of the Municipal Housing Department and the Community Architect Program visit vulnerable outlying communities to inform the populace of this opportunity and offer application advice.

Intuitively, these municipalities have adopted the approach of *inclusive local services with outreach to beneficiaries*, one of the basic tools of local equity policy that is practically unknown in Cuba. The logic underlying this procedure is that it is not enough to create a service (even one based on a real need and demand of a specific population or community) for the community to benefit from it. Frequently these opportunities are sought (and captured) by middle-class strata, while those most in need of the service make less use of it (due to lack of information, mobility, or self-esteem). The proposed remedy is to seek out prioritized beneficiaries and offer them the service, on-site and adapted to their means of real access. A wide range of such inclusive service mechanisms have been put into practice in Latin America, including micro-credit for disadvantaged sectors, flexible options for education and training, advice on accessing legal rights, care services for children, seniors and household members with health problems, etc. This could be quite powerful in Cuban conditions.

However, one of the least-developed themes in the process of reform and decentralization is local management of policies of social inclusion, targeted benefits, and affirmative attention to social disadvantage. Preliminary studies show that some measures applied in a primarily economic and productive sense (broadening private and cooperative work, private credit, land grants, and others) have yielded undesirable effects on social equity and, unintentionally, have generated processes of exclusion that affect historically disadvantaged groups and so reinforce old mechanisms of reproduction of inequality.

For example, only 26 percent of those employed in the small-scale private sector are women. The majority of working women (67 percent of them) are not independent proprietors or self-employed, but wage workers whose average earnings are less than those of men (Echevarría and Lara, 2012). Blacks and mixed-race individuals are under-represented in self-employment, whether as employers, in nonfarm cooperatives, or in the best-paid jobs (Espina, 2012). Policies for providing credit to the self-employed/small-business sector require loan guarantees from the borrowers (in the form of assets such as homes or jewels); this excludes the least-favored sectors and so accentuates equity gaps (Pajón and León, 2015).

The point to stress is that social policy continues to be centralized and homogeneous, thus ignoring diversity and the undesirable effects that arise when not all social groups or territories start from similar conditions. That assessment does not mean that all policies must be local, municipal, and decentralized, but rather that a coordinated combination of administrative levels and sources of financing as well as a combination of mechanisms (some universal, some targeted and affirmative) are essential to overcoming gaps in equity.

At the same time, international cooperation agencies, provincial governments, and municipal governments are implementing (even in the same locations in some cases) what are generically called "local development projects" centered on building local actors' capacities for self-management. These projects seek to strengthen local leaders' management skills on the understanding that municipal governments lack technical knowledge and practical experience in autonomous decision-making, a problem that is one of the most severe limitations to promoting local development. The tradition of centralized and sectoral public administration, with mechanisms for citizens participation through consultation and representation but few for direct participation in the design, monitoring, and evaluation of social policies or other public affairs, has generated this deficit that must be reversed in any process of transition toward municipalization (see Guzón and Hernández, 2015).

These select programs employ a variety of tools for decentralizing management, but for purposes of this study we will point out two:

Municipal Development Strategies (Spanish initials EDM). Designed by the Center for Local and Community Development (CEDEL) as part of the PRODEL project (Program for Strengthening Municipal Capacities for Local Development) supported by the Swiss Agency for Development and Cooperation (COSUDE), this mechanism seeks to build local governments' and other local actors' capacities for strategic action and the formulation and implementation of municipal programs and projects with an integrated, coordinated, and sustainable approach to development. It offers a methodological guide to the design process and a municipal strategy that includes diagnostics focused on social and gender equity, identification of goals, priorities and resources, sources of financing, coordination of actors (public, private, institutional, social organizations), and a variety of phases of citizen consultation and participation (Various authors, 2011).

Seventy-three Cuban municipalities are now using EDM, and PRODEL has trained 2,300 local officials and specialists in its use, as well as 57 national and 30 provincial officials. Local authorities involved in the project feel that design mechanisms of EDM have strengthened their capacities for autonomous decision-making, even within Cuba's restricted local administrative framework, and they feel it has allowed them to increase opportunities for citizen participation, administrative transparency, and representing popular demands in local government decision-making.[15]

Of course, the still-undefined municipal authority and scarce funding sources for local development limit the opportunities for EDM's implementation and spread and the potential for strategic management to translate into a stronger productive fabric, better municipal services, and concrete material benefits, particularly for disadvantaged groups. Still, the project has the effect of demonstrating that strategic decentralized development management is possible and advantageous in Cuban conditions.

Participatory Budgeting. An example of participatory budgeting is the initiative called *XtuBarrio*, carried out in a People's Council in the municipality of Old Havana as part of a cooperation project between the Office of the Historian of the City and COSUDE.[16] This initiative should not be seen as isolated because it is connected with other participatory mechanisms supported by the joint project. But it is the first such experience in the country, and in spite of it its departure from the usual practice of budgetary decision-making and appropriation, it operated with success and won support from local citizens.

A fund of 100,000 convertible pesos (CUC, donated by the Swiss agency) was made available to resolve community problems in line with citizen proposals. According to data from the Historian's Office, the project had more than 80 percent citizen participation, involving concrete, well-considered proposals; citizens demonstrated abilities to negotiate, offer arguments, and make collective decisions. The result of the exercise was the decision to rebuild a primary school in the neighborhood in 2014, still an ongoing project.[17]

A study of fiscal decentralization in Cuba argues that without competent officials it is almost impossible for the municipality to carry out its constitutionally defined role as the entity equipped to satisfy basic local needs and make autonomous decisions about applying the budget toward local development ends. The study also shows the dysfunctionality of the budget as a tool of territorial administration because of several factors: the Municipal Administrative Council's approval of the draft budget being a purely formal exercise; the lack of legal clarity with respect to the function of the Municipal Assembly in the budget approval process; the limited room for decision-making by that body in relation to budget implementation; and the absence of citizen input from the entire process of the budget's design, oversight, and implementation (Díaz, 2015). In such conditions it is very difficult to put a working participatory mechanism into practice, but still, the new authorization for subnational taxation indicates that, in the short run, local budgetary management with popular participation will be possible and relevant.

In sum, the balance of recent experiences is positive and shows that municipalization, although unfolding only slowly and still insufficiently practiced, allows for more local participation, for structuring localities and communities as sites for design and implementation of social policy, and for granting more importance to the role of micro-scale decisions in the social agenda, shaping policies that are more closely aligned to the needs of local populations.

Final Comments: Does Municipal Decentralization Demonstrate Potential for Reducing Poverty and Generating Social Inclusion?

This key question still cannot be answered because the answer would require information not yet available, such as levels and trends of poverty, inequality, and human development on a municipal scale. Cuba lacks these basic data to assess decentralization policy.

Attempting some approximate answers, one could say that the reform now under way is the introduction of a delayed inductive decentralization into a situation where the model of centralist planning and administration has been exhausted. The reform's leading actor, the national state authority, has established a general strategy that opts for decentralization so as to lighten the burdens on the central budget and to more efficiently mobilize local resources to satisfy the needs of the population and contribute to national development.

This perspective coincides on some points with the approaches and demands of other sectors (academia, civil society, local government, international cooperation agencies) that see local autonomy and citizen participation at the municipal level as an opportunity for democratization and sustainability of development, one that goes beyond crisis management and economic aspects and has the potential to stimulate social, political, and cultural progress.

For the moment, decentralization is limited to a mix of aspects in the political and taxation dimensions, and it partially loosens power concentration and implements some delegation without going as far as devolution. The level of municipal autonomy is still low, and the heavy influence of national, provincial, and sectoral decisions inhibits the leadership roles of local actors.

Taking note of the full range of actors who legitimate the idea of decentralization and their proposals and agendas, it can be inferred that the political conditions are present to imbue the process with greater dynamism and radicalness than it has had so far, so as to hasten the creation of necessary conditions and leverage the success factors identified by theory. The key for such radicalization resides in greater local autonomy and a system of guarantees to bolster it.

By way of conclusion, we can review the approaches advocated by actors in the academy and local government. What would be required to create the basic conditions for decentralization and to promote the factors that would contribute to its success? The answer is to move forward in at least four directions:

- Creation of the legal framework. Modification of the Constitution to overcome the existing constitutional interpretation that the local sphere is meant to satisfy *minimal* local needs. That understanding suggests that the municipality is not seen as a prioritized area for development, but only as a primary site for the solution of problems; the macro-governmental sphere is the problem-solver. A law of municipalities could offer clear designations of powers according to level of administration, in line with the principle of subsidiarity; it could guarantee local autonomy via fiscal decentralization. This would include granting the municipalities some levels of decision-making about the planning, supervision, and execution of capital spending.
- Increasing decentralization of spending, and enabling municipalities to implement social services according to local needs, with a focus on equity and inclusion. A first element of inclusive services would be broad visibility and easy access to information about job possibilities, social assistance, and services. Another is to set up skill-building and advising offices to help people find or generate employment in the new circumstances, giving preference (that is, creating favorable

conditions of access) to women, non-whites, rural dwellers, and others at disadvantage.

- Implementing mechanisms of financial equity and of inclusive and mutual-aid financing. Any effort to modify disadvantaged groups' living conditions requires financial resources to pay for needed services, and also help for potential beneficiaries to create undertakings that generate work and income. Loans could be offered at very low interest or no interest, through public support for the formation of community savings groups and loan funds, as well as community investment or enterprise groups built on neighborliness and trust. Public municipal institutions would provide incentives for such initiatives and offer financial and legal training and advice.
- Direct citizen participation. Generating more equity via decentralization requires agile and direct participatory tools, such as public meetings and consultation, participatory budgeting, and community diagnostics. These tools have the virtue of increasing local government's capacity to make contact with groups that do not participate through traditional channels, and to encourage emergence of diversity and of more diverse voices and demands, especially from disadvantaged sectors.

Notes

1. Analysis of the Cuban reform makes use of Castro 2008 a and b; Castro, 2016; and PCC 2011 and 2016.
2. See especially Guidelines 35–37, 120, and 121 (PCC, 2011).
3. This research does not assume that decentralization, local development, and local social policy refer only to the municipal level. There can be multiple subnational divisions (regional, provincial, municipal, inter-municipal, community, and division according to natural or economic units, among others). In the case of the current Cuban reform, though, the municipality is the organizational and administrative entity that, for reasons of convention and practicality, has been identified as the key stage for local development and the micro-link in the chain of decentralization. This is because the municipality is the country's smallest level of government and public decision-making. Also, in the Cuban constitutional tradition the municipality is recognized as the basic space for the exercise of citizen's rights and access to justice. For more on the topic of localities and territories, see Íniguez (2014), who suggests overcoming ". . . the assumption that local is synonymous with municipal . . ." Discussion of citizenship, rights, and the municipality in Cuba can be found in Pérez and Díaz, 2015.
4. Territory is defined as organized, delimited geographic space that is used as an element of administration. It includes the specific environmental

characteristics and natural, economic, social, and cultural resources that are based in and tied to that space, as well as the actors who interact there. Its size and level can range from the micro (settlements, communities, and municipalities), the mid-level (intra-national regions) and the macro (nations, international regions). See Alburquerque (1995, p. 3) and Íñiguez (2014, p. 46).

5. "Radicalness" refers to degrees and dimensions of decentralization that result in real autonomy and competencies acquired by actors and government levels that enable them to make decisions. In terms of the "degrees," *deconcentration—delegation—devolution* make up a scale with devolution at the high end. In terms of the "dimensions," radicalness alludes to complete or partial transfer of state functions to local governments.

6. Evaluating the success of decentralization and municipalization requires assessing the contribution of these processes to integrated municipal development (in economic, social, cultural, political and other aspects) through indices that permit comparative measurement over time and in relation to the situations of other municipalities. An example of this type of metric is the Municipal Development Index, which allows for identification of progress or deterioration in the municipal situation, combining economic, demographic, labor, and social dimensions. See Becerra y Pino (2014).

7. Sectoral management of the economy and social policies means a manner of designing and implementing policies and resource administration that views the economic-social system as made up of important interrelated sectors (e.g., agriculture, industry, education, and health) with the sector as the main focus of administration and interrelation as secondary. In contrast, integrated management sees the economic-social system in terms of its unity and internal interrelations (territories, communities).

8. Examples of NGOs involved in community and local affairs are the Centro Martin Luther King Jr. (devoted to grassroots education), Centro de Reflexión y Diálogo Oscar Arnulfo Romero (gender-based and domestic violence), Centro Félix Varela (ethics and environment), and CIERIC (local cultural initiatives), among others.

9. See, for example, Márquez, 2009; Accioly, 2014.

10. Identification of these ten prioritized problems and social policy proposals was based on an analysis of the results of recent (2010–15) research undertaken by the Cuban institutions most recognized for their study of inequality and poverty. Their conclusions led to the identification of a preliminary list of 21 problems and 60 general proposals on which these studies converged. This list was submitted to experts who, in a series of interviews, were asked to rank the problems in order of priority (in terms of the degree to which they threaten social equity and access to well-being by diverse social groups) and the proposals according to the criteria of what could and should most immediately be done to solve the problems. Twenty experts were interviewed: two officials of national institutions involved in economic and territorial planning;

two officials of provincial governments; ten municipal government specialists and officials connected to local development policy; and six scholars who research topics related to inequality and the implementation of cooperation projects. The ten problems and the associated proposals were then selected by assigning points according to the number of experts who placed them among their top ten priorities.

11. On this issue, consult the chapter called *Política social* in the *Lineamientos de la Política Económica y Social del Partido y la Revolución* (PCC, 2011).

12. See "Ley no. 113 del Sistema Tributario," approved in 2012.

13. See Resoluciones 17, 18 and 19 of 2016 from the Ministerio de Finanzas y Precios. MINJUS, *Gaceta Oficial* 2, 2016.

14. Artemisa and Mayabeque are two provinces in the western part of the country, each bordering Havana. Most of their municipalities may be classified as moderately developed (see García Pleyán and Sulzer, 2014). There are reasons for their selection for this experiment: as two recently created provinces that emerged from a new political-administrative division approved in 2011, they are easier sites to introduce a novel government structure; their proximity to Havana, the center of national political and institutional power, permits direct and systematic monitoring; both are sites of economic projects important to the country's development (the port and free trade zone of Mariel in Artemisa, expansion of oil-producing areas in Mayabeque).

15. Source: Ada Guzón, director of the Centro de Desarrollo Local y Comunitario (CEDEL).

16. Participatory Budgeting (PB) is a mechanism to manage financial resources based on inviting the citizenry to take part in decisions about the use and apportionment of an available amount of public budget funds for public institutions. It arose in the 1990s in Brazil and Argentina when left-wing parties won office in various city governments. PB's underlying assumption is that citizen participation and deliberation will increase the effective use of local resources and social equity in access to goods and services. This mechanism applies three principles: concentration on specific tangible problems; active participation by ordinary people affected by these problems as well as officials close to that population; and the deliberative search for solutions to these problems. See Fung and Wright, 2003.

17. Source: Maidolys Iglesias, specialist with the Grupo de Investigaciones Sociales del Plan Maestro, Oficina del Historiador de la Ciudad de La Habana.

Bibliography

Alburquerque, Francisco 1995. *Espacio, territorio y desarrollo económico local.* Santiago de Chile: ILPES.

———. 2004. "Desarrollo económico local y descentralización en América Latina." In *Investigación de la CEPAL,* 82:157–171.

Arocena, José. 1995. "El desarrollo local. Aspectos teóricos. Condicionantes. Actores." In *Fondos de CLAEH.* Montevideo: CLAEH.

Becerra, Francisco, and José. Pino. 2014. "Desarrollo socioeconómico local en Cienfuegos. Mediciones a escala municipal y estrategias de trasformación desde el territorio." In O. Pérez and R. Torres, eds., *Miradas a la economía cubana. Desde un perspectiva territorial.* Havana: Caminos.

Casado, Gabriel, (Ed.). 2005. *La financiación de los municipios. Experiencias comparadas.* Madrid: Editorial Dykinson, S.L.

Castro, Raúl, 2008a, "Discurso pronunciado el 24 de febrero," In *Granma;* 25 February.

———. 2008b. "Discurso de clausura del sexto pleno del PCC." In *Granma,* 23 April.

———. 2008c. "Discurso pronunciado en el acto por el 26 de julio." In *Granma,* 27 July.

———. 2010. "Discurso pronunciado en la clausura del Sexto Período Ordinario de Sesiones de la Séptima Legislatura de la Asamblea Nacional del Poder Popular." In *Granma*: 18 December. [Official English translation from http://www.cuba.cu/gobierno/rauldiscursos/2010/ing/r181210i.html.]

———. 2016. Discurso de apertura del VII Congreso del PCC. In *Granma,* 17 April. [Official English translation from http://en.cubadebate.cu/news/2016/04/18/7th-pcc-congress-central-report-presented-by-first-secretary-raul-castro-ruz/.]

Coraggio, José Luis 2003. *El papel de la teoría en el desarrollo local.* Quito: Universidad Andina.

Díaz, Ileana 2014. "Las nuevas medidas en empresas estatales: ¿cambios en la autonomía?" In *Memorias del Seminario Científico por el 25 aniversario del CEEC.* Havana: CEEC.

Díaz, Orestes 2015. "Descentralización fiscal y desarrollo local en Cuba: Ideas preliminares desde el derecho para la articulación del proceso." In L. Pérez and Díaz, eds., ¿Qué municipio queremos? Respuestas para Cuba en clave de descentralización y *desarrollo local.* Havana: Universidad de La Habana.

Dilla, Haroldo, et al. 1998. "Movimientos barriales en Cuba: un análisis comparativo. In Aurora. Vázquez and Roberto Dávalos, eds., *Participación social, desarrollo urbano y comunitario.* Havana: Universidad de La Habana.

Espina, Mayra 2008. *Políticas de atención a la pobreza y la desigualdad. Examinando el rol del Estado en la experiencia socialista cubana.* Buenos Aires: CLACSO.

———. 2012. "Procesos de diversificación social y desigualdades en Cuba hoy: nueve zonas de cambio." In ¡Que hay que tené boluntá! Memorias del VII Coloquio y Festival Internacional Nicolás Guillén. Havana: Universidad de La Habana.

Espina, Mayra, and Dayma Echevarría, eds. 2015. *Cuba: los correlatos socioculturales del cambio económico.* Havana: Ciencias Sociales.

Echevarría, Dayma, and Teresa. Lara. 2012. "Cambios recientes: ¿oportunidad para las mujeres?" In Pavel Vidal and O. Pérez, eds., *Miradas a la Economía Cubana III.* Havana: Caminos.

Finot, Iván. 2001. "Descentralización en América Latina: teoría y práctica. In *Serie Gestión Pública* 12. Santiago de Chile: ILPES-CEPAL.

———. 2003. "Descentralización en América Latina: cómo hacer viable el desarrollo local." In *Serie Gestión Pública* 38. Santiago de Chile: ILPES-CEPAL.

Fung, Archon, and Erik Olin Wright. 2003. "En torno al Gobierno Participativo con Poder de Decisión." In A. Fung and E. Wright, eds., *Democracia en profundidad. Nuevas formas institucionales de gobierno participativo con poder de decisión.* Bogotá: Universidad de Colombia.

García Pleyán, Carlos 2014. "Prólogo." In Omar Pérez and Ricardo. Torres, eds., *Miradas a la Economía Cubana. Desde una perspectiva territorial*. Havana: Caminos.

García Pleyán, Carlos, and Peter Sulzer. 2014. *Mapa de desigualdades territoriales.* Índice de desarrollo municipal. Havana: COSUDE.

Giddens, Anthony 1981. "Agency, Institution and Time Space Analysis. In K. Cetina and A. Cicourel, eds., *Advances in Social Theory and Methodology: Toward an Integration of Micro and Macro Sociologies*. Boston: Routledge and Kegan Paul.

Guzón, Ada, ed. 2006. *Desarrollo local en Cuba*. Havana: Academia.

Guzón, Ada, and Rider Hernández. 2015. "A propósito del desarrollo local en Cuba." In Lissette Pérez and Orestes Díaz, eds., ¿Qué municipio queremos? Respuestas para Cuba en clave de descentralización y *desarrollo local.* Havana: Universidad de La Habana.

Instituto de Planificación Física. 2012. *Procedimiento para la elaboración del Plan de Desarrollo Integral del Municipio.* Havana: IPF.

Íñiguez, Luisa 2014. "¿De quiénes son los territorios?" In Omar Pérez and Ricardo Torres, eds., *Miradas a la Economía Cubana. Desde un perspectiva territorial.* Havana: Caminos.

Jütting, Johannes, et al. 2005. "Decentralisation and Poverty in Developing Countries: Exploring the Impact." In *OECD Development Centre Working Paper*, Number 236. Paris: OCDE.

Llanes, Aizel 2015. "Desarrollo local y ordenamiento territorial en Cuba." In *Memorias de la XV Convención Internacional de Ordenamiento Territorial y Urbanismo.* Havana: IPF.

Márquez, Miguel, ed. 2009. *Programa de Desarrollo Humano Local. Lecciones aprendidas*. Havana: PNUD.

Matilla, Andry 2015. "Municipio y administración local: breves glosas al hilo del contexto jurídico cubano actual." In Lissette Pérez and Orestes. Díaz, eds., ¿Qué municipio queremos? Respuestas para Cuba en clave de descentralización y *desarrollo local.* Havana: Universidad de La Habana.

Mejía, Carolina, and Orazio Atanasio. 2001. "Descentralización en América Latina. Estudios de Caso." In *Documentos,* Number 30/08. Santiago de Chile: Instituto de Estudios Fiscales.

Ministerio de Finanzas. 2016. "Resoluciones 17, 18 y 19 de 2016." In *Gaceta Oficial*, No.2. Havana: Ministerio de Justicia.

Mulet, Yailenis 2015. "La descentralización en Cuba: la necesidad de una estrategia nacional." In *Economía y Desarrollo*. Number 155.

Núñez, Jorge 2014. *Universidad, conocimiento, innovación y desarrollo local.* Havana: Félix Varela.

PCC. 2011a. *Lineamientos de la Política Económica y Social.* Havana: PCC.

———. 2011b. *Documento Base. Primera Conferencia Nacional.* Havana: PCC.

———. 2016. *Conceptualización del modelo económico y social cubano de desarrollo socialista.* Havana: PCC.

Pajón, David, and Jessica León. 2015. "Nuevos actores y nuevas políticas en Cuba: rol del financiamiento en el proceso de reforma." Presented at LASA 2015, San Juan (Puerto Rico), 30 May.

Pérez, Lissette, and Orestes Díaz, eds. 2015. ¿Qué municipio queremos? Respuestas para Cuba en clave de descentralización y *desarrollo local.* Havana: Universidad de La Habana.

Rondinelli, Dennis. 1981. "Government Decentralization in Comparative Perspective: Theory and Practice in Developing Countries." In *International Review of Administrative Sciences.* 47:133–145.

Various authors. 2011. *Cataurito de herramientas para el desarrollo local.* Havana: Caminos.

Vázquez Barquero, Antonio. 1988. *Desarrollo local. Una estrategia de creación de empleo.* Madrid: Pirámide.

———. 2000. *Desarrollo económico local y descentralización: aproximación a un marco conceptual.* Santiago de Chile: CEPAL.

Zabala, María del Carmen, ed. 2013. *Algunas claves para pensar la pobreza en Cuba desde la mirada de jóvenes investigadores.* Havana: FLACSO-Acuario.

Zabala, María del Carmen et al. 2015. *Retos para la equidad social en el proceso de actualizació*n del modelo económico cubano. Havana: Ciencias Sociales.

5

Nonfarm Cooperatives in the Current Cuban Context: Challenges and Perspectives

Reynaldo Jiménez Guethón and Niurka Padrón Sánchez

This panoramic view of cooperatives in Cuba includes a brief historical survey of that sector on the island. The discussion is divided into five periods: 1930s–1958, 1959–1975, 1976–1990, 1991–March 2011, and beyond (from the Sixth Congress of the Cuban Communist Party on April 16 of that year to the Seventh Congress in April of 2016).

Undertaking this survey will help the readers to understand the successes and failures of the larger Cuban cooperative sector, looking at it from a political perspective with an economic base. Utilizing a qualitative research methodology, drawing on questionnaires, interviews, narratives, photographs, and written registries of all types, the authors have delved into the idea and formation of cooperatives, their actions, and the surrounding legal framework, challenges, and opportunities.

The research focuses on how cooperatives and their evolution fit within the model of updating of the Cuban economy, centering on the social relations of production and their economic base. Thus, we evaluate public policies in this area and their efficacy, as well as the objectives set in the course of several Party Congresses. We conclude with the major challenges and opportunities facing the new cooperatives today.

First Period: Cooperatives in Cuba from the 1930s to 1958

Spanish colonialism slowed the development of cooperatives in Cuba. The struggles for Cuban independence from 1868 to 1898, the absence of a numerically important working class and of large urban centers, and the weakening and impoverishment of the rural population by both war and large-planter domination prevented the formation of cooperatives.

Rapid growth of the sugar industry between 1900 and 1925 led to the creation of workers' organizations, including trade unions, whose main task for several decades was the defense of workers' rights. Not until the 1930s were the first Cuban cooperatives formed. They were stimulated by the influence of new waves of Spanish immigrants, who brought the cooperative model already established in Europe. Examples include the creation of mutual-aid health care facilities such as the Quinta Dependiente and the Quinta Covadonga; the mass transit cooperative Ómnibus Aliados, which was essentially a corporation; and some early, short-lived agricultural cooperatives of which very little evidence remains.

The Constitution of 1940, in its Article 75, recognized the possibility of a rise of cooperatives in all spheres, but by the 1950s the few such experiments there were suffered from a lack of cooperative culture and politics and from the impossibility of their developing without state support.[1] According to Avelino Fernández, during the pseudo-republican period in Cuba there was no real or legal development of the cooperative phenomenon, not even by way of creating a basic legal framework as the Constitution of 1940 had envisioned.

During the 1950–59 period, formation of cooperatives apparently stagnated due to the structural deformation of the Cuban economy, which was dependent on a sole product, sugar, sustaining a seasonal economy. Eighty percent of the non-sugar economy was concentrated in the western part of the country, in low value-added activities; there was no incentive for technological and scientific development, and the economy was oriented toward foreign markets and suppliers.

Second Period: Cooperatives from 1959 to 1975

From the first years after its triumph in 1959, the Cuban Revolution saw agricultural cooperatives as a form of cooperation that offered advantages for the modernization of crops and as a way to exploit the land in collective fashion.[2] The origins of this cooperative movement were based on democratization of land ownership, as effected by successive agrarian reform laws, given that cooperatives can exist only as associations of owners or usufruct grantees of land. Before 1959, this opening would have been impossible because of the high concentration of land ownership and the predominance of large plantations, with nine percent of farms accounting for 73 percent of arable land.[3]

On May 17, 1959, the First Agrarian Reform Law gave ownership of land to those who worked it and eliminated the plantations that had been in the hands of the domestic and foreign oligarchy by setting the maximum private farm size at 30 *caballerías* (402 hectares). This law established the principle that land was for the tiller, eliminating the exploitation that had previously prevailed.

In October of 1960, sugar cane cooperatives were created on the lands of former sugar plantations. In these entities, the state owned the land and the means of production, while the cooperative members exercised economic and legal power. The members of such cane cooperatives were agricultural workers, not small proprietors. According to economist Blanca Rosa Pampín, Cuba had 621 sugar cane cooperatives in 1960, with an average size of 1,409 hectares, and a total area of 876,142 hectares devoted to growing that crop.[4] Not until 1961 was the first peasants' organization created, the National Association of Small Farmers (Spanish initials ANAP), which promoted the active political and economic role of small proprietors and encouraged cooperation among them.

The first cane cooperatives lasted only a short while, from 1960 to 1962, suffering from serious errors in organization and management methods. The year 1962 saw the birth of Agricultural Societies, voluntary associations of peasants who combined their lands, equipment, and draft animals so as to farm the land collectively. These Societies disappeared in the 1970s.

According to the late Vice President Carlos Rafael Rodríguez, in the first years of the Revolution there were still not the necessary conditions for energetic development of cooperation among small and middle peasants.[5] Although there is a lack of literature that discusses these associative forms of landholding and work among the peasants, the history of Cuban economics and politics establishes that the government, in general, failed to recognize economic realities in its direction of the country. As Fidel Castro Ruz said in 1975 in his Main Report to the First Party Congress, "In guiding our economy, we have undoubtedly made some idealistic mistakes and have, now and again, ignored the reality of existing objective economic laws by which we must abide."[6]

In the decade of the '60s, the small farmers began to organize themselves into Peasant Bases that coordinated the distribution of inputs and material resources for agricultural production, received credit in a centralized fashion, etc. This led to the creation of the Credit and Service Cooperatives (CCS).[7] The CCS were later defined by Law 95 of 2002 as "the voluntary association of small farmers who hold title or usufruct to their land and other means of production and to the production they obtain. It is a form of agrarian cooperation through which to process and facilitate technical, financial, and material assistance provided by the state to increase output and facilitate its commercialization. [The CCS] has its own existence as a legal entity and is liable, with its patrimony, for its actions."[8] The CCS received decisive state support through long-term credits, differential interest rates, supply of equipment and inputs, housing construction, training programs, electrification, and service infrastructure.

In 1963, the Second Agrarian Reform Law reduced maximum landholding to 67 hectares and nationalized farms of greater size, thus increasing state participation in cane growing. This was also the period that gave rise to the creation of a political party that would answer to the revolutionary principles and objectives of the Revolution, becoming the single force for management and leadership of the economy and society. Thus, any deeper study of the cooperative sector requires consideration of the ruling party's relation to that sector.

On October 3, 1965, the first Central Committee of the Cuban Communist Party (CCP) was formed. The Cuban Constitution, in its Article 5, defines the Party as follows: "The Communist Party of Cuba, in the tradition of Martí's thought and Marxism-Leninism, the organized vanguard of the Cuban nation, is the highest leading force of society and the state, organizing and guiding the common efforts toward the lofty goals of the construction of socialism and progress toward a communist society."[9]

Third Period: Cooperatives from 1976 to 1990

At the time of the 1974 celebration of the fifteenth anniversary of the First Urban Reform Law, there was an evident need to seek new and better forms of agricultural production. This had to be done slowly, gradually, and on a voluntary basis. That understanding was the basis for the composition of an "Agrarian Thesis" dealing with relations with the peasantry. It was subsequently analyzed, discussed, and approved at the First Congress of the Cuban Communist Party in 1975.

The search for new forms of agricultural production led to the creation in 1976 of the Agricultural Production Cooperative (CPA), defined as "an economic entity that represents an advanced, efficient form of socialist production with its own patrimony and juridical personality, made up of the land and other assets contributed by small farmers, joined by other individuals to achieve sustainable agricultural production."[10] The CPA differed from the earlier Agricultural Society in that a CPA could have members who were not themselves small farmers. Also, property titles passed to the collective, so the assets ceased to be individual property, which had not been true of the Societies.

During this time, errors were committed in the agricultural sector. The existence of other forms of economic management such as state farms, multiple-crop enterprises, and others, did not permit the Ministry of Agriculture (MINAG) to devote much attention to the cooperative agricultural sector made up of the CCS and CPAs, which led to a loss of values and principles, failure to repay credits and other forms of aid, and failure to fulfill approved social objectives. These in turn negatively affected the operation of many of these units, which lost sight of the purpose for which they had been created, namely food production.

It is important to note not only the immediate legal framework of the cooperatives but the whole legal and institutional apparatus surrounding them. Article 20 of the 1976 Constitution recognized the right of small farmers to associate for purposes of agricultural production and gain access to state credits and services, and it specified that this right should be established and implemented by law. Thus, both types of agriculture cooperatives (the CCS and CPA), originated in the First Agrarian Reform Law, experienced an accelerated development following the First Party Congress. They are officially deemed an advanced form of socialist production; their mandate has been to foment the social development of peasant life as one of the principles of the Revolution's agrarian policy.

Law Number 36, the Law of Agricultural Cooperatives of July 22, 1982, governed the development of the Cuban cooperative movement for twenty years. This law constituted the indispensable legal underpinning of the orderly and voluntary transformation of individual small plot farming into collective forms of production. However, it was necessary to incorporate the positive experiences accumulated over the years and to take account of the socioeconomic and structural changes that had occurred in the country.

Fourth Period: Cooperatives from 1991 to 2011

At the beginning of the 1990s, as a result of the collapse of the European socialist model and the tightening of the U.S. blockade of Cuba, agricultural production decreased. Cuba lost its main suppliers; the availability of productive inputs dropped suddenly. As a result, the prevailing model of Cuban agricultural production based on the principles of the "Green Revolution" and consisting of extensive monoculture with heavy use of machinery and inputs of chemical fertilizers and pesticides suffered a true crisis. One example was the deterioration of all activities related to sugar production, a key sector of the economy. Causes included lack of fertilizer, fuel, and irrigation equipment and spare parts; reduction of planting and replanting; need to cut the entire crop without leaving any standing; lack of machinery and implements; decreased attention to the needs of agricultural workers and lack of repair facilities in general.

Many economic and rural development experts consider the year 1993 in Cuba to have been one of the most difficult moments within the entire development of the economy, and that economic crisis was sharpest in the agricultural sector. One the strategies adopted to confront this situation was the creation of Basic Units of Cooperative Production (UBPC), which represented an important transformation in Cuban agriculture, akin to a third Agrarian Reform Law. This transformation of property and production relations in the agricultural sector took place through Decree-Law 142 issued by the Council of State, which converted the majority of state farms used for sugar cane production into UBPCs.[11] The UBPCs thus emerged from an idea developed and birthed by the nation itself; MINAG and the sugar ministry MINAZ promoted the creation of this form of management.

According to the National Office of Statistics (ONE), as cited by Díaz, the creation of the UBPC radically changed the distribution of land ownership in Cuba. If in 1989, 82 percent of total land area and 73 percent of agricultural land belonged to 385 state enterprises, then in 2000, agricultural cooperatives of various types occupied 43 percent of total land and 61.3 percent of the agricultural portion. UBPCs alone occupied 28.7 percent of total land, and 40.6 percent of the agricultural portion.[12]

In 2000, the Ninth Congress of ANAP proposed to the National Assembly of People's Power new legislation concerning cooperatives. This legislation would promote the strengthening and continued development of sustainable agricultural production among cooperatives and small farmers and their families as an important means to contribute to the growth of the national economy.

Two years later, Law 36 was replaced by Law 95, the Law of Agricultural Production and Credit and Service Cooperatives, whose objectives were set forth in its Chapter 1, Article 1, namely, to:

a. modernize legislation relating to Agricultural Production Cooperatives and Credit and Service Cooperatives in response to the socioeconomic and structural changes that had taken place in the country;
b. contribute to strengthening cooperatives as socialist economic entities with autonomy, self-management, and social influence;
c. bring about sustainable growth in agricultural production with greater efficiency and quality;
d. promote greater exchange of actions and collaboration between cooperatives and local bodies of People's Power, that is, provincial and municipal assemblies; and
e. promote the creation of new cooperatives.

Article 3, in addition, provided that cooperatives should operate according to the following principles:

a. voluntary action: incorporation of new members and continuation of membership in the cooperatives is absolutely voluntary;

b. cooperation and mutual aid: all members work and unite their efforts toward the rational use of agricultural land and other assets that are the property or usufruct possessions of the cooperatives or their members;

c. contribution to development of the national economy: all cooperative plans and programs seek, and have as their fundamental goal, to work for the nation's sustainable economic and social development;

d. cooperative discipline: all members know, fulfill, and consciously abide by the provisions of this Law, its regulations, agreements made in the cooperative's own General Assembly, and other laws and regulations that apply to cooperatives;

e. collective decision-making: the rules governing the economic and social life of the cooperatives shall be discussed and decided in a democratic manner by its General Assembly and Leadership Council, in which the minority should adhere to and subordinate itself to what the majority approves;

f. territoriality: small farmers join and belong to the cooperative of the area within which their lands lie, so as to facilitate the best and most economical management of the cooperative in relation to its members;

g. welfare of members and their families: cooperatives work toward the rational satisfaction of the material, social, educational, cultural, and spiritual needs of their members and families;

h. collaboration among cooperatives: cooperatives collaborate among themselves buying and selling products for subsistence, breeding animals, sharing seeds and productive services, and exchanging experiences, and other legal non-profit activities;

i. human solidarity: they practice human solidarity among their members, workers, and other persons living in the communities where they are located;

j. social interests: all their measures and actions are toward the goal of social interests.

These proposals eloquently demonstrate the extraordinary importance of the cooperative sector in Cuban agricultural production, both in terms of production for domestic consumption and in terms of crops destined for export. Researcher Armando Nova asserts that the creation of the CCS, CPA, and UBPC shows an important expression of the country's

agricultural policy, confirming the cooperative movement as the funda-
ment base of the agricultural entrepreneurial economic system.[13]

However, the UBPCs did not develop as well as expected according to
the principles and design of the new form. Workers joined the entities,
but without a sense of individual or collective responsibility. Bank loans
made available for this form of management gradually disappeared. The
price ceilings imposed on agricultural products by the planned or centralized economy, along with a lack of needed inputs and raw materials, did
not support the economic or financial sustainability of this model. The
output achieved by many of these cooperatives was committed to meeting their debts, not providing income to their members. Apparently, the
autonomy of these units to administer their own resources and become
self-sufficient[14] was not completely achieved. Still, when their debts were
forgiven by the state, many UBPCs became successful while others did not.

Thus, in spite of the enormous effort made, the planned goals were not
fulfilled. According to studies of the cooperative sector carried out in 2015,
"some errors were committed in the process of creating the UBPCs, which
have become apparent in a group of them," as follows:

- The haste with which they were created did not allow for maturation
  of the idea or creation of the conditions, which would have accorded
  with the associative principles of the cooperative movement only
  with time and given the right conditions.
- Past practices of cooperative development were not taken into account.
- Since UBPCs were not recognized as true cooperatives, they remained
  stranded somewhere between the state farm and the CPA.
- The original endowments were economically overvalued; the initial
  working capital turned over by the state was assigned an elevated
  price that made it very hard to repay.
- The structure of the original state enterprises remained intact and
  subject to state control; they continued to function under state direction and could not achieve full autonomy.
- Fulfillment of the basic principles that had been approved did not
  become a necessary condition for the creation of the UBPCs.
- There appeared various elements that deformed the essence of the
  UBPCs, especially pertaining to economic aid, wage guarantees, and
  emergency funds granted by the state banking sector through agricultural enterprises.[15]

The UBPCs thus never acquired sufficient autonomy because of the
close ties they had to maintain with the state enterprises to which they are

subordinated. These state enterprises are the ones that craft and assign the UBPCs' technical economic plans and locate the resources needed for production. One problem that has particularly affected the process of agricultural production is the number of non-productive personnel of the state structure, a payroll at the cost of harvests or breeding stock. Only since 2010, as part of the updating of the economic model, did the Council of Ministers (July 2012) approve 17 measures for the state agriculture sector that give more flexibility and autonomy to the UBPCs:

1. Modify the legal provisions that establish the General Regulations for the operation of the UBPCs (Resolutions No. 629/04 and 525/03).
2. Develop an emergency program for preparing and training the administrators and Administrative Councils of UBPCs to deal with new powers and attributions, economic issues, planning, finance, legal issues, contractual relations, as well as administration and management.
3. Develop training courses for Enterprise Directors and the State Cadre of MINAG, including staff from other agencies as well, about legal topics and contractual relations related to the UBPC.
4. Compile a compendium of documents to use as a tool by UBPC administrators and entities in MINAG, the Sugar Group, and other agencies.
5. Revoke the rules of Resolution 499/01 that relate to application and control of personnel policies for UBPC administrators within the MINAG system; propose new procedures to regulate this activity in the future that correspond to the new General Regulations.
6. Establish direct contractual relations between UBPCs and input-supplying agencies of MINAG and the Sugar Group, without any intermediary bodies.
7. Establish direct contractual relations between MINAG's UBPCs and FINCIMEX, the financial arm of Corporación CIMEX, which operates under the Ministry of the Armed Forces (MINFAR), for acquisition of fuel.
8. Bring figures of the economic plan down to the UBPC level, thus allowing the creation of contracts between UBPCs and their supply agencies so as to directly commercialize inputs and services.
9. Issue instructions to other state bodies to eliminate current restrictions that impede provision of services and sale of inputs directly to the Basic Unit, in recognition of its existence as an independent legal entity.
10. Establish financial arrangements that will allow a UBPC, within a specific time frame, to rectify its productive, economic, and financial

situation so as to resolve its accumulated debt to the banking, fiscal, and enterprise sectors, and the losses accumulated in previous years. For this purpose, the following measures were proposed:

a. As a source of budgeted financing for capitalizing the UBPCs, establish a tax of five percent of gross income. Proceeds will be used for financing via the state budget, through a subsidy for losses and working capital toward specific ends, especially paying down of bank debt, irrespective of deadlines, and during the time foreseen for amortization of the same.

b. Set up financial arrangements to cover UBPCs' losses of previous years that remain active in groups I and II (332,100,000 pesos).

c. Set up financial and accounting arrangements for unguaranteed bank debts.

d. The Central Bank will determine the interest rates to be applied within a range between one and three percent; the Committee on Monetary Policy will set the rate.

11. Develop a process for merging or dissolving those UBPCs that have no possibility of recovery.

12. Develop a process of assemblies in each Basic Unit to study the new General Regulations and draft new rules.

13. Proceed with housing units in various phases of construction (foundation, structure, and completion).

14. Incorporate the fulfillment of the new measures affecting the UBPCs into the monitoring system of MINAG and the Sugar Group.

Fifth Period: Cooperatives from April 2011 to August 2016

With the opening of the Sixth Congress of the Cuban Communist Party on April 16, 2011, the life of the people of Cuba entered a new phase of transformation and change, fourteen years since the previous Congress. The main agenda of this one was to approve the Guidelines of Economic and Social Policy of the Cuban Revolution, a document that had been previously discussed by the majority of the population and that contained an economic reform defined as an adaptation of socialism to new times, also called twenty-first century socialism. This included the approval of the creation of cooperatives in non-farm sectors as well as the expansion of self-employment, thus solidifying the non-state sector of the Cuban economy, while also affirming that the fundamental means of production would remain socialist property of the entire people and within the prevailing economic system.

The Congress's commission on economic policy had five major lines of work, one of which was the "systematic oversight of the agencies and institutions in charge of enforcing the decisions stemming from the Guidelines and evaluation of their results."

Non-farm Cooperatives (CNoA)

Since 2011, Cuba has embarked on a process of updating its economic and social model as outlined in the Guidelines of Economic and Social Policy of the Party and the Revolution that had been approved by the Sixth Congress.[16] The section on Cooperatives, in Chapter 1, Model of Economic Management, contained Guidelines numbered 25 through 29 dealing with the gradual creation of cooperatives in non-agricultural activities and the experimental regulations to govern them:

- Grade 1 cooperatives shall be established as a socialist form of joint ownership in various sectors. A cooperative is a business organization that owns its estate and represents a distinct legal person. Its members are individuals who contribute assets or labor. Its purpose is to supply useful goods and services to society. It covers its costs with its own income.
- The legal instrument that regulates the cooperatives must make sure that this organization, as form of social property, is not sold or otherwise assigned in ownership to any other cooperative or any non-state organization or any natural person.
- A cooperative maintains contractual relations with other cooperatives, companies, state-funded entities and other non-state organizations. After satisfying its commitment with the state, the cooperative may pursue sales operations free from intermediaries and in accordance with the business activity it is authorized to perform.
- Subject to compliance with the appropriate laws and after observance of its tax and contribution obligations, each cooperative determines the income payable to its employees and the distribution of its profits.
- Grade 2 cooperatives shall be formed, the partners of which shall be Grade 1 cooperatives. A Grade 2 Cooperative shall represent a separate legal person that owns assets. The purpose of this cooperative is to pursue supplementary related activities or conduct operations that add value to the goods and services of its partners (such as production, service and marketing operations) or carry out joint sales and purchases for greater efficiency.[17]

At first, framers of this initiative foresaw the creation of some two hundred associations throughout the country, concentrated in the sectors of transportation, food service, fishing, personal and domestic services, raw material recovery, production of materials, and construction services.

The non-farm cooperative now constitutes a part of Cuban society. It is an organization of collective property that has both economic and social goals, aiming to raise the standard of living of its members, the community, and the society. An autonomous legal entity, it operates with seriousness, professionalism, austerity, efficiency, and quality. It respects the socialist legal system, practices principles of solidarity, and acts in concert with the moral and ethical standards of the Revolution; building a cooperative should stem from the desire and will of individuals. Such cooperatives may be formed by a group of three or more people or by the workforce of a state entity approving a shift to this form of management, which we shall refer to as a cooperative induced by the state.

The members are the owners of all the income from their work They adhere to the following Cooperative Principles:

a. *Voluntary Action.* Incorporation of new members and continuation of membership in the cooperative is free and voluntary.

b. *Cooperation and Mutual Aid.* All members work, collaborate, and provide assistance to the others so as to achieve the cooperative's goals.

c. *Collective Decision-Making and Equal Rights.* Rules governing the economic and social life of the cooperatives are discussed and decided in a democratic manner by the members, who participate in that decision-making with equal rights.

d. *Autonomy and Economic Sustainability.* Obligations are covered out of income. Once established taxes have been paid, profits are shared among the members in proportion to the work they have contributed.

e. *Cooperative Discipline.* All members contribute work to the cooperative. They know, fulfill, and consciously abide by the provisions regulating its activity, as well as accords reached by its managing and administrative bodies and any further regulations that apply.

f. *Social Responsibility, Contribution to the Planned Development of the Economy and to the Welfare of Members and Their Families.* The goal of the cooperative's planning is to contribute to the nation's sustainable economic and social development, protect the environment, carry out activities in a non-speculative manner, and guarantee the disciplined fulfillment of tax and other obligations. Members strive to promote cooperative culture and to meet the material, educational, social, cultural, moral, and spiritual needs of their members and families.

g. *Collaboration and Cooperation among Cooperatives and Other Entities.* Cooperatives collaborate among themselves and with other state or non-state entities by means of contracts, collaboration agreements, exchanges of experience, and other legal activities.

The body of laws governing development of nonfarm cooperatives consists of the experimental Decree-Laws of the Councils of State and Ministers published in the *Gaceta Ordinaria No. 053/12.*

Beginning in 2013, the state budget will cease financing the UBPCs except in cases of compelling state interest.

Table 5.1: Characteristics of the Cuban Cooperative Sector

Cuban Cooperatives	Characteristics
Credit and Service Cooperatives (CCS) Created in the 1960s	Groups of peasants who maintain title to their lands and other supplies.
Agricultural Production Cooperatives (CPA) Created in 1976	Groups of peasants and other individuals who surrender their land and other supplies, which become collective property.
Basic Units of Cooperative Production (UBPC) Created in 1993	State workers who unite to become agricultural cooperative members and receive land and other supplies in usufruct for an indefinite period.
Non-Agricultural Cooperatives (CNoA) Created in 2012	Collective property. In some cases members retain property rights to goods they have supplied, while in others they work with property and supplies rented from the state (without right of transfer), and still others work with both types of property, as their members may decide.

Source: Constructed by the authors, 2015

Cooperatives were typically created during a Communist Party Congress. Their type and their characteristics are displayed in Table 5.1. We thus conclude that this most recent form of economic management, the CNoA, is the most ambitious and integral because it includes the entire population aged 18 or more, whether professionals, technicians, farmers, or others, and it leaves room for decision-making by its members, who do not lose rights to their assets. It may be considered the most democratic model of all the cooperatives in Cuban society.

According to legal and administrative data from the National Office of Statistics and Information (ONEI), at the end of March 2016 the nation had 5,475 cooperatives, comprised of 383 CNoA, 1,690 UBPC, 894 CPA, and 2,508 CCS. Of the total, 93 percent were so so-called classic or agricultural cooperatives, of which 76 percent fall under the jurisdiction of the Ministry of Agriculture, 18 percent tof the Sugar Group, and 6 percent of other state agencies.[18]

If the total number of entities is compared to the cooperative sector, this sector includes 33 percent of the total number of officially established organizations[19]; however, it should be noted that although 498 CNoAs have been approved, 115 are not yet in operation. The activities of all approved 498 CNoAs are classified as follows in the list below, whereas Table 5.3 focuses on the cross-year evolution of cooperatives actually in operation.

Table 5.2: Number of Cooperatives by Activity Type

Activities	Quantity
Farmers' markers	101
Passenger transport	11
Auxiliary transport services	6
Waste recycling	2
Construction	69
Commerce, food service	246
Industry (production, repairs, printing, design)	32
Ornithology	17
Food production	3
Energy	5
Accounting services	6
Total	**498**

Source: Constructed by the authors, 2015

Table 5.3: Cooperative Organizations in Operation, 2011–2016

Year	CNoA	UBPC	CPA	CCS	Total Cooperatives
2011	0	2165	1002	2644	5811
2012	0	2038	1006	2644	5688
2013	198	1811	909	2502	5420
2014	345	1754	903	2504	5506
2015	367	1699	897	2510	5473
2016	383	1690	894	2508	5475

Source: Constructed by the authors with data from ONEI, March 2016

With the approval in 2013 of Decree-Law 305, the number of CNoA cooperatives began to rise, while the older forms—UBPC, CCS, CPA—began to decline. There were 2,165 UBPCs in 2011, while by the end of March 2016 there were only 1,690, a decrease of 475. In the case of the CPAs, the decline amounted to 108 (see Table 5.3).

These figures show the impact of the cooperative sector. Recall that the majority of these forms of production arose out of small private property holdings (small farmers, in the case of the CCS and CPA), but with the emergence of the CNoA in 2013, a majority arose from the initiative of the state itself, which decided, following the Party's programmatic platform, to divest itself of a great variety of service activities that had been carried out by state enterprises. This does not mean that those economic entities turn into cooperatives, but rather that this former state sector confers some of its basic units, workshops, premises, and spaces for the formation of cooperatives by renting them out.

The percentage distribution of Cuban cooperatives as of March 2016 may be seen in Figure 5.1. The greatest share is still that of the CCS, productive units whose members retain title to land and supplies.

Figure 5.1: Percent Distribution of Cuban Cooperatives by Type

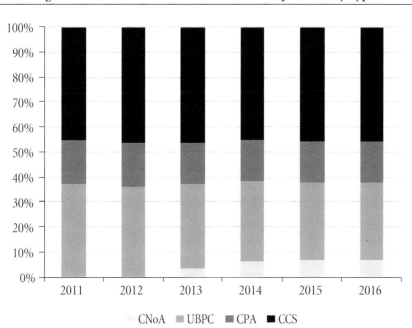

Source: Constructed by the authors with data from ONEI, March 2016

The geographic context in which the new non-farm cooperatives arose matters greatly. They first appeared as part of the updating processes under way in two provinces, Artemisa and Mayabeque, new provinces that had more than two years' experience with a new experimental political-administrative structure. The largest number of CNoA are in the provinces of Havana and Artemisa, followed by more than ten in the provinces of Matanzas, Mayabeque, and Pinar del Río, as shown in Table 5.4.

Table 5.4: Cooperatives in Operation by Province

Province	Total	CNoA	Total A.	UBPC	CPA	CCS
Pinar del Río	386	12	374	67	71	236
Artemisa	275	67	208	59	54	95
La Habana	323	208	115	27	0	88
Mayabeque	277	15	262	68	20	174
Matanzas	260	19	242	87	58	96
Villa Clara	427	8	419	127	70	222
Cienfuegos	190	4	183	82	32	72
Sanctí Spíritus	325	8	320	101	55	161
Ciego de Ávila	221	4	221	79	50	88
Camagüey	443	8	435	172	84	179
Las Tunas	279	2	280	117	43	117
Holguín	544	4	541	136	105	299
Granma	517	7	513	182	97	232
Santiago de Cuba	590	9	583	255	84	242
Guantánamo	390	5	385	123	70	192
Isla de la Juventud (special municipality)	28	3	25	8	1	16
Total	**5475**	**383**	**5092**	**1690**	**894**	**2508**

Source: Constructed by the authors with data from ONEI, March 2016. "Total A." refers to the sum of all forms of agricultural cooperatives.

The total distribution of cooperatives of all types in the country, as evident in Table 5.4, is characterized by homogeneity in the agricultural sector, because all provinces except Havana, Cienfuegos, and the special municipality Isla de la Juventud have more than 200 cooperatives, yielding an average of 365 per province (dividing the total of 5,475 by the number of provinces, 15). These patterns also show that each province has its own characteristics, which should always been borne in mind when crafting public policies. For instance, the fact that Havana has 208 CNoAs in operation need not mean that the same number should be approved for the province of Holguín; what works in one province need not apply to others. Still, we believe that wherever real applications and opportunities exist to establish new CNoAs, based on professional economic analysis, more CNoAs should be created and approved because people seem to want them; indeed, many such applications currently remain pending in the offices of various agencies throughout the country.

Table 5.5: CNoA in Operation by Economic Activity, June 2015 and March 2016

Economic Activity	Non-agricultural cooperatives	
	June 2015	March 2016
Manufacturing	49	49
Construction	61	60
Electricity, gas, and water supply	4	4
Transport, warehousing, and communication	6	6
Commerce and household appliance repair	130	131
Hotels and restaurants	87	102
Business services, real estate, and renting	6	7
Other personal and group service activities	8	24
Total	351	383

Source: Constructed by the authors with data from ONEI, June 2015–March 2016

At the end of March 2016, CNoAs actually in operation were engaged in the range of activities that can be seen in Table 5.5. Table 5.5 shows an increase in some sectors: one each in commerce and repairs and in business services, real estate, and renting; fifteen in hotels and restaurants; and sixteen in miscellaneous service activities. Regarding tourist services, Cuba offers a range of services to foreigners at very accessible prices, including health tourism, medical services, educational services, and others. It also guarantees the safety of its citizens, with the lowest incidence of violence in its region, thus offering the tourist sector a positive context for its products.

Cuba has 28 central agencies of which 43 percent (12) have now formed cooperatives in the non-farm sector, as is reflected in Table 5.6, which shows the central state administration agencies that have been active in creating non-farm cooperatives since 2012.

Table 5.6: CNoA by Ministry or Other Central Administrative Agency (Created since 2012)

Ministry or Other Agency	CNoA
MINDUS (Ministry of Industries)	28
MINEM (Ministry of Energy and Mines)	5
MINAL (Ministry of Food)	3
MICONS (Ministry of Construction)	68
MITRANS (Ministry of Transportation)	9
MINCIN (Ministry of Domestic Commerce)	2
INDER (National Institute of Sports, Physical Education, and Recreation)	1
MINTUR (Ministry of Tourism)	18
MINFAR (Ministry of Armed Forces)	1
People's Power (provincial government), Havana	126
People's Power (provincial government), other provinces	96
Other Agencies	26
Total	**383**

Source: Constructed by the authors, March 2016

The fundamental source of employment for Cuban citizens has long been the state, the center of economic activities. Therefore the new growth in cooperatives has come primarily out of that seedbed. The consequences of such centralization of the economy are worthy of further discussion, but in any case there is a need to diversify the economy with new economic actors, inevitable in any type of system, given that the state cannot take charge of all aspects of social life.

The state now promotes the creation of cooperatives in many of its establishments (cafeterias, restaurants, hair salons, clock and watch shops, repair shops for other small appliances, and more). At no time has the state dissolved an entire enterprise to convert it into cooperatives; these units have continued to function, renting out their facilities to the cooperatives. The real estate remains state property, regulated by Resolution 570 of the Ministry of Economy and Planning, which empowers the state enterprises to rent it.

Cooperatives continue to show signs of becoming a steady source of employment in many sectors of the economy. They are destined to occupy a very important place as an organizational and productive alternative within the updating of the nation's economic model. One valuable example is that the tax payments of the twenty non-farm cooperatives in the province of Matanzas now exceeds 18 million pesos.[20]

The creation of the new CNoA cooperatives authorized by Decree-Law 305 represents a step forward in the development of Cuban society, which may help to introduce efficacy and efficiency into the country's economic activities and processes. Many obstacles need to be overcome in order for this new form of cooperative in various approved sectors to succeed, and it is necessary to acknowledge and learn from the mistakes made in the earlier agricultural cooperatives so as not to repeat them.

The legal framework for creation of Grade 1 cooperatives in various sectors of the national economy, resulting from implementation of Guideline 25, also establishes the economic parameters for this collective form of productive property. Some cooperatives do not fulfil these parameters, violating rules to which they are required to adhere in order to function in an orderly and transparent way. Violations range from those related to social objectives, through those having to do with Cuban standards for accounting, internal oversight, taxes, banking, and contracts, to those related to the internationally practiced principles and values of the cooperative movement that are implicit in Guideline 25. We base our judgments on various sources. One is the investigation carried out by members of the National Assembly Commission on Services in 11 provinces and 88 municipalities in the first half of 2015, looking into operational practices in wholesale and retail commerce, new management models, quality, crime, illegality, and corruption. That investigation was not focused on cooperatives, but they were included in the broader inquiry. In the deficiencies uncovered across sectors, what most stands out is weak application of the system of internal oversight and the action plans, as well problems with the quality of products, etc.[21] Another source is an investigation that the Ministry of Industries (MINDUS) carried out among 89 percent of its CNoAs, which discovered 344 deficiencies; these figures became public in discussions by Cuban National Assembly Deputies on December 26, 2015, during a session of its Commission on Industry, Construction, and Energy.[22]

Violations of principles and standards, particularly those pertinent to the establishment of economic order. create an environment that is likely to lead to the dissolution of a cooperative. The common denominator of the causes is cooperative members' lack of preparation and training. An additional problem is the lack of preparation of many of the officials whose job is to guide the cooperatives and insure their conformity with established rules.

Positive Developments Arising from This New Form of Non-State Management (CNoA)

- Increased supply of goods and services for the population.
- Extended work schedules and greater opportunity for working people.
- Growth in autonomy and self-management, increasing workers' sense of belonging and ownership.
- Members become the owners of the economic results, which allows for reduction in costs.
- Participatory democracy becomes the guiding principle of operation.
- Improved appearance and architecture of many buildings that had deteriorated with time and lack of maintenance.

Challenges Facing the Process of Creation and Operation of Non-farm Cooperatives

- Delays in the process of approving or denying the creation of cooperatives.
- Implementing the full autonomy of the cooperative members.
- Not enough participation by actors (both members and supervisory officials) in the courses about cooperatives that various institutions have offered.
- Absence of a wholesale market.
- Vulnerability of the financial tools for this form of management.
- Absence or limited dissemination of radio or television programs or spots to promote and publicize good examples of successful cooperatives in the country.
- In many cases, individuals who hope to become part of a cooperative do not have sufficient access to legal advice. The option of becoming a cooperative member is not attractive to many people for lack of a true culture of cooperatives on a national level.

Future Outlook for the Cuban Cooperative Movement

Further development of the CNoA form requires systematic training programs both before and after the creation of a cooperative, for those interested in forming the cooperative or for those who have already become members, to counter the general lack of knowledge in this area. It is also necessary to speed up the creation, promotion, and development of wholesale markets throughout the country, as an indispensable mechanism for cooperatives to acquire raw materials and inputs. Cooperatives should also be permitted to form and maintain relations with other cooperatives in their sectors outside the country. A good example is the ornithological (chicken and other poultry) cooperatives, which so far are the only ones with authorization to import and export.

One area of public policy requiring further analysis is whether in a given province or locality it is more appropriate to charge a one-percent local development tax or to make a cooperative responsible for a school, daycare center, or nursing home, etc. The authors judge the latter to be more sensible and humane, linking people with their local environment and shaping values in an integral way rather than impersonal money transactions. This could be a means to establish real and effective education about cooperative principles in all types of Cuban cooperatives.

The Cuban cooperative movement was widely raised in the work sessions of the Seventh Congress of the CCP in April 2016. Further development of the CNoA experiment was prioritized, with emphasis on activities that offer solutions to local development and on beginning the process of creating Grade 2 cooperatives as well.

In closing, we should also note that the guidelines approved at the April 2016 Seventh Congress of the Party mandate the continued development of cooperatives in the country. Implementation of this mandate will allow for further study of their evolution and performance.

Notes

1. Valdés Paz, J. 2009. *Los procesos de organización agraria en Cuba 1959-2006.* Havana: Fundación Antonio Núñez Jiménez de la Naturaleza y el Hombre.
2. Rodríguez, Carlos Rafael. 1983. *Cuatro Años de Reforma Agraria En Letra con Filo. Tomo II.* Havana: Ciencias Sociales.
3. Jiménez, Reynaldo. 2006. "Educación para la participación social de las Unidades Básicas de Producción Cooperativas (UBPC). Estudio de Caso." Doctoral thesis, Universidad de La Habana.
4. Pampín, Blanca Rosa. 1996. *Los Cambios estructurales en la agricultura cubana.* Havana.
5. Rodríguez. 1983.
6. Castro Ruz, Fidel, 1975. Informe Central al Primer Congreso del Partido, 17 December 1975. Official English translation from https://archive.org/stream /FirstCongressPCC/First%20Congress%20PCC_djvu.txt.
7. Martín, Adelfo. 1982. *La ANAP dos años de trabajo.* Havana: Medios de Propaganda de PCC.
8. Ministerio de Justicia. 2002. Ley No.95 de las Cooperativas de Producción Agropecuaria y de Crédito y Servicios. Artículo 4. In *Gaceta Oficial de la República* (2002, 3). Havana: MINJUST.
9. http://www.cuba.cu/gobierno/cuba.htm.
10. Ministerio de Justicia. 2002.
11. Jiménez. 2006.

12. Díaz, Beatriz. 2005. "Migraciones Este-Oeste en Cuba. Las cooperativas agríco-las como vía de inclusión social." Presented at the IX Congreso Internacional UniRcoop, Rio de Janeiro, October 2005.

13. Nova, Armando. 2004. *El Cooperativismo línea de desarrollo en la agricultura cubana 1993-2003.* Havana: CEEC, Universidad de la Habana.

14. MINAZ. 2003. *Reglamentos General de las UBPC.* Havana: MINAG.

15. Monzón, Ricardo. 2015. "Producción Agropecuaria," *Cooperativas y Sociedad: un enfoque múltiple*, ed. Beatriz Díaz. Havana: Editorial Universitaria del Ministerio de Educación Superior, chapter 1.

16. The Guidelines of Economic and Social Policy are the expression of the people's will, contained in the policy of the Party, state, and government of the Republic of Cuba, to update the Cuban economic model with the objective of guaranteeing the continuity and irreversibility of socialism, the country's economic development, and the improvement of the population's standard of living, in concert with the necessary shaping of the ethical and political values of our citizens.

17. Partido Comunista de Cuba, Comité Central. 2011. "Lineamientos de la Política Económica y Social del Partido." Havana. [Official English translation from: "Sixth Congress of The Communist Party of Cuba, Resolution on the Guidelines of the Economic and Social Policy of the Party and the Revolution," consulted 3 September 2016 at http://www.cuba.cu/gobierno/documentos/2011/ing/l160711i.html.]

18. Oficina Nacional de Estadísticas. 2016. www.one.cu/ryc/organizacioninstitucional/orginst_1603.pdf.

19. Oficina Nacional de Estadísticas. 2016 www.one.cu/ryc/organizacioninstitucional/orginst_1603.pdf.

20. Agencia International de Noticias. 2015. "Cooperativa en Matanzas muestra éxito de gestión no estatal." http://www.cubadebate.cu/noticias/2015/10/21/cooperativa-en-matanzas-muestra-exito-de-gestion-no-estatal/.

21. Céspedes, Lauren. 2015. "Servicios, cooperativas, precios." http://www.granma.cu/cuba/2015-07-11/servicios-cooperativas-precios.

22. Castro, Yudy. 2015. "Avanza la experiencia de las cooperativas no agropecuarias en los sectores de la industria y la construcción." http://www.granma.cu/cuba/2015-12-26/avanza-la-experiencia-de-las-cooperativas-no-agropecuarias-en-los-sectores-de-la-industria-y-la-construcción.

PART

III

Social Policy Issue Areas: Education, Health Care, and Environment

6

Education and Employment in Cuba: Congruity or Disequilibrium? The First Fifteen Years of the Twenty-First Century

Dayma Echevarría León and Mayra Tejuca Martínez

From the start of the Cuban revolutionary process, it became clear that education was a key to development, so it has always been prioritized in social policy. In the last fifteen years, however, there have been many modifications in educational policy, particularly as it relates to preparation for work. To analyze if educational policy has satisfied labor market demands from 2000 to 2015, we focus particularly on the relationship between education and employment in two particular periods of the country's recent history: the so-called Battle of Ideas and the process of updating the economic and social model.

The idea of education as not just a basic universal right but also as a basic component of development and economic growth has gained growing academic and political support (Ranis and Steward, 2002; Cribeiro, 2011; Torres, 2013; López, 2012). In the case of Cuba, education, long viewed as one of the keys to development, has undergone important changes in the current century. Especially education for the workplace—understood as preparing individuals to find their places in the labor market (Jacinto, 2014)—has changed in terms of both strategies and priorities. Hence we examine the question of congruity-versus-disequilibrium in this area as one of the main elements that may contribute to economic development and may favor either the promotion of social equity or the growth of inequality.

Various international institutions have studied the relationship between human development and economic growth. The Economic Commission of Latin America (CEPAL) has demonstrated a close connection between them. Countries that have achieved good indicators in health and education, through public spending devoted to those spheres, have greater possibilities of showing positive economic growth. By contrast, countries whose priority is economic growth, and where public spending on health and education is seen as a derivative of that growth, rarely succeed in improving human development (Ranis and Steward, 2000).

There is no consensus, however, about what *type* of education best contributes to economic development. Some studies find expansion of primary education to be the main contributor to increased productivity (Schultz, 1975; Welch, 1970; Rosenzweig, 1995; Foster, 2000; all as cited by Ranis and Steward, 2002). Others emphasize the tertiary level as the main contributor to the development of basic sciences, adoption and adaptation of technology, and domestic development of new technology (Ranis and Steward, 2002), all much-desired results in underdeveloped economies. In this century, it has been argued that the useful effects of primary and secondary education have not increased at the same rate as access has been universalized, probably because improvement in quality has not matched growth in quantity; conversely, the opposite is true in higher education (Carnoy, 2005). The relationship between education and work also appears to be stronger in economies in which basic education is universal (Formichella and London, 2012).

Disequilibrium between education and employment[1] has repercussions at the individual, organizational, and national levels, and thus has a broad relation to human development. At the individual level, such incongruities are evident in the low wage and salary levels of individuals who are overqualified for a given post, or who express dissatisfaction with their jobs. At the organizational level, low productivity and high turnover are the most expensive effects. At the national level, sustainability of the system requires some rate of return on the investment made in education; also, failure to take advantage of qualified personnel represents a loss of potential opportunities for growth (Farooq, 2011:1).

In terms of equity, these incongruities have differential effects, such as gender gaps in levels of education, educational specialties, and occupations.[2] Men's and women's choices and labor market locations are differentiated, characterized by feminization of higher education and masculinization of technical education,[3] a tendency toward feminization of social sciences and masculinization of technical ones, and females in lower-level service occupations as compared to males in primary and industrial sectors, especially in technical and management posts. Several studies point to wage and salary gaps stemming from the different educational levels and specialties of women and men (Corominas et al., 2012;

Carnoy, 2005; Machín and Puhani, 2003). At the same time, the life cycles of women and men differ: women's biological and social maternity has a great effect on their work trajectories, because the time devoted to care of young children results in employment plateaus during the same period when male co-workers, in general, are in the process of adding skills and seeking better jobs (Echevarría, 2008; Heller, 2010; Maurizio, 2010).

Growth in educational availability and quality is often cited as a factor in development, but in order for these factors to operate, especially in terms of education for future careers, there have to be sufficient job opportunities, access to well-paid work, and equitable access to professional development. Several studies show that an increase in graduates does not necessarily result in greater advantage being take of their skills as a contribution to development, unless policies are oriented by that vision (Moreno-Brid and Ruiz, 2009; Palladines, 2008).

A more specific investigation seeks to focus on what sort of education contributes to graduates' occupational lives. On an international level, study of this area has paid particular attention to the college and university level, and so this field of research has become entangled in debates about the mission of the university and has come down on the side of the "utilitarian mission" (Íñigo, 2005); that is, the university's capacity to educate professionals with the skills needed to meet societal demands over the medium and long term. A debate around the relationship between years of instruction and the workplace skills developed is still underway (Bassi, et al., 2012). At the same time, Moreno-Brid and Ruiz (2009) argue that to strengthen the tie between the university and the labor market requires not just advances in the quantity and quality of graduates, but also sufficient job opportunities as well as institutions that link academic and research groups with firms participating in the labor market.

However, such ties are not easy to build. Marta Novick (2004) argues that education and industry follow different logics, so that their linkage requires a well-considered strategy. Their relationship may also turn out to be cyclical, because efforts to promote education and training grow in the upswings of economic cycles and weaken rapidly or disappear in downturns (Novick, 2004).

The social sciences have accumulated theoretical and empirical evidence about the link between education and employment and its effects on development, but this field has not been sufficiently explored in Cuba. This chapter provides a first approach to that topic. We look at two periods of recent Cuban history characterized by different emphases in social and economic policy. We assess the real and potential contribution of workforce-oriented education to human development and its specific implications for education and employment policies.

The period known as the Battle of Ideas[4](approximately 2001–2009) was marked by a central focus on individuals' educational advancement and an attempt to improve the living conditions of the populace (Escandell, 2006). The process of updating the economic and social model began in approximately 2010 and has continued since. In 2011, the Sixth Congress of the Cuban Communist Party (Spanish initials PCC) defined its direction more clearly regarding the programmatic basis of the Guidelines of Economic and Social Policy. In this second period, an emphasis on recovery of efficiency and productivity predominates.

The chapter's next section is a discussion of the major transformations in education for careers and in employment since 2000. Next, we analyze the relationship between education and labor market demands as a process and offer final reflections on this topic.

The Main Changes in Education and Employment in Cuba, 2000–2015

Key Elements to Understand Education in Cuba and Its Relation to Careers

Various studies describe Latin America as the most unequal region of the planet (Oxfam, 2015) in spite of a considerable decline in poverty since the 2000s (CAF-FLACSO, 2014). While the % of children and adolescents in primary and secondary school rose, the percentage of 9th grade graduates remains low, about 50% for young people between 15 and 19, and the percentage of 12th grade graduates among those younger than 24 is about 40% (Bassi, et al., 2012:4). The average number of school years completed varies from nine to twelve among the countries studied (Bassi, et al., 2012: 3).

Cuba's situation is quite different, with indicators better than the region's: graduation rates over 99% for completing the primary school cycle, 94% completing junior high school (ONEI, 2015) and an overall average of 11.5 years of schooling among population of 25 or more years old (PNUD, 2015). These results are largely owing to the equity orientation that has guided Cuba's social policy since 1959. Cuba also shows positive indicators related to health, education, and labor market access[5]compared to Latin America and the Caribbean. In Human Development Index rankings, Cuba has consistently been among the countries with "moderately high" human development, and it was ranked among the "very high" countries in 2014 (PNUD, 2014).

These results stem from the application of social policies based on the principles of universal, free-of-charge access to basic services such as education, health care, and employment, combined with a broad social safety net. However, the crisis of the 1990s led to reduced spending in these areas. Yet the state maintained its role as the primary regulator and implemented various social protection policies for the most vulnerable groups. As a result of reform measures taken to respond to the crisis, a degree of economic relief began to appear in the middle of the 1990s, as verified in gross domestic product (GDP) growth starting in 1995 (Pérez, 2004:13).

Education in Cuba is entirely a state function, free at all levels, and obligatory through ninth grade. When students finish what is called *secundaria básica* (roughly equivalent to U.S. junior high school) at the end of ninth grade, they choose between attending technical education (*Enseñanza Técnica-Profesional*, see endnote 3) or going on to pre-university study. Technical education prepares either skilled workers (*obreros calificados*) or mid-level technicians (*técnicos medios*), with educational levels equivalent to ninth grade and twelfth grade, respectively. Its graduates are ready to enter the work world in a wide variety of specialties. Access to the various types of education for junior high graduates depends on their ranking on a grade-point average scale, on their results on entrance exams if required, and on the number of available slots in the option they request.

The pre-university system, also known as the higher-middle level (*nivel medio superior*), runs through twelfth grade. Its mission is to prepare its graduates to enter the higher education system. The most important types of schools in this system are: Urban Pre-universities (IPU), Pre-universities in the Countryside (IPUEC), Vocational Pre-universities for the Exact Sciences (IPVCE), Vocational-Pedagogical Pre-universities, and Camilo Cienfuegos Military Schools, which prepare students for careers as military officers.

The process of granting junior-high graduates access to the various forms of continuing study seeks to harmonize their vocational interests, their academic achievements so far, and the economic and social needs of the country and particularly of each geographical area, as expressed in the demand for skilled labor calculated by the Ministry of Labor and Social Security. The entrance application decisions are made and implemented at various levels: provincial, municipal, or in the school.

For students who complete pre-university studies, those who want to go on to higher education must take college entrance exams. A formula combining in equal proportions this result with pre-university grades determines a student's standing on the scale used to award enrollment spots in various university majors (the *carreras*, or "careers," in which they specialize from the beginning of their university studies). Student decisions about applying for the various majors or careers generally take into account their interest in the specialty in question, their academic scores, and the number of slots available according to the announced enrollment projections. These projections are determined by the Ministry of Labor and Social Security in coordination with the educational system, on the basis of demand for qualified professionals as estimated by municipal and provincial governments and agencies of the central state apparatus. Students who complete pre-university and do not want to continue with university courses are offered the opportunity of further study in the technical education system.

The modalities of study in Cuban higher education system are: regular daytime courses, directed independent study (*cursos por encuentros*), and distance education. Pre-university graduates usually enter the regular daytime courses. The directed study and distance education courses enroll workers and students who do not win admission to higher education in the regular application process following pre-university. At times, the directed study courses have also been subject to merit-based access criteria, with more or less rigor depending on factors including the balance of supply and demand for these slots. The most rigorous period was that between the 2010–11 and 2015–16 academic years, when entrance exams were required for access to all modalities of higher education, including distance education.

Changes in Education Policy: Main Effects

In terms of educational policy, the period between 2000 and 2009 and the one from 2010 through today are clearly defined. The 2001–02 academic year marked the beginning of the Battle of Ideas in higher education, while the second period is associated with the updating process; in the field of education, it began in the 2010–11 academic year.

Social policy played a central role in the so-called Battle of Ideas. This process tried to develop the country through education and culture, taking advantage of the potential of Cuba's educated human resources and trying to incorporate some groups that had been excluded from the opportunities for access offered by universal policies.[6] More than 200 programs in the fields of education, health, culture, and IT/communications were begun to upgrade access and the quality of these services (Escandell, 2006). Escandell identifies a group of underlying problems that this process attempted to reverse, including:

> . . . an exodus of teachers to emerging sectors of the economy and a drop in the number of young people enrolling in the country's

teachers' colleges; hundreds of classrooms in Havana and the rest of the country with more than forty students, resulting in serious effects on the process of teaching and learning; highly specialized teachers with fifteen or thirty years' experience teaching just one subject, while the junior high schools were suffering a lack of staff; an elitist enrollment system at the pre-university level,[7] less material being covered in various subjects, and students interrupting continuation of their studies for multiple reasons (Escandell, 2006:4).

Out of the set of new measures that went into effect in the area of education, we will deal only with those related to technical education and the universities, because those are the main sectors involved with career education, that is, producing the professionals who will join the labor market once their studies are over.

Studying the relationship between school and work in Cuba involves a methodological problem, because public statistics on education provide indicators of the level of study completed but not necessarily of the acquisition of skills. Our research has utilized indicators such as enrollment and graduation totals disaggregated by type of institution or branch of science, as well as figures that show efficiency and graduation rates. Although these indicators do not directly show the kinds of abilities that education develops, they do offer clues about levels of knowledge and about specialties, which can be more or less oriented toward the skills required from the employment point of view.

In Cuban technical education, the changes sought to make the programs a better match for the demands of the venues that were looking for workers (Mena, 2006). Therefore, the time spent on basic education was reduced, while that for internships and other direct learning in workplaces increased. Also, new programs and textbooks and more use of information technology tools were introduced. For students in their senior years, this distribution of time fostered the tightening of links between study and work to develop abilities and skills for the kinds of work that graduates would be doing. Thus, 85% of their time was assigned to specific occupational education and training under the supervision of specialized instructors within workplaces (Mena, 2006).

This policy of moving schooling further into the realm of the workplace accompanied a drop in the number of schools devoted to technical education. In the 2007–08 academic year, there were 107 fewer such institutions than in 2002–03 (ONEI, 2008); enrollment had been relatively stable until 2006–07, but it then dropped at an annual rate of 7% beginning in

2007–08 until it stabilized again at the beginning of the next decade. Initial enrollment[8] in 2011–12 was 65% of what it had been in 2006–07, and it remained relatively stable at that level in the following years. Though the drop in technical education enrollment involved both men and women, the decline was particularly steep in the number of women (Figure 6.1, Panel A). Similarly, men made up a majority of the graduates from this

Figure 6.1: Enrollment (Panel A) and Graduates (Panel B) from Technical Education and Higher Education, by Gender

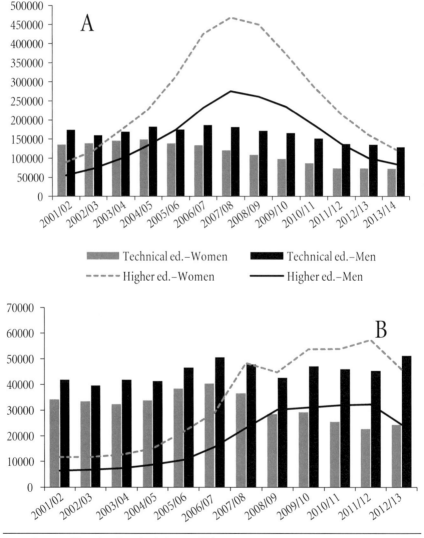

Source: Constructed by authors from data in ONEI, multiple years

type of study (Figure 6.1, Panel B). This trend was probably related to the broadening of other educational options more attractive to women, such as access to higher education. Stereotypes about technical education persist, mostly implying that technical tasks are "typical of men"; this is one factor making the higher education alternative more attractive to women. At the same time, the graduation rate[9] rose during the period, from 63.5% in 2002–03[10] to 88.1% in 2009–10 (Figure 6.2).

Figure 6.2: Patterns of Graduation Rates in Technical Education and Efficiency* Rates in Higher Education (%)

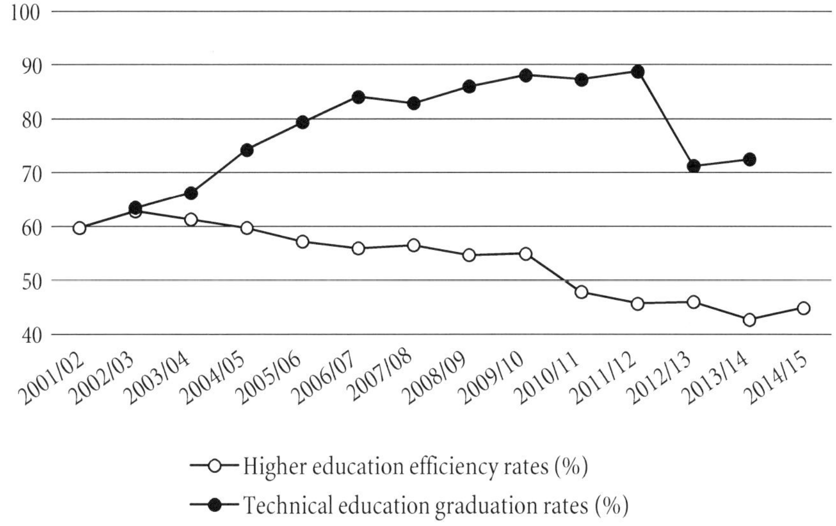

—○— Higher education efficiency rates (%)

—●— Technical education graduation rates (%)

Source: Constructed by authors from data in ONEI, multiple years, and Ministerio de Educación Superior (MES), 2016

*Translator's note: *Eficiencia académica*, an indicator used by the Ministry of Higher Education, is an approximate measure of the annual promotion rate of an entering class or cohort of university students. The estimation of this indicator considers the over-all promotion rate of each year through which a cohort passes. Since many students tend to take time off and then reenter the university, it is difficult to keep close track of cohorts, which is why the measure is only approximate. This chapter renders it literally as "academic efficiency."

In higher education, new efforts were made to broaden university access to all social groups in all regions of the country and include those who had been excluded for various reasons. This process, known as "universalization," led to the opening, in the 2001–02 academic year, of Municipal University Branches, local institutions subordinated to the central universities. These branches offered nearly fifty majors from almost all fields of study offered in Cuba, with the participation of thousands of production and service professionals who passed through an evaluation process to be certified as university teachers. This alternative favored enrollment by a larger proportion of children of workers and peasants, and of blacks and mixed-race people (Martín and Leal, 2006). Higher education reached its maximum enrollment in 2007–08, with 743,979 students, five times as many as in 2001–02 (MES, 2015). This growth is also reflected in the rise of the gross rate of high education enrollment,[11]which reached 66.2% in 2007–08.

Figure 6.3: Gross Rate of Higher Education Enrollment (%), 2001–2015

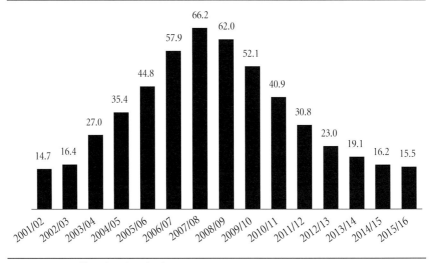

Source: Constructed by authors from data in MES, 2016

The specialties with highest enrollment in 2007–08, categorized by broad areas of study, were, in order, medical sciences,[12]social sciences and humanities, education, physical education, economics, technical sciences, agricultural sciences, and finally natural sciences and mathematics (MES 2015).With the exception of natural science and mathematics, all of these categories showed enrollment above their figures for the beginning of this period, 2001–02.[13] Some (such as social sciences and humanities, medical sciences, physical education and economics) surpassed the peak figures reached in the 1980s, while others (education, and technical and agricultural sciences) approximately recovered the levels of those years.[14] To make room for the increased number of students, the total number of university sites and branches reached 3,150 (ONEI, 2005).In order to sustain this higher level of service, the education budget for 2005 totaled 169% of what it had been in 2000, behind health care (196%) and science and technology (298.3%) (ONEI, 2006).

As the figures show, this period was characterized by an emphasis on broadening access to higher education, demonstrated by the growth in enrollment in many fields and the physical extension of universities to more areas of the country. The principal beneficiaries were blacks and mixed-race students, whose proportions increased in the student body. Also, there were more students whose parents were not university graduates, professionals or officials (Martín and Leal, 2006). Women continued to be in the majority, and this was the first time that higher education enrollment exceeded that of technical education. However, starting in 2007–08 for the technical level and 2008–09 for the universities, enrollment has declined, particularly in higher education. The drop is not explainable by the decrease in population during this period, as will be seen below in discussion of the gross rate of school enrollment.[15]

This occurs in a context in which Latin America and the Caribbean have seen accelerated growth in tertiary education enrollment, especially rapid in the 2000–10 decade (Rama, 2009; OREAL/UNESCO, 2013). According to UNESCO, the number of students in higher education per hundred thousand inhabitants in the region[16] rose from 2,316 in 2000 to 3,328 in 2010, an increase of a little more than 40% over the decade. The UNESCO report also shows that this positive trend was present in all the countries studied, but it was more accelerated in some; it points to Cuba as an example. In Cuba, the number of students in higher education per hundred thousand inhabitants[17] rose from 1,145 in 2000–01 to 4,210 in 2010–11 (authors' calculation from data in MES, 2016), for an increase of 268%.

In 2003, near the beginning of the decade, total university enrollment in Latin America and the Caribbean reached nearly 14 million, yielding a gross rate of enrollment[18] of 28.5% in the region as a whole and 15.3% in the Caribbean (Didriksson, 2008).[19] In Cuba, in the 2003–04 year, the gross enrollment rate reached 27.04% (Figure 6.3), but this indicator kept increasing at an accelerating pace until reaching 66.2% in 2007–08. In fact, according to Rama (2009)[20], enrollment in comparison to the population aged 20–24—the same parameter used by Didriksson—reached 31.8% in 2005, and was predicted to reach 35% by 2008. Both values were exceeded by the gross enrollment rate achieved by Cuba in 2005–06 and 2008–09, respectively (Figure 6.3). These results together show that while growth in higher education characterized the first decade of this century in Latin America and the Caribbean, the extent of universalization and growth of the municipal university branches in Cuba had a special impact on access to higher education, which much exceeded the regional trend.

The fields of study receiving the greatest impetus were social sciences and humanities, partly as a response to the need to understand the social changes underway, and partly because these disciplines have lower technology and infrastructure demands than, for instance, natural sciences and mathematics.

This expansion occurred in a context initially characterized by a recovery of GDP, which continued rising at an accelerating rate until 2006 (a year in which it rose 12.1% over the previous one), after which its growth rate fell consecutively: 2007, 7.3%; 2008: 4.1%; 2009, 1.4%. Between 2000 and 2006, annual investments devoted to education always constituted more than 12% of the total for all sectors of economic activity. However, this prioritization of education also created problems for the economy from the perspective of efficiency and economic productivity, which would become the key concerns of the next period.

The second decade of the 2000s represents the beginning of a different era. The updating of the economic and social model, formally begun in 2011, places more emphasis on promoting labor productivity and efficiency, introducing various modifications in social policy and amounts and apportioning social spending, among other measures. This set of changes began in a context of mild recovery of GDP after the slowdown in its growth at the end of the previous decade. In 2010, GDP stood 2.4% above the level of the year before (ONEI, 2014).

In general, since 2011 the share of the national budget devoted to health, education, social security and social assistance has remained above 43% of total spending—except for 2012, when it was 39.7%—and around 49% of operational spending, with the exception of 45.4% in 2012 (authors' calculations based on data from ONEI, 2014). This spending pattern shows a commitment to maintaining social guarantees for the population in sensitive areas. However, there has been a certain drop in absolute amounts, which to a large degree conforms to the policy of using more targeted social assistance, concentrating health care services, and reducing the number of boarding schools, among other measures proposed by the Guidelines of Economic and Social Policy (PCC 2011, #143, 148, and 155).

In the education sector, initial enrollments in higher education have continued to drop since 2010 (Figure 6.1, Panel A), but the number of new entrants[21] has shown a discrete rising trend since the minimum recorded in 2011–12 (MES, 2016). Meanwhile, enrollment in technical education has stabilized from 2011–12, at around 64–65% of that 2006–07 total.

In 2009, Resolution 109 regarding technical education brought changes in the structure of specialties. Two new categories of specialties under the rubric of Petroleum and Transport were added (made up mostly of new courses), and the total number of specialties increased by nine, including some completely new ones such as Human Capital Management and Beauty Services. In this new configuration more oriented toward trades, young women continue to have little motivation to enroll and graduate; this has resulted in a drop in female enrollment and graduation (Figure 6.1, Panels A and B).Graduation rates in the technical education system continued their upward trend until 2011–12, when they peaked at 88.8%. As Figure 6.2 shows, in 2012–13 and 2013–14 this indicator dropped to 71.3% and 72.5%, respectively.

In higher education, in contrast to the previous period of universalization, the changes implemented have sought to assure the quality of the graduates in all modalities of study. At the end of this century's first decade, *continuidad de estudios*[22] (a modality of study associated originally with the municipal university branches) began to lose priority within the study modalities; in effect; in the 2010–11 year there were no new enrollments in it. In the middle of the second decade, initial enrollments in higher education continued to drop, but at a much slower rate, tending rather to stabilize;[23] this pattern can also be seen in the gross rate of enrollment (Figure 6.3).

Additionally, changes in the admissions system were introduced in the 2009–10 academic year, going into effect for 2010–11 entrants. It had become obligatory to pass the university entrance exams to gain access to any modality of study within the Cuban higher education system. Problems in student preparedness had become evident in the system in general and especially among those studying in the municipal branches.[24]

At this level of education, enrollment is notably lower than it was in 2007–08,[25] and technical majors predominate over social sciences, which had been prioritized in the previous decade. In 2014–15, in terms of the broad categories of specialties, medical sciences had the highest enrollment, followed in order by technical sciences, education, social science and humanities, economics, physical education, agriculture, and finally natural sciences and mathematics. With the exception of natural sciences and mathematics, all these categories showed drops in enrollment. However, the shrinkage was not proportional across fields of study; for instance, for every ten students enrolled in social sciences in 2007–08, there is only one today, while for technical sciences that ratio is ten to seven.[26]Meanwhile the higher education system continues to enroll more females than males and to graduate more females as well,[27] even as these two indicators dropped for both genders (Figure 6.1, Panels A and B). The proportion of whites and of children of university graduates, professionals, and officials has increased (Tejuca, Gutiérrez, and García, 2015).

Academic efficiency has followed a gradual downward trend since 2002–03. The figure for 2002–03 was 62.8%, while in 2013–14 it was only 42.8% (Figure 6.2). However, in the most recent complete academic year, 2014–15, the indicator rose slightly to 44.9%, which can be explained by the improved promotion rate of the cohort in its first year of study.[28]

In summary, in the first decade of the 2000s, preparation of students for careers was characterized by emphasis on broadening access to higher education and an explicit intention to facilitate access to it for people who for various reasons had not been able to enter the tertiary level before. Since 2008, this situation changed; enrollment gradually began to fall. In the current period, there has been greater emphasis on technical and medical sciences, more consistent with the declared demand for employment; that change has been influenced to a large degree by greater linkage of the numbers of slots for new students to the numbers of expected jobs for graduates.[29]However, as we shall see, the majority of graduates from these levels of education entered the labor market in very different circumstances from those that prevailed when they began their studies.

The Cuban Labor Market, 2000–2014

According to Guillermo Labarca, understanding the dynamic of the labor market and its relationship to the processes of developing human resources requires analysis of the specific characteristics of economic development and technological innovation in the region or country in question (Labarca, 2004).Labor markets in Latin America in this period were characterized by employment growth and a decline of about 7% in unemployment (OIT, 2011). In spite of these advances, gender inequalities persisted, as reflected in differing labor force participation rates for women and men, continuing lack of occupational and income parity, and differences in job security and the distribution of non-paid work time for women and men (CEPAL, 2013; CEPAL/OIT, 2015). Toward the end of this period, a slowdown in the growth of Latin American economies cast doubt on the likelihood of maintaining the accomplishments of recent years of narrowing the persistent gaps in access to decent jobs. It remains unclear to what extent those accomplishments were due to changes in productive patterns and subsequent inequalities (OIT, 2013). Recent reports by CEPAL and the International Labor Organization (OIT) show that participation rates declined more than unemployment rates (CEPAL/OIT, 2014 and 2015). Moreover, both indicators are expected to worsen in the coming years due to the diminished capacity to generate formal paid jobs, even though 2014 saw a moderate increase in real wages (CEPAL/OIT, 2015).

In Cuba, Ricardo Torres has pointed out problems affecting the country's development, such as: insufficient use of natural resources, which generates dependence on foreign ones; failure to make use of human resources, which stems from the structure of exports and from characteristics of the industrial and service sectors; loss of capacity in the knowledge-dissemination networks; not enough diversification of the productive matrix and exports; low levels of productive investment; weak development of contemporary technological platforms; and low availability of research resources (Torres, 2013:34). In this framework, potential employers had few opportunities to make use of the human resources that came onto the labor market, especially in the first decade of the 2000s when large numbers of students graduated from the universities into the world of work.

Until the 1990s, the main source of employment in Cuba had been the state sector, which accounted for more than 90% of jobs. Thus, use of the term "labor market"—in the sense of an exchange between the supply of people with education and training and the demand from potential employers—came to make sense only following the reforms implemented in that decade. The concept of "economic multi-spatiality"[30] to a large degree explains the reality of the labor market of those years, characterized by a diversity of economic actors (Martín, 2007; Nicolau and Campos, 2007). Also, the commitment to full employment as a principle of labor market policy made the state responsible for guaranteeing employment for all.

In the first decade of the 2000s, the labor market[31] showed a certain decrease in the diversity of economic opportunities, especially in the private sector. In that decade as well, employment grew steadily in the sector of social, community, and personal services (including health care and education). Although there were also increases in mines and quarries, transportation, and electricity, gas, and water, their share of total employment is smaller, so these increases were not as visible. The rest of the sectors trended downward. The sector of community, social, and personal services then had to absorb the majority of graduates of the various educational initiatives related to the Battle of Ideas. Thus the labor market had a supply of abundant human resources, with excessive homogeneity in their education and training. In the framework of full employment policies, they did not always find jobs in line with their education.

In subsequent years, the process of updating the economic and social model has promoted the development of a growing non-state sector, with non-farm cooperatives as the main new development alongside an increase in private employment. The pattern can be seen in the evolution of employment totals as shown in Table 6.1.

Table 6.1: Employment According to Type of Firm, 2002–2014 (Thousands of Employees)												
	2002	2003	2004	2005	2006	2007	2008	2009	2010	2011	20 2	2013	2014
State-owned and mixed entities	4088.4	4163.3	3694	3785.6	3888.6	4036.13	4112.3	4249.5	4178.1	3873	368⊏3	3627.6	3591.3
Cooperatives	316.9	292.7	280.1	271.3	257	242.1	233.8	231.6	217	208.7	21⊏6	227	231.5
Private businesses	152.9	151	667.6	665.6	609	589.5	602.1	591.3	589.4	928.5	100⊏3	1064.2	1147

Source: Constructed by authors from data in ONEI, multiple years

The highest unemployment rate of the period under study came in 2000, with a rate of 5.4 %, after which it began to drop until it reached 1.6% in 2008. After that, the rate began to increase again, up to about 3.5% in 2012, and then dropped in 2014, to about 2.7%.[32]Indices of the economically active share of the population hit a low point in 2000 at 64% (ONEI, 2005), then rose until 2011, and declined to 71.9% in 2014, with a lower female rate (56.3%) and a higher male one (86.2%) (ONEI, 2015).[33]

If we categorize the numbers of institutions offering jobs according to type of entity, cooperatives predominate; in the period under analysis, there have been more cooperatives than state enterprises and other state-budget entities (ONEI, 2014). Until 2013, these were all agricultural cooperatives, with several different sorts of property tenure and relationship to the state.[34]Moreover, since 2012 there has been a number of changes in the state sector as a consequence of the restructuring of the state apparatus. This restructuring set up Organizaciones Superiores de Dirección (OSDE) and turned existing state enterprises into Unidades Empresariales de Base, thus reducing enterprise autonomy (Díaz, 2014).In terms of sectors of economic activity, the dominance of community, social, and personal services continues, to the detriment of more technology-intensive or knowledge-based economic activities (ONEI, various years).

The main sources of employment for recent graduates have been shifting from mostly state firms toward the cooperative and private sectors, although the state still predominates. In sectorial terms, social and personal services remain the main source of employment, without any evident increase in more knowledge-based sectors that could take better advantage of the contributions of higher-education graduates; presumably, the latter sectors are those that can contribute the most to developing basic science, achieving more flexibility in the adoption and adaptation of technology, and generating new technologies.

The retreat from the principle of full employment and the dismissal of workers in the state sector had evident effects by 2014; since 2010 it had over 51,000 fewer women working there, even though women's share of the working-age population had risen.[35]Overall, women were leaving the economically active population (those who are looking for work, studying, or employed). Some changes may also be seen in the structure of employment according to occupational category, in favor of operators, administrators, and officials, while technical and service personnel decreased. Also there was a drop in the absolute number of those employed (categorized by sector) in agriculture, hunting, forestry, fishing, and manufacturing, while an analysis of relative patterns shows that women have particularly been leaving the "male sectors": in agriculture, construction, and transportation, women dropped by between two and four percentage points from 2010 to 2014.[36]

In terms of pay,[37] some studies show that average monthly salary has little effect on the performance and qualifications of the labor force, because wage and salary policies favor pay equality irrespective of sector, geography, and occupational or qualification categories (Galtés, 2015). The occupational categories that imply quality and complexity of work, and that presumably depend on the level of educational qualifications combined with experience accumulated in a specific job, do not show contrasts in remuneration because the spread between minimum and maximum salaries is very narrow (Galtés, 2015). While sector of economic activity could make a difference in terms of salary, the cited study finds little evidence of such differentiation.

These processes occur in a context in which the average monthly salary in state and mixed enterprises has been growing, to the point where in 2014 it was 2.3 times what it had been in 2000. However, the consumer price index for markets in domestic currency[38] in 2014 was 3.5 times that of 2013, while the average monthly salary grew by only 1.2%. Thus, increases in nominal wages still do not cover the cost of Cuban daily life.

In sum, nominal salaries do not provide sufficient economic incentive for changing occupational category, increasing educational level, or shifting economic activities. According to Galtés (2015), the main such incentives are associated with seeking additional income outside the basic salary, additional earnings from secondary activities,[39] and moving outside the state sector. This other labor market confronts career education graduates with new exigencies and places women in the most vulnerable positions. Although the state sector and social and community services still provide the bulk of available jobs, the non-state economic sector is increasing. As a result, new individual skills and new concepts of career education could be required in the short and medium term.

Congruities and Incongruities between Education and Jobs since 2000

The study of congruities/incongruities between education and employment in Cuba presents certain methodological challenges. In the first place, as noted already, years of study, level of education, type of education, and field of knowledge can all serve as proxy values for abilities, skills, and capacities to perform different types of jobs, but these dimensions do not, in themselves, directly tell what variables make an individual most employable (Bassi et al., 2012). Assuming that technical education is more oriented toward jobs with moderate or low levels of complexity while higher education allows for formation of capacities for analysis and adaptation that favor a wider range of job offerings, one may infer that those graduating from the tertiary level should have better opportunities for getting jobs and succeeding in them.[40] Also, workforce insertion policies have facilitated job placement of recent graduates of that level, so they can count on a secure job when they leave the educational system.[41]

Another challenge is posed by the lack of longitudinal research (conducted or published) that would follow the graduates. Some research centers have carried out systematic analyses of the process of labor market insertion, but there are no results about graduates' workforce trajectories, which could prove useful for assessing the results of career education beyond the question of initial entrance into employment. The Center for Research on Higher Education (CEPES) of the University of Havana has carried out a number of studies to follow the labor market insertion of university graduates (Íñigo, Vega, and Delgado, 2014). The results show that, compared to periods analyzed previously,[42] the university-workplace relationship has been strengthened, although there are still things to be done, such as "the need to systematize and generalize a period of training that would complement the graduates' education and facilitate their adaptation, and the insufficient technical-economic authority and its implications for the graduates' effective professional and social development" (Íñigo, et al.:3).

This study shows that although 90% of university graduates are doing work related to their specialties, 30% have changed jobs or want to do so. Also, both their direct supervisors and higher officials of their employing agencies point to deficits in basic competencies such as foreign language mastery, evaluation of economic consequences in professional work, ability to make opportune and well-founded decisions, capacity to manage projects and involve others in them, and orientation, organization, and monitoring of the work of others. They acknowledge, however, university graduates' appropriate theoretical grounding, up-to-date information, technical mastery, ability to adapt quickly, wide knowledge of advanced technology, ability to multitask, good study habits and capacity for professional self-development, good work attitudes, and sense of responsibility, among others (Íñigo, et al.:7).

Meanwhile, a study carried out by the Institute for Research on Work that followed technical education graduates in two provinces found that some of the reasons those who were unemployed did not have jobs were dissatisfaction with the place and/or content of work (García and de la Torre, 2006). A methodological seminar carried out by the National Institute of Social Security (INASS) in 2005 reported that a not-insignificant share of technical education graduates had no job and were not attending school, and the same was true of graduates of trade schools (INASS, 2005).

As a way of responding to these problems, the 2013 Labor Code modified the state's responsibility for placing graduates of the technical and trade schools, who from then on would only have to fulfill the requirement for two years of mandated social service jobs that had already been solicited by employers.[43] This general rule modified what was previously stipulated in Resolution 9/2007 ("Regulation on the treatment of recent graduates during the process of workforce training"), which said that recent graduates of this type of education should be placed according to the centralized distribution plan approved by the provincial and municipal administrative councils. According to 9/2007, the salaries of the graduates were to be paid out of the training budget of the entity receiving them.

The 2013 modification explicitly recognized the labor system's inability, for several years, to provide jobs that matched the hopes and preparation of technical education graduates and the obligatory nature of their social service period even when the assigned job was outside their area of interest. However, it transferred the responsibility to seek more adequate jobs to the young people and their families. Also, as noted above, the current configuration of the job market locates the main opportunities for skilled work in the non-state sector, where most likely these graduates can find work only as employees because they lack the capital to set up a business and the practical abilities and experience in their specialties.

According to compiled figures on estimated workforce demands for 2014–18[44] by levels of education, as shown in Table 6.2, for graduates of higher and *técnico medio* education, a predominant tendency is toward more available jobs than available graduates. The excess of trade school graduates represent a certain bottleneck. On the education side, their numbers represent an expected trend in the country, but on the labor-force demand side there is no representation of the private sector. That is still not seen as an actor in development, not only in terms of generating employment but also as a source of capital, technology, innovation; the sector is not taken into account in the model of demand. Thus it would seem that those who graduate as skilled workers are not considered covered by the requests assembled by the state bodies, but they may find sufficient jobs in the non-state sector.

Table 6.2: Balance of Demand and Availability, 2014–2018						
Educational Level **Demand-Availability**	**Total**	**YEAR**				
		2014	**2015**	**2016**	**2017**	**2018**
Higher Education						
• Demand	168129	43483	34076	31424	29615	29531
• Availability	92757	29243	18872	14606	14714	15322
• Difference	−75372	−14240	−15204	−16818	−14901	−14209
Mid-Level Technician (*técnico medio*)						
• Demand	102059	28325	25502	25372	22860	—
• Availability	98077	38865	18207	22243	18762	—
• Difference	−3982	10540	−7295	−3129	−4098	—
Skilled Worker						
• Demand	57116	28984	28132	—	—	—
• Availability	77385	38064	39321	—	—	—
• Difference	20269	9080	11189	—	—	—
Totals						
• Demand	327304	100792	87710	56796	52475	29531
• Availability	268219	106172	76400	36849	33476	15322
• Difference	−59085	5380	−11310	−19947	−18999	−14209

Legend: − deficit of graduates
+ graduates for whom there is no demand

Source: Office of Training and Development, Department of Employment, Ministry of Work and Social Security (MTSS). December, 2013.

While improvements remain to be made in the determination of workforce demand, given that it is limited to the state sector,[45] the projections show that the growth in graduates solicited on the workforce has still not been met by enrollment or graduation numbers for technical or higher education, because the demand for graduates over the next few years is higher than their availability from the relevant types of education. The educational policy in effect through mid-2015 led to a contraction in enrollment, especially in higher education, which is reflected in a lower gross rate of enrollment, as was seen in Figure 6.3.

Bear in mind, however, that the numbers of employed Cubans with high school or university educations have been growing over the past fifteen years, reaching 51.9% and 21.4% of total employment, respectively.

Women present a more favorable situation, because in these groups they constitute 53.4% and 32.1%, respectively, of all women employed in the same period. These data indicate the existence and availability of qualified workers within the employed population. However, during 2013 more than 58% of the employed were more than 40 years old,[46] so the role of recent graduates in guaranteeing the succession and continuity of the labor force should not be forgotten. What does not appear to be a problem in 2015—the reduction in number of middle- and higher-education graduates—could affect the qualifications of the labor force within the next fifteen years if the current downward trend continues.

Analyzing the career graduates (the total graduates from technical and higher education) by gender shows a relative balance of women and men throughout the period, with women making up the majority of graduates from 2005 and 2012. However, this parity does not directly affect women's entry into the work world because the female economic activity rate[47] is below 61% of women of working age, while for men it exceeds 86%.[48]

In 2015 some of the changes announced in Cuban higher education (Rodríguez, 2015), will have an impact on access. The change in the procedure for admission to directed study and distance education courses, the incorporation into these programs of the objectives that are usually evaluated in entrance exams, the diversification of specialties that may be studied in these modalities, and the wider number of admission slots are measures that will likely have a positive impact on access to higher education; as a result, there should be more university graduates. As part of the changes, the number of available slots for directed study and distance education have been placed in the hands of the universities. These institutions are currently responsible for the design of plans that will respond to their regions' needs for professionals and to the capacities of each university, including the main campuses, the municipal branches, and other branches. The first impact of these measures may be seen in the 59,866 total slots offered for distance education for 2016–17 (Ramón, 2016).

At the same time, there is a plan to create a new level of education called non-university higher education, or short-cycle higher education (two or three years of duration) to prepare students for specific workforce occupations. The hope is that these graduates' entry into the labor market will to some degree reduce the disequilibrium between qualifications and occupations in the form of underutilization of the qualified workforce. Also, the Higher Education Ministry has undertaken a reform of the university curriculum to make room for broadly conceived majors that will focus on the solution of general and basic problems of the professions. This will also allow for reduction in the length of university careers, so that students graduate more quickly.

Final Considerations

The education-work relationship is a key element for thinking about the development of a country or region. In the case of Cuba, that relationship is not yet seen as strategic in spite of the individual, organizational, and social costs of that lack of vision.

Career education policies instituted in the 2000s promoted broader access to education and especially to higher education, but were generally not linked to labor market demands and suffered from an excessive emphasis on social sciences. Given the ongoing full-employment policy, this incongruity was not reflected in rising unemployment, but it did find expression at the individual level in a disjuncture between education and jobs, qualifications and jobs, and field of study and jobs. At a broader social level, expected productivity increases did not materialize.

The changes in education and training policy that have been taking place within the process of updating the economic and social model have emphasized trades and technical specialties and a structure of educational specialties that favors medical and technical sciences. The purpose of these changes has been to respond to disequilibria between the supply of skilled labor and the demands of the labor market, but this has not yet been achieved. In addition, we believe that the imbalance in the number of graduates between the various branches of the sciences, this time favoring medical and technical sciences, does not contribute to the country's development over the middle and long term.

Women experience the most severe incongruities between education and jobs. Although the totals for women are similar to those for men, this does not produce an increase in their rate of economic activity (participation rate). Also, the expected configuration of the labor market—trending toward trades and high-productivity sectors—does not offer women many opportunities because there still tend to be fewer female graduates in trades and technical specialties. The non-state sector still lacks the level of development that would absorb enough graduates from various levels of career education, especially those coming from technical schools.

Although the changes in educational policies in the two periods analyzed have had different effects on enrollments, numbers of graduates, and graduation rates, in neither case were they oriented toward improving abilities and skills for the workplace, and they encouraged insufficiently diverse graduate profiles—first, university graduates with social sciences degrees, and now technical-education graduates, especially skilled workers and technical specialists. At the same time, the changes in employment policy have not changed the occupational structure to any large degree, whether in terms of type of property of the employer, or economic activity sector, or economic incentives.

The changes in state-sector regulations and the growth of the non-state sector both threaten the guarantees for workers that prevailed before the updating period. Therefore it is likely that education will need to develop students' competencies in dealing with uncertainty, adapting to new circumstances, and exercising autonomy and responsibility in the search for jobs. Entrepreneurial and proactive capacities will be one of the requirements of the new context.

Institutionally, new models of both career education and employment policy are needed. In education, it would be advisable to have a full range of graduates in terms of both specialties and levels of education, governed not only by short-term labor market demands but also by looking farther into the future. Competencies such as entrepreneurship, proactive abilities, and other socio-emotional skills need to be promoted. The development of information technology systems that can follow various categories of graduates over time could facilitate the assessment of skills, abilities, and competencies fostered by their education. Another priority is dealing with people who do not succeed in entering any of the career education systems, which prejudices their ability to find jobs.

On the employment policy side, close attention to changes in the labor market will be vital to matching the supply and demand for qualified workers over the short, medium, and long runs. It is important to promote links among local development actors to establish a good match. No less important will be links between educational policy and proactive employment policies, so as to facilitate the insertion of vulnerable groups into the workforce.

Matching people to the job market should unfold in parallel with development of a productive and social fabric that fosters productivity growth based on taking best advantage of educational capacities. However, the improvements we have discussed need to constitute elements of the country's general development strategy; they need to be criteria for implementing economic policies, not merely areas in which economic growth can be assumed to trickle down to the social sphere.

Notes

1. A disequilibrium between education and employment shows up in three relationships: between educational level and employment, between qualifications and employment, and between field of study and employment. The first compares the number of school years completed to the number required for a given occupation or post. The second consists of the extent to which workers think their skills and abilities match their jobs; this analysis results in seeing workers as over- or underqualified. Another frequently used method measures the worker's real abilities versus those required in the specific job, which are assumed to have to be learned. The third, the relationship between field of knowledge and employment, refers to the relevance or irrelevance of a worker's field of knowledge to the content of his or her work. For more, see Farooq, 2011.

2. Other variables at the individual level also affect choices and opportunities in these spaces. These variables include skin color, area of residence, and social class.

3. Translator's note: The Cuban term *enseñanza técnica-profesional* is best translated in U.S. terms as "technical educational" or "vocational education" because it does not prepare students for what are most commonly regarded as "professional" jobs in the United States. See the authors' subsequent definition in a later section of this chapter. This chapter uses "technical" rather than "vocational" because it is closer to the Cuban term, broader in a U.S. context, and it avoids confusion with the high schools called *vocacional* in Cuba, which are college-prep institutions; see subsequent discussion of the IPVCE schools in Cuba.

4. The Battle of Ideas was a political movement initiated by a Fidel Castro speech at the closing session of the Seventh Congress of Young Communist League on December 10, 1998. Fidel asserted that, while the danger of armed aggression against the country had not completely disappeared, the main task at this time was to engage in a Battle of Ideas rather a military one (Castro, 1998). Even so, the event that marked the beginning of the movement was a march to the U.S. Interests Section in Havana by participants in the Seventh Congress of Youth Technical Brigades on December 5, 1999. The demonstration demanded the return of the child Elián González. This march turned into a process of changes guided by more than 200 programs directed at raising the population's standards and conditions of living. The programs focused on six main areas: education, culture, social attention and development, political-ideological work, investment, and health.

5. A high life expectancy: 78.45 years; a low rate of infant mortality: 4.2 per 1000 live births; higher education: 14.14% of all school graduates in the 2013/2014 academic year were in higher education, 65% of whom were women. Unemployment rates hovered around 3.3%. (Source: Authors' calculations on basis of information ONEI, 2015).

6. See Rodríguez, et al., 2000.

7. This system of access resulted from educational policies that try to correct disequilibria that had become evident in the late 1980s between the number and specialties of graduates at all levels and the country's economic needs. These policies led to lowered enrollments in higher-education institutions and higher ones in polytechnic schools (Domínguez and Díaz, 1997). In the 1992–93 school year, two out of every three ninth-grade graduates enrolled in technical education, and one out of three in pre-university, with admission decisions taking academic achievement in consideration. Additionally, at that time there were essentially two alternatives for pre-university studies: the IPUEC (boarding schools in the countryside, which were the most numerous) and IPVCE (with highly competitive entrance requirements in terms of academic achievement). The IPVCEs were the most desired because of the quality of students and professors, the design of the curriculum, and the value they placed on laboratory work, all of which in turn guaranteed success on university entrance exams (Domínguez y Díaz, 1997); however, there was only one IPVCE per province. The result was a stratification of the student body at the high school level. A 1991 study found more white students and children of intellectuals in the more academically demanding schools such as the IPVCE, an imbalance that continued in later years. Less academically demanding schools, such as those that trained skilled workers, had higher percentages of black students and of students with working-class parents (Barreras et al., 1991).

8. See note 23 for definition of this term.

9. Translator's note: *Retención escolar,* a statistic used by the Ministry of Education, is defined as the percentage of graduates as compared to the number of new enrollees in the first year of that graduating class's cycle. It also reflects promotion rates, i.e., students who graduate without having to repeat any grade (ONEI, 2014: Educación, Notas metodológicas). This chapter renders it as "graduation rate" rather than "retention rate," to be more in line with the meanings of those two terms in U.S. educational statistics terminology.

10. There is no available graduation rate data for the 2001–02 academic year.

11. The gross rate of enrollment expresses, as a percent, total enrollment of higher education students with respect to the entire Cuban population aged 18–24. It is an approximation of the net rate, a more precise indicator of what share of youth between 18 and 24 are in fact enrolled in higher education (i.e., the net rate excludes students over 24).

12. Enrollment trends in medical science specialties have resembled those in most other fields, except that in medical science it has been far higher than in other branches of the life or physical sciences, even in the post-2010 period. That trend is related to the political determination to develop this sector in response to both domestic and international demand for these professionals. The Integrated Strategy for Export of Services, approved in 2011, highlighted four potential sectors of services: health care, tourism, information

technology, and telecommunications. The whole service sector now represents two thirds of the country's total exports (Sosín, 2014). This has had an effect on education in the second decade of the twenty-first century; since the trough reached in 2011–12, there has been an annual increase in initial enrollments in medical sciences.

13. The biggest increases were in social sciences and humanities, 16.5 times what they had been in 2001–02. Authors' calculations from data in MES, 2015.

14. The first enrollment peak in Cuban higher education came in the 1980s. The maximum reached in this period, in 1987–88, was 293,722 students (MES, 2015).

15. The gross rate of school enrollment for technical education, as a proportion of the Cuban population aged 15–18, was estimated by the authors. This indicator showed gradual but sustained downward trend in the period under analysis (data not presented here), so here too the drop cannot be explained by reduction in size of the demographic group.

16. The study included 30 countries of Latin America and the Caribbean.

17. Unlike the enrollment rates cited above, this indicator compares enrolled students to the population as a whole, not to a particular age group.

18. Defined by Didriksson, the total higher-education enrollment as a percentage of the population agcd 20 to 24.

19. At this time, according to Didriksson (2008), the indicator for North America and Europe stood at 57%.

20. Of the 19 countries in this study, two were Caribbean: Cuba and the Dominican Republic.

21. Initial enrollment refers to the total number of students who are enrolled at the beginning of an academic year, including those in all phases of their major; whereas new entrants, as the term indicates, are those who, in a given academic year, enroll in their first year of study. Historical series for the two indicators yield similar graphs, but the later one is more sensitive to changes in access policies.

22. See note 6.

23. Between 2014–15 and 2015–16, enrollment dropped by only 7,372 students (MES, 2016), while between 2007–08 and 2008–09, it dropped by 33,001.

24. To improve the preparation of those entering and studying in the higher education system, various measures were adopted. Problems with mastery of the Spanish language led to the use of diagnostic tests—considered as requirements for graduation—in the municipal branches and for the medical science majors in the main university centers as well; these tests were administered in the 2008–09 and 2009–10 academic years. (Resolution No. 92/09). New standards and grading formulas for spelling were mandated for all forms of study (Instruction No. 1/09), as were new attendance rules for workers enrolled in the Municipal University Centers (Instruction No.2/09). The Municipal University Branches of the Ministry of Education and the National Institute of

Sports, Physical Education, and Recreation were reorganized and placed under the Ministry of Higher Education's methodological supervision.

25. In 2014–15, overall enrollment represented 23% (173,298 students) of that for 2007–08 (MES, 2015).

26. However, looking at new entrants, from the minimum reached in the 2011–12 year, there has been an upward trend in medical sciences, and a discrete growth in education and physical education (MES, 2016).

27. In the period analyzed, women's share of university enrollment fluctuated between 61% and 65%, and their share of graduates between 60% and 68% (MES, 2015).

28. These students entered higher education in the 2010–11 academic year, so the majority of them had to pass entrance exams to be admitted. A greater increase in the parameter is expected for the cohort that will graduate in 2015–16, all of whom had to pass the entrance exams. Promotions after the first and second years in this cohort exceeded those in the previous one. The succeeding cohorts (those who entered in 2012–13, 2013–14, and 2014–15) show a trend toward stabilization in promotion in the first years of study.

29. See Guidelines #97, 131, 172 in PCC, 2011.

30. This category was created in 2007 by a team of researchers at the Centro de Investigaciones Psicológicas y Sociológicas (CIPS) dealing with the issue of Work. It refers to the diversity of situations present at that moment in the labor sphere, in all forms of property and management. The researchers identified five such spaces: revived state, non-revived state, mixed, cooperative, private, and residual. For more information, see Nicolau and Campos, 2007, and Martín, 2007.

31. In this chapter, we characterize the Cuban labor market according to a classification of institutions based on form of property and management, number of employees, sectoral distribution, occupational categories, and pay rates.

32. The unemployment rate is calculated by taking the number of individuals who have stated in the National Employment Survey that they are seeking jobs (whether for the first time or because of losing a previous job), dividing it by the total economically active population, and multiplying by 100. This indicator depends on current economic circumstances; in market economies, where supply and demand govern the labor market, it is useful to predict the future of labor issues. However, in Cuba, until 2010, this indicator reflected the political commitment to full employment, as a result of which low unemployment rates could be hiding underemployment and informal off-the-books jobs. Possible reasons for the higher unemployment rate for women include women more readily expressing a desire to seek work, women not finding jobs as quickly as men, and men getting discouraged quicker than women, which leads them to give up the search for a job.

33. Research data from the authors' current research using employment statistics from ONEI show an increase, among the female population of working age, of

women who do not study, work, or seek employment—a group that has been growing since 2008.

34. Agricultural cooperatives can be Credit and Service Cooperative (Spanish initials CCS) made up of individual land-owning peasants who associate for joint access to credit and inputs, or Agricultural Production Cooperatives (CPA), made up of individual peasants and their descendants who, in the 1970s and 1980s, combined their lands into larger units that they farmed as cooperatives. Since 1993, many state farms were converted to a third type of cooperative called Basic Units of Cooperative Production (UBPC).

35. Labor laws allow women to remain on the rolls of paid workers while taking advantage of maternity leave both before and after giving birth. However, several cultural factors assign to women the caretaking roles that require them to miss work more often and cast them as less able to perform certain kinds of jobs. See Echevarría, 2014.

36. Authors' calculations based on data from ONEI, 2015.

37. Cuba's statistical annuals provide data only for the state sector and the mixed one; they do not include the cooperative and private sectors, which have grown significantly in this century.

38. Consumer price index data refer only to goods and services sold for the domestic currency (CUP), not those sold for the convertible CUC, although the latter market now accounts for a significant share of the main goods and services sought by consumers.

39. The 2012 census shows a decrease in the number of people declaring they have a second job, as compared to that of 2002. In 2002, 1.86% of the employed had a second job, compared to 0.9% in 2012. This pattern could reflect improved salaries and other additions to personal income.

40. Bassi et al. (2012) report a broad debate about the difference between years of education, quality of learning, and skills/abilities required in the working world. In Latin America, increased access to education and greater promotion or graduation rates do not lead to significant returns on the investment unless both cognitive and non-cognitive abilities (perseverance, motivation, self-control) are effectively developed in the graduates.

41. This placement occurs through the system of social service employment, which has historically been required of students when they graduate from their program, whether on the secondary or tertiary level. It is seen as another phase of education and training, promoting the recent graduates' adaptation to the workplace and the additional concepts and skills they may need to take on permanent posts in the entities to which they have been assigned. It is also viewed as a means by which graduates repay the society for the investment made in them.

42. This work systematizes the results of an analysis of the workplace histories of a historical series of nearly twenty graduating classes from universities that are part of the Ministry of Higher Education system, starting with the classes of

1980–84 and including '86–'90, '91–'95, '96–2000, and 2004–2010. Its methodological discussion covers through the end of 2014.

43. See note 46, above, on social service placement and employment.

44. The estimate of labor force demand is an annual process based on expected demand from the state sector, which in turn has a large influence on the supply of career education options at the provincial level; that is, given a certain level of demand, a certain quantity of total slots and slots in particular specialties are made available for applicants to technical and higher education institutions. The estimate tends to be made on a sectoral basis; it is coordinated with the Departments of Work and Education at the provincial level. Thus far, the needs of the non-state sector are not included. Source: Authors' interviews with officials of Ministry of Work and Social Security at the national level in the province of Artemisa, May-September 2014.

45. In interviews, specialists from the employment departments of provincial and municipal administrations in Artemisa say that labor force demands usually are estimated at the sectoral level. Each ministry presents an estimate of the graduates it will need, taking into account technological and production changes within its sector. However, in the provinces of Artemisa and Mayabeque, which are in the midst of experimental government decentralization, the estimate of demand is made at the enterprise level, taking into account the development plans of the organization and the expected attrition, whether from retirement, transfer, or other causes. According to the interviewees, however, this estimate is still not precise because the enterprises are often unsure about the main development strategies for the coming years.

46. Authors' calculations based on data from ONEI, 2013: Table 7.9.

47. The rate of economic activity shows, as a percent, the relationship between the active population (those employed or seeking work) and the working-age population, which is considered to be women between 17 and 55, and men between 17 and 60 (ONEI, 2014).

48. Authors' calculations based on data from ONEI, various years.

Bibliography

Alpízar, M. 2012. "La educación superior cubana y su financiamiento: situación actual y perspectivas para su desarrollo." In *Pedagogía Universitaria*. Volume XVII, No. 5:142–155.

Barreras, Karelia, Orlando García, Daysi González, and Blanca González. 1991. *La raíz socioestructural de la universalización de la educación en Cuba.* Havana, Fondo del CIPS, unpublished.

Bassi, M., Matías Busso, Sergio Urzúa, and Jaime Vargas. 2012. *Desconectados. Habilidades, educación y empleo en América Latina.* Washington, United States, Banco Iberoamericano de Desarrollo.

CAF-FLACSO. 2014. *Tendencias de las políticas sociales en América Latina y El Caribe.* II Boletin.

Carnoy, M. 2005. "La búsqueda de la igualdad a través de las políticas educativas: alcances y límites. In *Revista Iberoamericana sobre Calidad, Eficacia y Cambio en Educación.* Volume 3, No. 2:1–14.

CEPAL. 2013. *Panorama social de América Latina.*Santiago de Chile: Naciones Unidas.

CEPAL/OIT. 2014. *Coyuntura Laboral en América Latina y el Caribe. Formalización del empleo ydistribución de los ingresos laborales.* Santiago de Chile: Naciones Unidas.

———. 2015. *Coyuntura Laboral en América Latina y el Caribe.Protección social universal en mercados laborales con informalidad.* Santiago de Chile: Naciones Unidas.

Corominas, E., et al. 2012. "Construcción de un Índice de Calidad Ocupacional (ICO) para el análisis de la inserción profesional de los graduados universitarios." In *Revista de Educación.* Number357:351–374.

Cribeiro, Y. 2011. "Fuerza de trabajo calificada y crecimiento económico." Doctoral thesis, Universidad de La Habana.

Díaz, I. 2014. "Nuevas medidas a empresas estatales: retos para el crecimiento." In Various authors, *Economía cubana: transformaciones y desafíos,* pp. 390–412. Havana: Ciencias Sociales.

Didriksson, A. 2008. *Contexto global y regional de la educación superior en América Latina y el Caribe en Tendencias de la educación superior en América Latina y el Caribe.* IESALC-UNESCO. http://www.iesalc.unesco.org.ve, consulted 17 November 2015.

Domínguez, María Isabel, and María del Rosario Díaz. 1997. *Reproducción social y acceso a la Educación Superior. Situación en los 90.* Havana: Fondo bibliográfico del CIPS (unpublished).

Echevarría, D. 2008. *Estilos para Dirigir: Los Factores Personales y la Cultura Organizacional desde la Perspectiva de Género. Estudio de Caso En Empresas Cubanas.* Doctoral thesis, Universidad de La Habana.

———. 2014. "Trabajo remunerado femenino en dos momentos de transformación económica."In*Revista Temas.* Number 80:4–10.

Escandell, V. E. 2006. *La Batalla de Ideas: fundamento estratégico para el desarrollo de una economía del conocimiento en Cuba.* Available at www.rebelion.org/docs/145614.pdf.

Espina, M. 2007. *Reajuste y movilidad social en Cuba.* Havana:CIPS.

García, A., and P. de la Torre. 2006. "Monitoreo sobre la aplicación de las normativas de la política de empleo a los egresados de la enseñanza técnico profesional." In *Revista Hombre Trabajo.* Number 2.

Farooq, S. 2011. *Mismatch Between Education and Occupation: A Case Study of Pakistani Graduates.* Islamabad: National University of Science and Technology.

Formichella, Maria Marta, and Silvia London. 2013. "Empleabilidad, educación y equidad social." In *Revista Estudios Sociales* (Bogotá). Number 47:79–91

Galtés, I. 2015. "Diferenciación salarial y productividad en Cuba." In *Economía y Desarrollo.* Special Issue.

García, L. 2004. *Situación de la formación docente inicial y en servicio de la República de Cuba.* Havana: UNESCO.

Heller, L. 2010. "Mujeres emprendedoras en América Latina y el Caribe: realidades, obstáculos y desafíos." In CEPAL, *Mujer y Desarrollo93.* Santiago de Chile: Editorial CEPAL.

Instituto Nacional de Seguridad Social. 2005. "Preparación Metodológica a coordinadores de la superación del INASS." Havana: Centro de Capacitación, Información y Archivo, MTSS.

Íñigo, E. 2004. "Experiencias en el estudio de los jóvenes profesionales en Cuba." Havana: Fondos de CEPES (article available).

Íñigo, Enrique, Juan Francisco Vega, and Yeny Delgado. 2014. "La formación de profesionales: seguimiento metodológico desde el mundo del trabajo." Presented at the conference *Universidad 2014,* CEPES, Havana.

Jacinto, Claudia. 2004. *¿Educar para qué trabajo? Discutiendo rumbos en América Latina.* Argentina: CLACSO.

Labarca, G. 2004. "Educación y capacitación para mercados del trabajo cambiantes y para la inserción social." In C. Jacinto: *¿Educar para qué trabajo? Discutiendo rumbos en América Latina*, pp. 25–72.CLACSO: Argentina.

López, A. 2012. "Educación superior y crecimiento económico, un análisis econométrico de la tasa de cobertura y financiamiento de la educación superior en México y su correlación con el PIB*per cápita* 1996–2000." Thesis, Universidad Tecnológica de La Mixteca, Huajuapan de León, Oaxaca.

Machin, Stephen, and Patrick Puhani. 2003. "Subject of Degree and the Gender Wage Differential: Evidence from the UK and Germany."In *Economics Letters.* Volume 79:393–400.

Martín, E., and M. Leal. 2006."El acceso a la educación superior. ¿Cómo lograr la equidad?" In Various authors, *Avances y perspectivas de la investigación universitaria.* Havana: Editorial Félix Varela, La Habana.

Martín, J. L. 2007. *El reajuste de los 90 y sus consecuencias sociales.* Havana: CIPS.

Maurizio, Roxana. 2010. "Enfoque de género en las instituciones laborales y las políticas del mercado de trabajo en América Latina." In CEPAL, *Serie Macroeconomía del desarrollo.* 104. Santiago de Chile: División de Desarrollo Económico.

Mena, J. A. 2006."La formación profesional de los bachilleres técnicos: Responsabilidad a compartir entre la escuela politécnica y las entidades laborales."In *Revista Mendive.* Volume 5, Number 19:1–6. Obtained from: www.revistamendive.rimed.cu/nfuentes/num19/pdf/Art_6_Juan.pdf.

MES. 2008, 2015, 2016. *Prontuario de educación superior en Cuba*, various years. Havana: MES.

Moreno-Brid J.C., and Pablo Ruiz. 2009. *La educación superior y el Desarrollo Económico en América Latina.* Mexico City: Naciones Unidas.

Nicolau, J.L., and J.C. Campos. 2007. *Repercusión del reajuste en la realidad laboral cubana.* Havana: CIPS.

Novick, M. 2004. "Transformaciones recientes en el mercado del trabajo argentino y nuevas demandas de formación." In C. Jacinto: *¿Educar para qué trabajo? Discutiendo rumbos en América Latina*, pp. 73–83. Argentina: CLACSO.

OIT (Organización Internacional de Trabajo). 2011. *Panorama Laboral 2011. América Latina y el Caribe.* Oficina Regional para América Latina y el Caribe.

ONEI (Oficina Nacional de Estadisticas y Información). 2005, 2006, 2008, 2013, 2014, 2015. Havana: *Anuario Estadístico de Cuba* (various years).

OREALC/UNESCO. 2013. *Situación Educativa de América Latina y el Caribe.* Santiago de Chile: UNESCO. Available at: http://www.unesco.org/new/fileadmin/MULTIMEDIA/FIELD/Santiago/pdf/situacion-educativa-mexico-2013.pdf. Consulted 15 februrary 2016.

Oxfam. 2015. *Privilegios que niegan derechos. Desigualdad extrema y secuestro de la democracia en América Latina y el Caribe.* www.oxfam.org, consulted 12 October 2015.

Paladines, C. 2008. "Educación y Desarrollo Económico." In *UNIVERSIDAD VERDAD, Revista de la Universidad de Alzuay.* Number 45:173–190.

PCC. 2011. *Lineamientos de la Política Económica y Social del Partido y la Revolución.* Havana: Partido Comunista de Cuba.

Pérez Villanueva, O. E. 2004. "La situación actual de la economía cubana y su retos futuros." In O. E. Pérez, Ed.,*Reflexiones sobre economía cubana*, pp. 11–48. Havana: Ciencias Sociales.

PNUD. 2014. *Informe Sobre Desarrollo Humano.* http://www.undp.org/content/dam/undp/library/corporate/HDR/2014HDR/HDR-2014–Spanish.pdf. Consulted January 2015.

———. 2015. *Informe Sobre Desarrollo Humano.Trabajo al servicio del desarrollo humano.* www. dr.undp.org/sites/default/files/hdr_2015_report_sp.pdf. Consulted September 2016.

Rama, C. 2009. "La tendencia a la masificación de la cobertura de la educación superior en América Latina." In *Revista iberoamericana de educación.* Number 50:173–195.

Ramón, María del Carmen. 2016. "Parlamento cubano debate sobre ingreso a Educación Superior. *Cubadebate*, http://www.cubadebate.cu/noticias/2016/07/04/parlamento-cubano-debate-sobre-ingreso-a-educacion-superior/#.V3u-9btFBhg, consulted 5 July 2016.

Ranis, G., and F. Steward. 2002. "Crecimiento económico y desarrollo humano en América Latina." In *Revista de la CEPAL*, pp.7–24.

Rodríguez, J.L., M. Millares, and O. Martínez. 2000. *Cuba: resultados económicos y proyección para el* 2000. Havana: Editora Política.

Rodríguez, Lissy. 2015. "La Educación Superior en Cuba se transforma." In *Granma Internacional.* http://www.granma.cu/cuba/2015–09–07/la-educacion-superior-en-cuba-se-transforma, consulted 25 December 2015.

Sosin, Eileen. 2014. "La apuesta cubana de exportar servicios.In *Havana Times.* www.havanatimes.org/sp/?p=98794, consulted October 2014.

Tejuca, M., O. Gutiérrez, and I. García. 2015."El acceso a la educación superior cubana en el curso 2013–2014: una mirada a la composición social territorial." In *Revista Cubana de Educación Superior,* Number 3:42–61.

Torres, R. 2013. "Algunas contradicciones del desarrollo económico cubano contemporáneo." In O. E. Pérez Villanueva, *Miradas a la economía cubana: entre la eficiencia económica y la equidad social,* pp. 31–40. Havana: Caminos.

Tristá, B., A.Gort, and E. Íñigo. 2013. "Equidad en la educación superior cubana: logros y desafíos." In *Revista Lusófona de Educação.* Number 24:117–133.

Vidal, P. 2012. "Desafíos monetarios y financieros." In O.E. Pérez Villanueva, *Miradas a la economía cubana: entre la eficiencia económica y la equidad social,* pp. 97–112. Havana: Caminos.

7

Looking at Health Care in Cuba: Social Policy in a Context of Widening Social Inequality

Susset Fuentes Reverón

The existence of a single, universal, and free health care system is of tremendous importance in thinking about equity in Cuba. Still, examining equity in health care requires a wider perspective that puts it in the larger context in which public health institutions operate. Over the past two decades, Cuba has undergone widening gaps in equality, polarization of monetary income, and growth of poverty and social vulnerability. Therefore, an analysis must look at factors that present problems for equal access or equal results among certain groups with inherited or recently arisen disadvantages.

Starting Points

The Cuban government has maintained its public health sector as a non-commercialized right, offering universal services free of charge. Both the official political discourse and part of the scholarly one often state that access to health care services "is independent of monetary income" and offers "equal opportunity" for the entire population.

This chapter seeks to explore conflicts and hidden facets of this situation. During the past 25 years, growing economic inequality and increased and intensified poverty have weakened the ability of the health care system to provide free and universal services. Given the problems handicapping the system, along with the wider role of income and markets in meeting the needs of the population, many responsibilities have fallen to the domestic-family sphere, itself dependent on the personal resources of individuals and families, which are unequally distributed.

The research embodied in this chapter seeks to explore some "weaknesses" in the study of social policy in Cuba: the existence of a degree of triumphalism that limits the depth of critical analysis, and the scant consideration (as an object of study) of the points of view of those who are receiving services (Espina, 2008a). This chapter attempts to maintain a critical and responsible balance that allows us to identify successes and accomplishments of the Cuban system as well as its insufficiencies and blind spots.

Points of Debate

A controversy about how to understand and carry out social policy has been expressed as an opposition between "targeted or selective policy" and "universalization."[1] As Mayra Espina points out, that debate is carried out on a theoretical-evaluative level. It should be enriched with empirical studies that document and explain the efficacy of one or the other style of social policy in specific contexts. In my opinion, the issue itself is poorly framed because, a priori, it identifies "universalization" with a guarantee of social rights and social integration, and "targeted policy" with residual effects (Espina, 2008b).

Similarly, the World Health Organization (WHO) regards as a "common misunderstanding" the belief that health systems intended to achieve universal access are by definition equitable. WHO warns that universality is a necessary but not sufficient condition for achieving equity (OMS, 2008).

In this century there has been a tendency toward seeing universalization as a model based on the affirmation of social protection as a right of every citizen (CEPAL, 2010). But the pathways to universalization are not without conflicts and intricacies, because political equality among citizens can be limited in real terms unless there is recognition and action to respond to inequalities in material and symbolic resources. For that reason, it is necessary to go beyond the formal, legalistic level and work from a principle of "real or substantive equality" that makes citizens' rights into effective ones (CEPAL, 2010).

The effectiveness of universalism can be undermined in at least two ways. First, as a common rhyming refrain in Spanish puts it, the road from words to deeds can be a long one. This implies that what is required in order for universal services to be truly effective is an analysis of their concrete implementation. Second, even when the normative and effective orientation of social policy offers social rights and opportunities to the whole population, in practice individuals still have different starting points from which to take advantage of those rights and opportunities. There are still mediating factors between the structure of opportunities and access to them.

In the case of Cuba, its political and academic discourses generally present the "spaces of equality"[2] in health and other services as such by definition, because medical care and other forms of social attention are free of charge and thus *per se* a generator of equity. That conclusion is shared by Fleitas, who after an extensive review of research by social scientists and health care experts, asserts that all sources agree on "an understanding of health care as an area that is protected and free of contradictions, associated with free access to services and a high level of spending by the state" (Fleitas, 2013:103). Proof of the massive and equitable nature of access to health care in Cuba is usually provided in the form of national statistics that show very satisfactory indices with little geographic variation.

This vision is questionable, however, if one takes into account that statistical medical indices can hide noteworthy differences, and general indicators tend to mask the persistence of inequalities, so that general advances are not always reliable in terms of specific impacts on disadvantaged groups (Espina, 2008b).[3] Additionally, questions related to accessibility (time required to get to the location of services, waiting time, ways and means of access, quality of service, degree of satisfaction) are aspects of great importance that are little treated in the statistics used to assess the Cuban situation—hence the need to develop indicators capable of reflecting the quality of services provided (Gálvez, 2003). In general, assessments of equity in health care, although they recognize the importance of social determinants of health, do not concede the same importance to all those determinants. They tend to privilege a perspective centered on the health care system and its accomplishments,[4] to the detriment of other determinants.

Insufficient consideration of such issues has privileged a macro-social perspective that takes as its main information sources the social policies put into practice and their evaluation through corroborating general indicators. This fails to take into account other levels of analysis that recognize the importance of micro-practices, daily life, and its social relations and processes. The conclusion fails to problematize those spaces, which are viewed only in terms of their formal structure without looking into the complex intersections between macro-level design and real daily functioning.

Thus, inequalities and conditions of vulnerability, and their concrete effects on people's lives, appear disconnected (or at least insufficiently explicit) from their possible implications for access to these services, and for opportunities to satisfy demands for care and attention associated with situations of poor health.

Trajectories of Social Policy in Public Health: Changes and Continuities

After the triumph of the Cuban Revolution in 1959, a series of import-ant reforms led to the creation of a single, integrated, universal, and free National System of Public Health (Spanish initials SNSP)—the first in Cuba's history and in that of Latin America as a whole. This system embodied the right of every citizen to health protection and care, without charge, with universal coverage and accessibility, and with the state taking responsibility for that right.

An overall accounting of successes in the health sphere during the first three decades of the Revolution confirms its significant contribu-tion to the progressive development of equity, enormously narrowing health gaps that had stemmed from income and geographic location. As a result of the decisive priority the government placed on improving the people's health, by the 1980s the country occupied an outstanding rank within Latin America in indicators of health status, available material and human resources, and services.

The effects of the economic crisis of the 1990s brought many challenges and difficulties to the SNSP, part of an overall troubling outlook for pre-serving social conquests,[5] despite the government's steadfast determina-tion not to abandon these. In the midst of the crisis and attendant reforms, the health sector was prioritized by the Cuban government. Despite the country's severe economic contraction, the health care system maintained its broad coverage and free access, not only to basic services but also to highly complex specialized ones, unlike what happens to health care under economic pressures in Latin America.

Nonetheless, the crisis did affect the quality and performance of health services as well as the social determinants that affect the populace's state of health. Given the intense financial contraction that impacted delivery of all services, which were compromised by a lack of needed resources and inputs, the negative effects on health services were real and signifi-cant. Some other effects, less noted by researchers, occurred in the areas of human capital, working conditions, and service organization and man-agement. The economic slide was also reflected in the deterioration of liv-ing conditions for Cubans, which in turn affected their health. Particularly important to stress are the deterioration in environmental and sanitary conditions[6] and the profound effect on nutrition.[7]

Economic recovery then led to new investments in social policy includ-ing, in the early 2000s, the Revolutionary Health Programs[8] intended to reform the system in general. While the measures taken to counter the negative effects of the economic crisis and economic reforms bore positive fruit and stimulated an important recovery of the health care sector, certain deficiencies associated with both objective and subjective factors remained. An internal analysis by the Ministry of Public Health noted a complex of problems such as inadequate use of material resources, lack of discipline, low productivity and failure to make full use of working hours, and lack of economic supervision and growth in criminal activity, among others. All these have had negative effects on service quality and led to attendant grassroots complaints (MINSAP, 2010).

From the perspective of users of the services,[9] a number of dissatisfactions also emerged: difficulty in getting prompt access to complementary services; problems obtaining medicines; deficiencies in the physical and sanitary condition of facilities, and in inputs needed for medical care and for keeping up inpatient rooms and services in hospitals; disorganization and other management problems; irregularities and lack of coordination among different levels of medical services; waste of state resources; disorder and lack of discipline among both patients and providers; unofficial privileges in access to services stemming from personal connections or economic interest; absence or rapid turnover of family doctors and specialized polyclinic personnel; ethical breaches by some personnel, manifested in bad treatment, laziness, and, in general, failing to meet standards of attention to patients; need to improve the working conditions of health care staff. In general, such issues compromise the Ministry of Health's declared responsibility for guaranteeing that every patient be received by the system and given quality care.

The current era of new reforms has brought further changes to the health system. The 2011 Guidelines of Economic and Social Policy of the Party and the Revolution include a section specifically addressing this sector (Guidelines 154–160), summarized in number 154: "Increase service quality to the satisfaction of the population; improve working conditions and health care employee support; make sure that resources are efficiently utilized and saved, and unnecessary expenditures are eliminated" (PCC, 2011:24).

In 2009, President Raúl Castro had declared that, while free-of-charge services would be maintained in vital areas such as health care, education and others, there was a need for budget decisions to eliminate unsustainable and ineffective spending (Castro, 2009). In this context, in late 2010 the authorities proclaimed a "Reorganization, streamlining, and regionalization of health services." Its goal was to obtain a more efficient and rational use of resources to guarantee the sustainability of services. Its adoption stemmed not only from economic motives but also from a pressing need to achieve higher levels of efficiency and quality so to improve the population's health and satisfaction with services[10] (MINSAP, 2010).

In early 2014, the directors of the Public Health Ministry (MINSAP) made public the results of the ministry's evaluation of the first stage of that policy (2010–2013) and its impacts. The evaluation found that the goals had been fulfilled because the reform had contributed to improving the population's health, the quality of services and public satisfaction with them, and the efficiency and sustainability of the system (Cubadebate, 2014). MINSAP's presentation displays a perspective that emphasizes achievements; although deficiencies are not named as such, there is emphasis on the need to devote "special attention" to the functioning of services (Cubadebate, 2014, author's emphasis).

Non-official sources (scholarly ones and those based on public opinion research) offer a more complicated image of the current changes in the SNSP and their possible impacts on service delivery. Íñiguez calls attention to what may be the major obstacles to achieving the objectives laid out in the heart of these reforms. Highlighting service accessibility, she says this is "a factor the can restrict the accomplishments expected to come from regionalization, in terms of satisfaction and others" (Íñiguez, 2012:119).

These issues have been confirmed in practice by researchers in various parts of Cuba who interviewed users; they reveal that the reorganization of health services has produced a geographic redistribution of first- and second-level institutions. While it is economically advantageous to move them farther away from local communities and neighborhoods, the new locations have limited the geographic accessibility of services for part of the population, which has affected their care (Gómez, 2014; Hernández, Íñiguez, and Gerhartz, 2011).

Similarly, Skeen (2015) collects the opinions of residents of municipalities within the Cuban capital about quality of care and attention to patients in the health services that was most affected by the reform process, and identifies the major perceived problems: instability of personnel, lack of adherence to official work schedules, deficiencies in sanitary conditions in the facilities, organizational problems in the services, unnecessary delays, lack of equipment, lack of specialized services, lack of role models and loss of values among the personnel—all of which affect the quality, efficiency, and effectiveness of patient care.

These investigations show some negative results and unfavorable impacts brought on by the restructuring of the health sector, as well as the persistence of many problems the reform was designed to overcome. All of this reaffirms the need for studies that take on these issues and evaluate this process in all its complexity.

While it is necessary to bear such problems in mind for critical, committed analysis of health services in Cuba (the purpose of this chapter),it is also important to remember that they coexist with important accomplishments in this area, which are also recognized and appreciated by the Cuban populace.[11]In spite of economic limitations and the effects of the harsh U.S. economic blockade, the country can take satisfaction in indicators superior to those of developing countries and close to those of developed ones.[12]

The documents approved[13] by the April 2016 Seventh Congress of the Cuban Communist Party declare the right to health to be one of the principles of Cuban socialism that are the basis for the updated model (PCC, 2016a).They reaffirm the goal of consolidating the Revolution's accomplishments in access to health care (PCC, 2015b:18), guaranteeing the universal policies of that sector (PCC, 2016b:24), keeping it free of charge and with internationally recognized standards of quality (PCC, 2016a:13), and continuing to increase the efficiency of resource utilization as well as improve the quality of services (PCC, 2016b:24).

The Changing Context of Social Inequality

During the first three decades of the Cuban Revolution, the socialist socio-economic transformations for the most part promoted homogeneity with respect to many dimensions of the people's welfare. Various types of influence coincided to produce that result. On the one hand, state-sponsored redistribution was decisive in meeting needs, as was the great expansion in consumption guaranteed by social spending and services, which became the main mechanism for universal access to goods and services, the majority of them free of charge. The state played a leading, centralized, and nearly absolute role. Simultaneously, disparities in monetary income were greatly reduced, thanks to the deep structural transformations affecting property, reinforced by state action affecting wages and salaries through centralized and uniform pay policy with very little spread between minimum and maximum salaries.

The model of providing for citizen welfare applied in Cuba from 1959 on was characterized by a lesser role for individual and family incomes in meeting needs, as compared to the leading role of social consumption (Espina, 2011; Nerey, 2005). The results were evident in reduction of poverty and the elimination of extreme need through direct action (Espina, 2008a).

In the 1990s, a number of domestic and external factors unleashed an intense economic crisis. The catalyst was the disappearance of the Soviet socialist bloc, and the effect was sharpened by the tightening of the U.S. economic blockade. The Cuban response was to implement a process of reforms. This Cuban readjustment contrasted with the neoliberal reform orientation that predominated in Latin America in that era, because the Cuban changes occurred with the state maintaining its leading role without privatizing basic social services, all of which reflected its intention to manage the costs of reform according to criteria of social justice. That decision meant that the impacts of the process, although quite significant, differed in magnitude and severity from the trends displayed by otherwise parallel reforms elsewhere.

However, that comparative perspective "toward the outside" should not obscure our understanding of the impacts of crisis and reform "on the inside," that is, in comparison with the previous era in Cuba. In that sense, what occurred was a drastic drop in the standard of living and welfare of the population, stemming from reduced access to goods and services in the quantities and qualities previously available. Despite the continuity of social policy, some areas of social integration suffered, affecting public services' quality and ability to satisfy needs (Espina, 2008a; Álvarez and Máttar, 2004; Mesa-Lago, 2010).

The combined effects of the crisis and reforms interrupted the logic of systematic expansion of social equality, giving rise to a new "social re-stratification" characterized by widening inequality; a change in the structural hierarchy of the factors affecting equality and inequality; polarization of monetary incomes; and more and deeper poverty and social vulnerability (Espina, 2003). The income-consumption model[14] underwent substantial change, displaying a radical shift in the distribution of individual and family incomes.

The reform also implied that the job of satisfying a wide range of needs would shift from the public sector (where the goods and services had been free or subsidized) to the distributive mechanism of the market. This shift, alongside the fall in the purchasing power of workers' real wages and the increase in consumer prices, has turned income and the market into mechanisms with strong differentiating power[15] (Espina, 2011). In this new era, the role of individual and family monetary incomes in meeting needs and access to consumption has changed, so that income now plays a fundamental and decisive role (Espina, 2008a). To put it another way, many and important needs must now be satisfied in the private sphere through family and personal income, placing many people at a disadvantage. These purchases include a substantial part of food and transportation, clothing and shoes, personal hygiene products, leisure activities, and home repair, among others. In that framework, an important part of the population lacks access, or has restricted access, to those markets, as is shown by the emergence of exclusive distributive mechanisms that now generate inequalities in the area of basic needs (Espina, 2003).

These changes in the roles of the state, market, and family in the generation of social protection are reinforced—and to a degree legitimized—by the updating of the Cuban economic and social model. Some important changes related to social policy occur in budgeting for social spending[16] (which must be limited to the real financial resources generated by the country's economy), the elimination of excessive free and subsidized goods and services, and the decrease of consumption associated with the state service sector[17] (Espina, 2012).

The modifications in the model of social policy are also associated with changes in the conception of social equality, as expressed in more use of tools specifically targeting vulnerabilities (Espina, 2012; Voghón and Peña, 2013). The Guidelines state that it is necessary to "ensure that social security protection is received by those really in need; *that is to say, the individuals unable to work and with no relatives to provide for them*" (Guideline 166, author's emphasis).

The developments just summarized, when taken together, reveal a relative retreat by the state from its role of producing citizen well-being. In official discourse concerning the reforms, this is regarded as a necessary step that, along with a growth in labor productivity, will allow for "gradually resolving the existing distortions in the wage system" (Castro, 2008). However, it is important to note that the measures related to eliminating "excessive subsidies" have been the first to be implemented as part of the Guidelines, and they affect the entire Cuban population; the actions addressed to raising salaries have been slower and more specific, so they have not affected all sectors equally.

The retreat of the state from certain areas, whether intentional or not and whether explicit or implicit, has awarded the market more importance as a satisfier of needs. One of the goals put forward as part of the updating of the model is to restore work-based income as the main means for satisfying personal and family needs (Guideline 141), to the extent that work can be remunerated according to its quantity and quality. That goal has led to a process of restructuring employment and salaries, expressed in piecemeal measures such as legalization of multiple job holding, reducing state sector payrolls, broadening and loosening self-employment, and determining the sums destined for workers' wages and bonuses in accordance with their results, in both state enterprises and cooperatives[18] (Guidelines 19, 20, and 28).

Although work and the income it produces have been given a central role as a mechanism of social protection in the new reform era, in practice such employment and income have not accelerated sufficiently or in equitable form across socio-occupational groups and economic sectors. Because of the complexity of this dynamic, its implementation has been particularly delayed in relation to that of other parts of the Guidelines, and there have been warnings against false hopes in this respect (Castro, 2014).

This analysis shows that the reforms now underway transfer more responsibilities to the individual/family sphere to the extent that they produce a shift to that sphere in the social protections that the state previously provided (Peña, 2014). This implies that the degree to which the domestic-family sphere can meet those responsibilities will depend on family assets, which—as is now clear—are unequally distributed in the society.

Some Research Results

Fuentes (2016) explored the possible synergies that—in a context of growing inequality, impoverishment and social vulnerability, and some weakening of social services—might arise between inequality in families' material conditions and their access to health services or, particularly, their ability to meet needs for care when in poor health.[19] The research study examined thirty households or families, selected (given the intention to undertake a comparative study) for diversity in material living conditions,[20] including extreme and contrasting situations[21] (Appendix 7.1). Selection also followed a criterion of relevance: recent or current experiences of illness and/ or access to health services (Appendix 7.2).

Access to Health Care Services

In principle, access is universal and free of charge regardless of any other factors. This is a crucial underpinning, but it does not in itself guarantee social protection or health equity. Given the possible gaps between "formal access" and "real access" to services, we look beyond intentions and legalisms so as to focus on practice. This allows for better understanding of how real access to opportunities occurs, what difficulties there may be, and what strategies the actors use to confront them. Such understanding would provide important data for rethinking the topic of equity and a social service system's real capacity to provide protection.

The subjects interviewed for the study expressed very positive feelings about the existence of the system of free health care and the guarantees it offers for their medical care. They see it as an important source of protection. Their own experiences reflect their opportunities for access irrespective of the material conditions in which they live:

> . . . right now I'm dealing with lung cancer, and everything . . . all the care I've received is free . . . They sent me for chest x-rays, ultrasound, and all sorts of analyses, and the x-ray showed a shadow, so the radiologist ordered a CT-scan, which confirmed that there was a tumor in the upper part of my left lung, and the next week I was admitted, they were doing all the tests, they did a biopsy that turned out to be positive, and right away they sent me for a cycle of four IV chemotherapies. (Case 10, G-2; female, 69, white, technical school graduate, housewife.)
>   . . . they've done tests on me that I didn't even know existed, even a device that lets them look at my eye in three dimensions . . . really, every machine that exists or will exist! I think there's hardly anything they've got that that I haven't been tested with already. . . (Case 6, G-4; male, 61, white, junior high graduate, retired.)

Nonetheless, alongside this positive impression, interviewees also immediately mention obstacles and barriers to access. They allude, in general, to material problems: deterioration of physical conditions and cleanliness in health facilities at various levels; absence or intermittent supply of some medications; lack or shortage of supplies for examinations or analyses, broken medical equipment, etc. Other deeply felt problems are in the sphere of quality of attention provided by doctors and other staff; that is, problems of human resources, especially the relation between providers and users. The interviewees report very diverse experiences: some very favorable, where what stands out are the dedication, concern, friendliness, professionalism, and consideration shown by the staff, especially the doctors; others extremely negative, with reports of lack of interest, mistreatment, and lack of respect for patients.

For the interviewees, accessibility (given its importance in the experience of using medical services) is the main difficulty, not in terms of gaining entrance to the system, which is assured, but more in terms of what happens inside it: lack of supervision of material and human resources, lack of discipline on the part of both staff and clients, poor organization and planning, long waiting times (whether for primary or specialty care or for exams and tests), and difficulties in making contact with specialists and thus lesser chance of appropriate follow-up and treatment. In regard to the complex of problems in the area of material and human resources and the management and organization of services, interviewees expressed opinions about the state's limited power to solve these problems and meet users' needs. However, their experiences are very diverse, not only from household to household but even within the history of a given individual. Although some problems are quite widespread (shortages of resources and supplies, for instance), the issues of organization, operation, supervision, and quality vary across facilities and doctors.

Thus, although free and universal services exist, the paths to take advantage of these opportunities can be plagued with obstacles that lessen the quality of the process. Guarantees of citizens' rights to health care can be realized to greater and lesser degree depending on the combination of ease and obstacles in using the services, and these can depend very much on circumstances.

Families have developed strategies to deal with obstacles that arise. Alongside the formal, established channels, they also commonly make use of "informal channels"that involve having and using economic or social capital. For the former, this is through direct and illegal payment for some type of service, or indirectly by offering gifts to medical personnel in hopes of obtaining benefits and preferences. For the latter, it is through seeking contact with people who work in health care facilities and can provide easier access to them. Access through these routes tends to bring benefits in terms of speed, quality, and effective meeting of needs, when compared to formal routes and the difficulties associated with them.

Mechanisms of informal access to the same services and resources offered in the same state institutions exist, but in this case it is through privileged attention propitiated by friendship, economic benefit, or other forms of interest—in contrast to what is formally and legally established by the state and to guarantees the state defends and offers to the citizens. The existence of such "alternative" mechanisms testifies to a process of informal restructuring of the means of access and control of resources, by way of unwritten rules, thus reproducing inequalities and favoring inequities.

In the experiences reported by the research subjects, the most common practice is making use of relationships with people who work directly in health services; those relationships constitute are source of great value in getting faster and better response to care. In general, the distribution of this type of social capital tends to be fortuitous, and not necessarily related directly to material living conditions. This may constitute a source of protection for all types of families, including those with the most difficult living conditions.

Another strategy involves investing economic capital in the creation of social capital by way of frequent gift-giving to health care personnel, with the intention of including them in one's more or less stable network of relationships, so as to be able to call on them whenever necessary and to enjoy the benefits this kind of tie can provide.

Also, the interviews reveal examples of direct payments for some health services, or for removing obstacles to the use of those. This too operates in opposition to the guarantees established by the state and to its effort to maintain the valuable resources of Cuba's health sector for the use of all citizens. Such use of payments involved dental services, buying medicines that are supposed to be reserved for inpatient use in hospitals, getting exams, ambulances, oxygen tanks, wheelchairs and hospital-type beds, and paying health care personnel not only for access to a facility but also to get them to fulfill their regular duties.

We see, therefore, how limitations in state services can impel individuals and families to search for alternative means of protection, which in turn depend on the quantity and quality of resources they can muster, which are unequally distributed. Whether those resources are social or economic capital, the situation implies a break with the criteria that should define equity in health care, which, according to Whitehead (1991), are: equal access to available care for equal needs; equal utilization for equal needs; and equal quality of attention to all. Whether access is being mediated by social or economic capital, their use suggests unjust privileges as well as disadvantages and possible exclusion of groups whose assets are insufficient.

Still, lack of such resources does not automatically imply a closed door when difficulties and obstacles arise. Poor operation and management of services are not universal and can depend on chance; there are services that function correctly and offer an effective alternative without any extra payment. Also, even when obstacles are present, the fact of medical attention being free of charge and a citizen right still provides a floor, a basic level of protection and possible pathway to care.

On the other hand, when lack of economic resources is combined with limited social networks, and when barriers to access to established health services increase, a family may be exposed to a high degree of insecurity and thus find itself in a situation of vulnerability. A limited range of assets that can be wielded to get access to a structure of opportunity that has undergone informal reconfiguration, while not implying a closure of all avenues to medical care, does leave a household dependent on only a single avenue: the use of established channels. When these channels are littered with difficulties, the result can be exhaustion, distress, and possibly inadequate diagnosis, care, and follow-up. These have logical implications for the patient's health.

In sum, managing to access health services often depends on a family's assets. The fewer the resources that can be deployed to access the structure of opportunity, the less the capacity to confront obstacles and the greater the level of vulnerability.

Care and Attention in the Family Setting

The interviews with people who have direct experience with current or recent illness (whether their own or that of a family member) frequently highlight needs that arise or sharpen during illness and demand the deployment of various resources by the families and other institutions. Issues such as improving diet, getting to the health care facility, providing the attention and company the sick person requires, acquiring specific supplies or devices according to the type of illness, and finding and managing medications are among the worries shared by those facing such situations.

State institutions have created a support system for such cases, either free or at subsidized prices, to which those in need can potentially gain access.[22] But in the cases studied, the experiences with those mechanisms of state support vary widely. In general, the insufficiency and scarcity of the resources offered, instability in supply, delays, quality issues, and lack of information about the existence of the mechanisms constitute obstacles that limit their real capacity to offer solutions.[23]

To judge by the interviewees' reports, the state sphere cannot satisfactorily meet all the needs that arise in the home when a member of the household is ill. In none of the cases studied is state support sufficient, although its existence does constitute, to some degree, a relief for the family, especially to those with the worst living conditions, for whom help from Social Assistance, for instance, is very important.

Given the weaknesses, gaps, and insufficient social protection from the state, the search for solutions turns to spheres where the individual or family have the primary responsibility: the market and social networks. Again, therefore, solutions to problems related to illness have to do with economic resources and social capital. Significantly, interviewees repeatedly state that their main source of protection comes from family and informal support networks that, with whatever they have, always try to offer material and spiritual support in case of illness. These networks include various kinds of resources (in-kind, money, help in carrying out certain tasks and caring for the sick person) that are vital to confronting such situations.

While social networks contribute to dealing with illness, that contribution varies. For people in better economic circumstances, social capital is one among several resources, while for others with weaker economic capacity, drawing on social networks offers almost the only option. Also, it is worth noting that the networks of the most disadvantaged households are made up mostly of people in similar circumstances, with limited quantity and quality of resources. In contrast, families with higher standards of living tend to have more valuable and abundant resources circulating within their networks.

At the same time, the great majority of the cases studied needed to have recourse to the market, to some degree, to meet needs linked to situations of poor health and the new or increased demands that these impose. It is unanimously recognized that "being sick costs money," a comment that refers fundamentally to spending in the domestic-family[24] sphere. Some households have high income and/or savings that facilitate such spending, but most interviewees say they do not have this kind of foundation.

Because of inequality in standards of living, treatment of illness may be faced with more or fewer limitations depending on the size and strength of family resources. Not all the families are in the same geographic proximity to services, or can afford the cost of improved or adjusted diets. Not all have the proper conditions in their homes to make special physical arrangements that may be required, nor can they acquire certain supplies needed to care for people who are ill.

The families that have sizeable economic resources (not only in terms of income but also in terms of an economic cushion, and good material living conditions) can count on many more alternatives to confront needs or demands linked to health and illness. They still suffer reverses, but deploying their resources allows these to be overcome more easily. Other families have no "extra" resources to devote to confronting illness, beyond what is normally used to minimally meet daily needs. For these families, unless additional resources come from other sources, it becomes harder to attend properly to cases of illness.

We will consider two examples with two specific types of health problems—bedridden patients and diabetes—and the differing family capacities to confront them, as based on available resources. The study sample includes four cases of bedridden patients who need special and intense attention from their caretakers because of limited bodily functions. In two cases (with optimal material living conditions), a great quantity of family economic resources have been deployed, with monthly spending of 3,036 and 5,400 pesos, respectively, devoted to buying food, paying private caretakers, buying disposable diapers or urinals, paying for transportation to health care facilities, etc. Also, these families have good housing conditions, with enough space and a range of domestic appliances in working condition, all of which makes it easier to carry out the tasks of care. They also have networks of support that provide important resources such as money and supplies.

In another case (with average material conditions), economic resources have also been devoted to care, coming from savings and from economic aid sent by relatives abroad, but the sums have been smaller than in the first two cases, and devoted mostly to food and necessary supplies, without enough to buy disposable diapers or pay private caretakers. Thus this family finds it more difficult, for instance, to handle incontinence and the implications for the sanitary condition of the patient, which demand more time and effort from family caretakers. They have met other needs through social network support: bedsores medications, wheelchairs, hospital beds, etc. Also, their dwelling is small and inferior, which makes it much harder to provide specific kinds of care, such as bathing, for a non-ambulatory patient.

Finally, there is one case with poor material living conditions that cause multiple problems in caring for the sick person. Practically the only available resources are those from state support (some supplies, free medical attention, etc.), which cannot meet all the needs in the quantity and quality required. All areas associated with care are affected: diet is deficient and poor; sanitary-hygienic conditions are deficient because of the lack of cleaning and bathing supplies, urinary incontinence, and no running water inside the home; the physical conditions of the home are very bad and some appliances are lacking (there is no washing machine, no fans, and no blender), which further damages the ability to meet the demands of this kind of illness and further affects the patient's quality of life.

The presence of diabetes also reveals unequal family abilities to face a disease that requires a specific diet, medications to control blood sugar level, and some supplies such as hypodermic needles (for those dependent on insulin shots) and glucometers. Although the state is supposed to completely guarantee the medications, in practice there are difficulties associated with interruptions in supply and not enough quantities necessary for treatment. That shortage generates gaps that, if not covered by the families' own resources, compromise the patient's medical care. For other needs such as food and other supplies, state mechanisms offer partial but insufficient support, so that the responsibility again falls on the shoulder of families to meet through their own resources. Not all such cases can adequately deal with the disease according to the requirements for proper care.

> My mom needs a super-special diet, in general she has to eat fruit but what's especially recommended are apples . . . I buy the apples

twenty at a time, which means they cost between forty and sixty cents apiece, CUC [convertible Cuban pesos, with equivalence to foreign currency] . . . The medicine comes from the state, but when there's not enough I have to go out and look for it in the black market! Right now she's entitled to ten bottles a month and she's only getting two, because they aren't covering all the medicine—and those other eight, I have to buy them on the street where I'm getting charged 2.50 CUC per bottle! . . . Also I have to buy the strips for the glucometer, and a little pack of fifty of them costs 37.60 CUC in the international pharmacy. (Case in optimal economic conditions.)

Not long ago my foot was in pretty bad shape, they even told me I was going to lose it . . . but then there's the problem of shoes. I wear these not because I like them, but because they're what I've got, and I can't afford the luxury of buying a pair for 20 or 30 or 40 dollars . . . I have to buy one that's not too bad, but it's not good either! Usually they're sneakers with flat soles—but eight or nine dollar sneakers, so you can imagine, and even that's a sacrifice because I make only 200 pesos a month [pesos, equal to a bit over 8 dollars or 8 CUC] . . . so these are the shoes I have to wear, and my foot gets bad every so often because these aren't the right shoes for someone like me. . . The balanced diet for a diabetic, all day long, it's breakfast, snack, lunch, snack, dinner, snack, and there's no way I can do that! . . . and vegetables, forget it, I like them and I'm happy to eat them, but do you know how much vegetables cost? I can't buy vegetables every day or in the amount that I need, and the same for fruits and other things . . . The state provides me a special diet of chicken and milk but that's not enough to begin to cover my needs . . . So, since I can't comply with the diet I have to take the disease as it comes, what else can you do? . . . There's no other solution. (Case with poor material living conditions.)

Given widening economic inequality in Cuba, private buying, public services, and poorly paid work combine in different ways according to people's places in the socioeconomic structure. This demonstrates the existence of contrasting realities in which some families have multiple options for risk management, and others have very few options and quite limited room to maneuver.

There are, therefore, real limitations—with different degrees of gravity—that affect appropriate responses to situations of illness. The most alarming cases are those where serious health problems coincide with very low monetary income, little or no non-monetary proceeds, and lack of any notable accumulation of material goods. These can coexist with very problematic housing in poor physical conditions, cramped quarters, lack of some basic appliances, and meager or deteriorated furniture, which make it very hard to face situations of poor health.

Conclusions

In general, the state still has a greater capacity to generate health care services that resist the reproduction of inequality. In spite of difficulties in the functioning of these services and of mechanisms of informal access that are more available to people who possess certain types of capital, the contribution made by universal, free public services continues to be very significant. It is precisely this sort of service that prevents the emergence of a one-to-one equivalence between economic and social-resource vulnerability and vulnerability in access to health services. Despite the existence of obstacles, these services always provide a possible path to social protection, to a greater or lesser degree.

In contrast, the area of care and attention within the domestic-family sphere is more adversely affected to the extent that satisfaction of these needs depends more directly on families' personal resources, the disparity of which may show stark contrasts that affect the families' ability to successfully manage situations of illness of one or more members. In general, the out-of-pocket costs that must be borne by families dealing with illness and care of the sick, along with the economic impacts and harm that these costs inflict on households, are more and more significant in understanding how, in practice, social protection in these situations is (or is not) generated; such costs and impacts must be considered in analyses of this issue.

Therefore, as other Cuban researchers have stressed, there is a need for a more integrated vision in the design of social policy to overcome the traditional compartmentalization of "prioritized areas" (such as health and education) and "lagging" ones (such as housing and employment-wages). Given the nature of the primary generating mechanisms of inequality, poverty, and vulnerability in contemporary Cuba, social policy design must accord greater importance, within social spending priorities, to those areas that directly impact the domestic-family sphere, broadening the elective capacities of families and individuals by way of the generation of their own assets and income. This would contribute to the attainment of social development in a systematic way, so that the great investments in some spheres, such as health services, are not limited or neutralized by inattention to other areas that also affect that sphere.

Appendix 7.1

Classification of Living Conditions	
Material living condition	**Number of households**
Very Good (G-1)	6
Good (G-2)	8
Fair (G-3)	7
Poor (G-4)	6
Very Poor (G-5)	3

Appendix 7.2: Situations of Illness in the Cases Studied

While the section on the family-domestic sphere deals primarily with the health situations of the families studied (the illnesses and other medical conditions present in their homes), the medical situations of family members who do not live in the same dwelling, yet with whom they are involved, are also important. Both contribute to the lived experience of the subjects in relation to illness and care.

The medical problems present among the members of families in the sample are:

20 cases of the following illness:	Hypertension
12 cases of the following illness:	Diabetes
11 cases of the following illness:	Bronchial asthma
6 cases each of the following illnesses:	Osteoarthritis, allergies
3 cases each of the following illnesses:	Cancers, mild itellectual disability
2 cases each of the following illnesses:	Hypothyroidism, anemia, hip fractures, gall bladder
1 case each of the following illnesses:	Stroke (mild), stroke (severe), severe intellectual disability, schizophrenia, psoriasis, senile dementia, colostomy, simple partial seizure, heart disease, migraines, multiple sclerosis, obesity

Source: Constructed by the author from research data

And those of non-cohabiting family members are:

1 case each of the following illnesses:	Cirrhosis, diabetes, hypertension, prostate cancer, breast cancer, Alzheimer's disease, lung cancer, brain cancer
2 cases of the following illness:	Bedridden elder

Source: Constructed by the author from research data

Although these data offer a general picture, the diseases are not distributed proportionally among the cases. There are variations in the numbers of persons in each household who suffer from health problems, the number of conditions per person (some suffer from more than one), and how chronic or serious the conditions are. Thus, each household in the study faced a scenario somewhat different from the others.

Notes

1. Of course, this is not an abstract debate; it parallels the region's very specific experiences and realities. Targeted or selective approaches have been linked to a neoliberal version of social policy.

2. Sociologist Mayra Espina defines this concept as "a mechanism for distribution through social consumption characterized by universality, massivity, free or otherwise enabled access, legally guaranteed right, centralized public design with guaranteed access, social participation, preponderance of collective solutions over individual ones, homogeneity, increasing quality, opportunities for social integration under equal conditions for all social sectors independent of income, and aspiration to equality of results" (2008a:144).

3. MINSAP's Dirección Nacional de Registros Médicos y Estadística de Salud, in its series of *Anuarios Estadísticos de Salud*, presents indicators organized in time series, by geographic area, by age cohorts, and by gender. The categories do not include skin color or economic stratum, although these are important variables in relation to social inequalities in today's Cuba. Health outcomes are not shown in relation to other variables such as educational level, although several studies have confirmed the importance of education in relation to health. By contrast, the WHO, in its annual series *World Health Statistics,* offers information on health inequalities that includes data on the distribution of health outcomes and health care services within countries and by subgroups of their population, surpassing Cuban domestic statistical media.

4. See De la Torre, et al., 2005, pp. 177–186.

5. During the existence of socialist bloc, Cuba received heavy Soviet subsidies which, to a large degree, made possible the construction and durability of the Cuban model of providing citizen welfare. However, with the collapse of that bloc, the need to generate income to sustain growing and complex social services emerged as a problem that was difficult to avoid. The insufficient economic sustainability of its social policy has been cited as one of the limitations of the Cuban social policy model (Espina, 2008b; Nerey, 2005).

6. One important factor was shortcomings in systems of water supply and sanitation, including sanitary control of excretions, reduced hours of water service, water treatment and potable quality, the degree of systematization of disinfection, etc. (CIEM, 1997). Such situations led to an increase in mortality from infectious and parasitic diseases and rising morbidity rates from some infectious diseases, associated with deterioration of environmental and living conditions.

7. Food scarcity led to an increase in malnutrition and excessive weight loss, as well as an increase in low birth weights (Fleitas, 2013). Also associated with the food situation was the outbreak of an epidemic of optical neuropathy that affected more than 53,000 people.

8. This included the Program for accelerated education of nurses, the Program for reconstruction and modernization of hospitals, and the Program for

reconstruction and modernization of polyclinics. The latter was intended to improve the deteriorated physical condition of those facilities and to broaden their offerings of services with greater accessibility and quality. The result was a new institution called an "integrated polyclinic" that offered an average of 20 different services.

9. This information is drawn from an analysis of the section of letters to the editor of the daily newspaper *Granma*. The section is published every Friday and reflects opinions of the Cuban populace. The analysis covered the period from the initiation of the letters-to-the-editor section in March 2008 through the year 2014, and the focus of attention was on letters with explicit reference to the health sector, and especially to health care services.

10. At the same time there was process of labor reorganization in the sector, carried out from 2010 to 2013, which resulted in the elimination of 109,000 positions and a reduction of 1. 9 trillion pesos in spending (Cubadebate, 2014). These savings, along with significant income from the export of health services (8.2 billion CUC in 2014, equal 64 percent of Cuba's total sales of services according to a statement by economy and planning minister Marino Murillo), provided the economic support for a salary increase in the health sector, announced in March 2014. Action has also been taken to maintain and repair health facilities at various levels of the system.

11. See opinions published in the *Cartas a la Dirección* section of *Granma*.

12. In Latin America, Cuba has the best indicators for infant mortality, mortality in ages of five years old or less, and doctors per inhabitant. It shares the leading positions for other indicators such as life expectancy at birth, births attended by qualified personnel, deaths in childbirth, and total health spending as a percent of GDP. Cuba's infant and child mortality indicators are comparable to those in developed countries. See MINSAP, 2015; CEPAL, 2014.

13. The reference is to the "Conceptualización del modelo económico y social cubano de desarrollo socialista" and the "Plan nacional de desarrollo económico y social hasta 2030: propuesta de visión de la nación, ejes y sectores estratégicos." Of the four documents approved by the Seventh Congress of the CCP, these are the two that have been widely distributed.

14. In this model, family incomes are defined by differentiated opportunities to participate in the production-consumption process, and also in the process of consumption not derived from productive activity but rather from economic aid by third parties and from the results of illicit activities. Thus differences in access and consumption do not necessarily depend on the values of work or job qualifications.

15. Also, this occurs in a context of market expansion and segmentation and a dual currency. The two currencies are the CUC (convertible Cuban peso) and the CUP (Cuban peso, also called *moneda nacional*, domestic currency). The purchasing power of the former exceeds that of the latter, at a ratio of 24:1; that is, 1 CUC=24 CUP.

16. The restructuring of the state budget, with gradual reductions in total spending, has affected such social policies as Social Assistance. Between 2009 and 2014, spending in that area dropped by 366. 5 billion CUP; the number of beneficiaries likewise dropped, from 426,390 to 169,778 (ONEI, 2015). The scarcity of information on who has ceased to receive Social Assistance support does not allow for a qualitative evaluation of this process and its real implications.

17. The process of gradual elimination of the ration book system (Guideline 174) has continued, as has the elimination of subsidies for some other goods and services; some products that had been subsidized for the entire population have shifted to unrationed sales at market prices.

18. All these measures have enabled the diversification of options for employment and income, thus opening up new opportunities for families to legally increase their earnings either outside the state sphere or in conjunction with it.

19. The issue was approached from the point of view of users of medical services on the basis of their experiences and social discourses. The qualitative methodological design stemmed from a judgment that this type of perspective was the most important for acquiring empirical evidence about the phenomena being studied.

20. In this study, "material living conditions" refers to the family's standard of living as expressed by income distribution, access to material well-being and consumption, and supply of resources and means to meet household needs. Material conditions are operationally defined by "economic conditions" (monetary and non-monetary income, assets in the form of goods and property) and "housing conditions" (type, physical condition, layout and use of living space, hygienic-sanitary conditions, fuel and lighting, and appliances).

21. To guarantee the sample's heterogeneity in this sense, the study used qualitative typologies that allowed selection of cases representing typical socio-structural situations with a degree of prevalence in Cuban social structure (Espina, 2003).

22. Some sick people are offered, through the ration-book system, an additional quota made up mostly of powdered milk, chicken, and root vegetables. There are also mechanisms within the public health system to supply equipment, supplies, and services needed for particular types of illnesses: taxi rides, disposable diapers, portable urinals, wheelchairs, hospital beds, oxygen tanks, prostheses, canes, orthopedic supports, catheters, glucometers, rubbing alcohol, swabs, gauze, and raw cotton. Additionally, institutions such as Social Assistance support households or individuals in extremely disadvantaged situations whose health problems can aggravate their already precarious situations. According to the specifics of each case, they may offer free medicine, supply bathing and cleaning products or other supplies, and they also offer the services of home-care workers paid by the state. In addition there are facilities such as nursing homes, elderly centers, and homes for the mentally ill, among others.

23. The effectiveness and problem-solving capacity of the state channels depends on how well those structures are functioning in each specific context and also on what resources the state has to devote to those ends, given the country's difficult economic situation.

24. Out-of-pocket expenses are considered part of private health care spending, in this case meaning all direct and indirect expenditures the family devotes to caring for the health of its members. That includes direct spending on various kinds of services and can also include indirect costs for transportation and other needs, loss of wages related to incidents of illness, etc.

Bibliography

Álvarez, Elena, and J. Máttar, eds. 2004. *Política social y reformas estructurales: Cuba a principios del siglo XXI.* Mexico City: CEPAL/INIE/PNUD.

Castro Ruz, Raúl. 2008. Discurso pronunciado en el Segundo Período de Sesiones de la VII Legislatura de la Asamblea Nacional del Poder Popular, en el Palacio de Convenciones. Havana, 27 December.

————. 2009. Discurso pronunciado en el Tercer Período Ordinario de Sesiones de la VII Legislatura de la Asamblea Nacional del Poder Popular, en el Palacio de Convenciones. Havana, 1 August.

————. 2014. Discurso pronunciado en las conclusiones del XX Congreso de la Central de Trabajadores de Cuba. Havana, 22 February.

CEPAL. 2010. *La hora de la igualdad. Brechas por cerrar, caminos por abrir.* Santiago de Chile: Naciones Unidas.

————. 2014. *Panorama social de América Latina 2014.* Santiago de Chile: Naciones Unidas.

CIEM (Centro de Investigaciones de la Economía Mundial). 1997. *Investigación sobre el desarrollo humano en Cuba, 1996.* Havana: Ediciones Caguayo S. A.

Cubadebate. 2014. "Las transformaciones en el sistema nacional de salud y sus impactos," panel discussion on the Cuban television show Mesa Redonda, 26 March.

De la Torre, Ernesto, Cándido López, Miguel Márquez, J. A. Gutiérrez, and Francisco Rojas. 2005. *Salud para todos sí es posible.* Havana: MercieGroup-ENPSES.

Espina, Mayra. 2003. "Efectos sociales del reajuste económico: igualdad, desigualdad y procesos de complejización en la sociedad cubana." Presented at LASA 2003, XXIV International Congress of the Latin American Studies Association, Dallas, 27–29 March.

————. 2008a. *Políticas de atención a la pobreza y la desigualdad. Examinando el rol del Estado en la experiencia cubana.* Buenos Aires: CLACSO-CROP.

————. 2008b. "Política social en Cuba. Equidad y movilidad." In *Working Papers* (DRCLAS-Harvard University), # 07/08-3.

————. 2011. "La política social en Cuba: resultados y retos." Presented at seminar, "La cuestión social en Cuba contemporánea," Center for Latin American and Latino Studies, American University, Washington, D.C., February.

———. 2012. Retos y cambios en la política social. In Pavel Vidal and Omar Everleny Pérez, eds., *Miradas a la economía cubana. El proceso de actualización.* Havana: Editorial Caminos.

Fleitas, Reina. 2013. *Familias pobres y desigualdades de género en salud: el caso del barrio de San Isidro.* Buenos Aires: CLACSO-CROP.

Fuentes, Susset. 2016. "El acceso a los servicios de salud y la capacidad de enfrentamiento familiar ante situaciones de quebrantamiento de la salud. ¿Un lugar desde el cual pensar la reproducción de desigualdades en la Cuba actual?" Master's thesis, FLACSO Cuba, Havana.

Gálvez, Ana María. 2003. "Economía de la salud en el contexto de la salud pública cubana." In *Revista Cubana de Salud Pública.* Volume 29, No. 4.

Gómez, Clarisbel. 2014. Pobreza, salud mental y desigualdad. Un acercamiento a los actores institucionales que median esta relación en un Consejo Popular cubano. In María del Carmen Zabala, ed., *Algunas claves para pensar la pobreza en Cuba desde la mirada de jóvenes investigadores.* Havana: Publicaciones Acuario.

Hernández, Wiliam, Luisa Íñiguez, and Adrian Gehartz. 2011. "Acercamiento geográfico al Sistema de Salud de la provincia de Pinar del Río." In *Novedades en población.* Number 15.

Íñiguez, Luisa. 2012. "Aproximación a la evolución de los cambios en los servicios de salud en Cuba." In *Revista Cubana de Salud Pública.* Volume 38, Number 1.

Mesa-Lago, Carmelo. 2010. "Cincuenta años de servicios sociales en Cuba." In *Temas*, Number 64.

MINSAP. 2010. *Transformaciones necesarias en el Sistema de Salud Pública.* Havana, MINSAP.

———. 2015. *Anuario Estadístico de Salud 2014.* Havana: MINSAP.

Nerey, Boris. 2005. "Cuba: desarrollo, estado de bienestar y política salarial." Master's thesis, Universidad de la Habana.

OMS (Organización Mundial de la Salud, English initials WHO). 2008. *Informe sobre la salud en el mundo 2008: La atención primaria de salud. Más necesaria que nunca.* Geneva: WHO.

ONEI (Oficina Nacional de Estadística e Información). 2015. *Anuario Estadístico de Cuba 2014 (Empleo y Salarios).* Havana: ONEI.

PCC. 2011. *Lineamientos de la Política Económica y Social del Partido y la Revolución.* Havana: 6to Congreso del PCC. [Official English translation from: "Sixth Congress of The Communist Party of Cuba, Resolution on the Guidelines of the Economic and Social Policy of the Party and the Revolution," consulted 3 September 2016 at http://www.cuba.cu/gobierno/documentos/2011/ing/l160711i. html.]

———. 2016a. *Conceptualización del modelo económico y social cubano de desarrollo socialista.* Havana: 7mo Congreso del PCC.

———. 2016b. *Plan nacional de desarrollo económico y social hasta 2030: propuesta de visión de la nación, ejes y sectores estratégicos.* Havana: 7mo Congreso del PCC.

Peña, Ángela. 2014. "La reproducción de la pobreza familiar desde la óptica de los regímenes de bienestar en el contexto cubano actual." Doctoral thesis, Universidad de La Habana.

Skeen, Marta María. 2015 "Las políticas sociales en el ámbito de la Salud Pública. Municipio Plaza de la Revolución. Atención Primaria 2010–2014." Master's thesis, FLACSO Cuba.

Voghón, Rosa María and Ángela Peña, 2013, ¿Reproducción de la pobreza en el contexto de políticas sociales universales? Encrucijadas y desafíos del modelo de protección social cubano. In*Persistencias de la pobreza y esquemas de protección social en América Latina y el Caribe* (collection). Buenos Aires: CLACSO-CROP.

Whitehead, Margaret. 1991. *Los conceptos y principios de la equidad en salud*. Washington: Organización Panamericana de la Salud.

8

Environmental Policy and Management of Water Resources: Challenges and Perspectives

Marta Rosa Muñoz Campos

Cuba's environmental policy is stated in a legal and institutional instrument delineating the use, regulation, protection, and conservation of environmental systems.[1] Its application implies access to natural resources, science, and technology; stimulus of community participation and social responsibility; and planning, protection, and sustainable use of the environment. In addition, the policy is necessarily linked to problems of development, particularly sustainable development. It is an instrument of both integrated and multifaceted nature whose main pillars are education, health, and employment, though it also involves food and nutrition, housing, sanitation, public safety, and social assistance.[2] This policy has gained international recognition because of its well-established organization throughout the country, well-educated human resources, and strong political commitment from decision-makers.

Researcher Leonel Vega[3] has surveyed environmental concepts reflected in social policies, identifying the environmental approaches present in this policy at the international level with its corresponding influences on the Cuban system. He offers a historical approach to understanding and action in this area, which he perceives occurred in stages, as follows:

Incidental. This approach consists of actions that are neither planned nor guided by a larger strategic plan, but rather are taken to confront specific environmental problems. Environmental degradation is seen as an isolated, sporadic, and inevitable phenomenon, caused by damaging behavior that occurs in the normal course of human activities. This type of environmental management predominated until the mid-twentieth century.

Operational. During this stage those in charge plan and carry out environmental programs and projects, but the programs lack coordination among legislative and regulatory mechanisms and the social actors who implement them. That drawback results from excessive bureaucracy that fails to consider the plans' viability, efficiency, and attention to real needs. Environmental problems are viewed as involuntary, yet caused by errors in policy, planning, and program execution. This is the dominant perspective today, characterized by command-control instruments (laws, regulations, environmental permits, impact statements, and taxes), in which environmental policy seeks to correct behavior without altering current economic, cultural, or institutional decisions. Internationally, this type of management became prevalent in the 1970s.

Systemic. In line with the concept of the environment as a whole system, efficient and effective management is structured by following certain ongoing processes: "What resolves [environmental] problems is the continuous process of designing, executing, evaluating, correcting, re-designing, and re-executing. In other words, a process of learning, feedback, and continual improvement is, in essence, the basic conceptual precept of the systemic approach."[4] This perspective arose in the 1990s, and it is the one closest to the conception of the Cuban system.

In this view, two fundamental objectives emerge: first, to maintain and improve environmental programs and supports (social opportunities to continue benefiting from environmental services), and second, to orient cultural movement toward sustainability. This appeal to the social sphere must be encouraged by inclusive policies that strengthen equal opportunity, and by attention to such issues as education, housing, health, socio-demographic trends, and economic activities throughout the country. Environmental sustainability is one of the fundamental aims of Cuban social policy, as structured by interrelated consideration of the economic, environmental, and social aspects of development; the centrality of the state; and encouragement of participation by and differential treatment of groups considered vulnerable to natural disasters such as floods, drought, and extreme climate events.[5]

The main expression of the view of environmental issues as part of social policy is the Law of the Environment (No. 81 of 1997), which states: "Environmental management applies environmental policy established by a multidisciplinary approach, taking into account cultural patterns, accumulated national experience, and public participation."[6] About the actors responsible for such management, it specifies, "environmental management is integral and trans-sectoral, involving the coordinated participation of state bodies and organisms, other entities and institutions, and society and its citizens in general, in accord with their respective jurisdictions and capacities."

Distinctive Characteristics of Cuban Environmental Policy

The basic mechanism of implementation of Law 81 is the National Environmental Strategy, which guides Territorial Environmental Strategies, especially the sectoral ones that cover all production and service sectors. Decree 138 of 1993 on Terrestrial Waters regulates the use, control, and protection of water supplies. Other legislation related to conservation of water and soil resources includes a variety of laws and resolutions about domestic water supplies (1993), pricing of water for irrigation (1999), and protection and rational use of water resources (1995). Important complementary instruments are Decrees 200 and 201; the former establishes regulations related to the Law of the Environment, while the latter includes provisions about the National System of Protected Areas.[7]

From the institutional point of view, the Law of the Environment defines the Ministry of Agriculture (MINAGRI) as the leading body responsible for the management, conservation, and improvement of agricultural and forest land, and for taking the necessary steps to fulfill that law in coordination with the ministries of Science, Technology, and Environment (CITMA), Basic Industry (MINBAS), Sugar (MINAZ), and other appropriate institutions. The institutions responsible for developing water and irrigation resources are the National Institute of Hydraulic Resources (Spanish initials INRH), MINAGRI's Institute for Research on Irrigation and Drainage (IIRD), and MINAZ's National Department of Irrigation and Drainage (DNRD). The INRH regulates the use of both surface and subterranean water supplies, and is charged with planning, executing, and exploiting new reserves and reservoirs in concert with changes in land use.

Scientific research and the encouragement of innovation are reflected in the various National Scientific-Technical Programs, which seek to apply science to problems of development, guiding the use of the state budget toward those ends. These include the National Program for Combatting Desertification and Drought, the Program for Rehabilitating Bays, the National Program of Hydrographic Basins, the National Program for Combating Pollution, the National Action Program on Water and Sanitation, and the program called "Climate Change in Cuba: Impacts, Mitigation, and Adaptation."

Work done by these programs has yielded important results: assessment of the impact of climate change in Cuba and the adaptation methods needed; development of new climate models; improvement and development of new and diverse Early Alert Systems for extreme hydro-meteorological events; modeling and assessment of scenarios of foreseeable sea level rise on Cuban coasts for 2050 and 2100; studies of the state of natural coastal resources; impacts on land and sea biodiversity; and evaluations of danger, vulnerability, and risk from various meteorological events at the local, provincial, and national scales.

A key element has been collaboration between domestic institutions and international cooperation bodies. These ties have made possible an infrastructural framework for carrying out the activities. At the same time, they have allowed for implementation of successful practices in relation to similar work in other parts of the world, have provided methodological advice about formulation and implementation of projects, and have put accumulated knowledge at the disposal of the country. According to the Cuban professor and researcher Willy Pedroso, the characteristics of this collaboration have been:[8]

- Orientation to national development goals and environmental priorities, taking as a starting point what is established in Cuban regulations and strategies, in accordance with the international agreements to which the country has subscribed.
- A multidisciplinary and multisectoral approach. This implies identification and formation of work teams made up of all the actors who, given their social objectives, can support implementation.
- Emphasis on knowledge management. This element consists of systematizing the learning and best practices generated during project implementation, for later expansion through various products.
- Emphasis on capacity-building. Sustainability and replicability require the entities taking part in team work to be in condition to continue this work independently.
- Emphasis on the local, that is, through Administrative Councils, the local offices of involved entities, leaders of representative organization (Committees for the Defense of the Revolution, Cuban Women's Federation, Union of Young Communists, National Small Farmers' Association) and informal leaders. The latter have a socio-cultural and communicative role to play in the shaping of environmental perceptions and, therefore, of community attitudes toward their surroundings.
- Communications management. This activity stresses producing content, making projects visible, and managing communications media in support of all dimensions of the work.

This collaboration has stimulated all aspects of environmental management in the country. Most prominent in the agricultural sector is the Local Agricultural Innovation Project (PIAL), supported by Swiss Agency for Development and Cooperation (COSUDE); within its focus on producing healthy food for Cuban families, it has developed important capacity-building activities for rural men and women, such as schools for farmers. Also in the area of rural development and sustainable agriculture, with support from the European Union, is the Program for Local Support for Modernization of the Agricultural Sector (PALMA), which seeks to increase local food production and access through an economically sustainable strategy centered on cooperatives, new usufruct landholders, and decentralized management of food production.

In the realm of confronting climate change, an important initiative is the project called "Assessment of the potential impacts of climate change on biodiversity and the development of adaptation strategies in two regions of Cuba with fragile ecosystems," which focuses on the national parks Jardines de la Reina and Ciénaga de Zapata, through cooperation between Cuba's Fundación Antonio Núñez Jiménez and the World Wildlife Fund. This initiative, known by the acronym CCamBIO, combines economic and social mechanisms to protect endangered species such as corals, four types of sea turtles, and the Cuban crocodile, and also designs adaptation strategies for the two sites. The United Nations Development Program has stimulated significant experiences such as the Sabana-Camagüey project, in coordination with the Global Environment Facility, resulting in the conservation and sustainable use of biodiversity in the archipelago of that name.

These are only some examples of the lines of work that have been opened with support of international organizations that have been the major mechanism for implementing and stimulating Cuban environmental policy, as seen not only in the results achieved but also in the high levels of communication with the populace. Thus, the country can count on high levels of expertise in environmental management and ability to carry out important initiatives, but the situation is not without challenges.

Policy and Environmental Problems in Cuba

Despite the country's achievements in environmental policy, important challenges to its sustainability stem from problems connected to management, implementation, and incorporation of an environmental dimension of development, and from other educational and cultural issues affecting health and quality of life, prioritized economic activities, particular regions, and highly fragile ecosystems.

A central element is attention to the main environmental problems described in the National Environmental Strategy, whose fundamental goal for the 2011–2015 period was "Prevention and systematic solution of the country's main environmental problems, and facing and quickly adapting to the impacts of climate change."[9] These include:

- *Soil Degradation:* The country's total agricultural land covers 6.7 million hectares, of which 3.3 million is arable. Erosion affects 71.23 percent, while 43 percent is cited as subject to severe or moderate erosion. A million hectares, or 15 percent of the agricultural total, are affected by salinization.

- *Damage to Forest Cover:* In general, Cuba has been able to continually increase forest cover, to a total of 3,897,423.8 hectares. However, problems persist in the majority of the natural forests, especially in the most important hydrographic basins, including low exploitation of biomass, presence of invasive plants. and failure to use forest planning.

- *Contamination:* This includes pollution by liquid and solid residues; atmospheric and sonic pollution; contamination by dangerous chemicals and waste flows from industrial facilities in urban areas; insufficient financial resources for capture and reuse of residues; and lack of an adequate monitoring system for atmospheric emissions or soil quality, and relating solutions to these problems to the decision-making process so as to improve the population's quality of life.

- *Loss of Biological Diversity:* The National Study for Biological Diversity identified the fundamental causes of loss of biodiversity as the transformation, fragmentation, or destruction of habitat. These are in turn associated with deforestation, changes in land use, and the use of inappropriate practices in fishing, harvesting, and preparing soils for planting, among others. Currently, out of 4,783 plant species examined, 314 are classified as being in critical danger of extinction, 336 in danger, 263 vulnerable, and 22 as extinct.

- *Water Scarcity and Quality:* Some parts of the country have a scarcity of water that has been aggravated by prolonged droughts, variations in seasonal patterns, and other variations induced by human activity; over-exploitation, saline intrusion, and contamination; and leakage in the supply system—all of which affect the real availability of water to a considerable degree.

- *Impact of Climate Change:* In relation to climate change, it is important to underline the population's vulnerability to rising sea levels.

In Cuba, as Figure 8.1 indicates, there are 246 human settlements in coastal areas, which means that 3.5 million people live within a few kilometers of the coastline.

Figure 8.1: Characteristics of the Cuban Archipelago

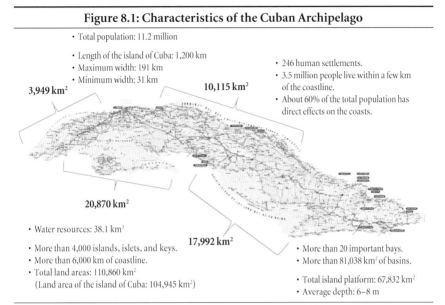

- Total population: 11.2 million

- Length of the island of Cuba: 1,200 km
- Maximum width: 191 km
- Minimum width: 31 km

3,949 km²

10,115 km²

- 246 human settlements.
- 3.5 million people live within a few km of the coastline.
- About 60% of the total population has direct effects on the coasts.

20,870 km²

17,992 km²

- Water resources: 38.1 km³
- More than 4,000 islands, islets, and keys.
- More than 6,000 km of coastline.
- Total land areas: 110,860 km² (Land area of the island of Cuba: 104,945 km²)

- More than 20 important bays.
- More than 81,038 km² of basins.

- Total island platform: 67,832 km²
- Average depth: 6–8 m

Source: Environmental Agency of CITMA (2015)

According to Cuban sociologist Ángela Peña, examination of environmental problems has not included a more integrated perspective that would consider vulnerability and poverty of some of the people concerned, principally on the periphery of urban areas. She says that in spite of the existence of a national preventive policy of managing social and physico-natural vulnerabilities, research has suffered from insufficient treatment of conflicts that would involve a more integral vision: differential access to natural resources, areas of vulnerability, and socio-environmental risks, as viewed from a multidimensional perspective.[10]

In this sense, environmental problems do not arise in isolated fashion, but in dialectic interaction with the social situation, especially the reproduction of conditions of poverty and vulnerability. Peña's research has identified the environmental conditions facing some poor families in Cuba. From the physico-natural point of view, she found housing units in critical condition, lack of sanitation and hygiene, and low strategic capacity to confront the negative effects of climate change. From the political point of view, she found a lack of effective opportunities to participate in decision-making processes.[11]

Environmental Policy and New Scenarios

Since 2011, when the country's new Guidelines for Economic and Social Policy[12] were approved, transformations have taken place that affect the implementation of Cuban environmental policy. These include:

- October, 2013: Distribution of idle land (potentially productive land not currently under exploitation)—1,500,000 hectares.
- Entire Year 2013: Authorization for juridical entities to buy goods and services from individuals, including payment in convertible currency (CUC).
- July, 2013: Creation of non-farm cooperatives. (Through late March of 2014, a total of 498 new cooperatives had been approved.)
- December, 2013: Approval of new regulations governing self-employment.
- September, 2013: Adoption of Decree-Law 313 regulating all aspects of the Mariel Special Development Zone (ZEDM).
- March, 2014: Approval of Law 118 on Foreign Investment. The section on protection of the environment was expanded (Chapter XV, Articles, 54–58).

The environmental implications of those changes are explained by Cuban geographer and environmentalist José Manuel Mateo, who underlines new trends affecting sustainability:[13]

- New forms of enterprise self-management and of social, community, and collective appropriation and control of space and environmental systems, such that the sense of belonging corresponds to that of ownership.
- Increased consumption and consumerist vision, accompanying the satisfaction of basic needs, which corroborates the humanist dimension of the socialist project.
- Growth of socio-cultural models imposed by globalization, simultaneously with intensified cultural policy intended to strengthen patriotic and national identity, socialist and revolutionary values.
- Intensification of the use of natural spaces and resources stemming from increased opportunities to use fossil fuels and greater use of technology and agrochemicals, alongside growing use of renewable resources, increased energy savings, and the incorporation of environmentally conceived technologies.
- Presence of new and varied non-state actors in the use and administration of environmental goods and services, motivated in large part

by competitiveness and desire for short-term profit, which will bring a new and higher level of tension to spatial and environmental systems.
- Greater spatial concentration of impacts and actions such as urbanization, tourist facility development, and industrial reconversion, parallel with spatial deconcentration and increasing autonomy of geographic regions, provinces, and municipalities.

We agree with this author that the major challenges to Cuban environmental policy are dealing with developmentalism, and incorporating an environmental dimension into the development process. There is a contradiction between the needed stimulation of economic development (tourism, agricultural production, mining) without consideration of possible negative impacts on the environment (Mateo calls this "short-term mentality"), and the positions established by national institutions (tension between policy and the process of implementation).

In bringing environmental concerns to the development process, the problem is to supersede a protectionist/conservationist vision in order to move to a vision of environmental adaptation and rationality. Thus environmental policy has to generate new approaches and ways of making use of the environmental that do not deny or limit social uses (offering alternatives to economic-productive or sociocultural activities that degrade their surroundings). This will be possible only through multidimensional mechanisms of policy implementation.

Regarding participation, Cuba is moving toward decentralization in the management of development, which raises the challenge of how to make national capacities, interests, and decisions about the environment mesh with management mechanisms that are more geographically decentralized. This requires efforts to spread awareness and education, make cultural and structural changes, and dialogue with the citizenry.

Returning to the Guidelines for Economic and Social Policy of the Party and the Revolution, Article 133 in the section on Science, Technology, Innovation, and Environment states:

> Comprehensive research studies must be conducted and sustained to help protect, preserve and remediate the environment and adapt the environmental policy to the new economic and social projections. Priority will be given to research studies that address climate change, and in general, Cuba's sustainable development. Emphasis will be made on the preservation and rational use of natural resources such as soils, water, beaches, the air, forests and biodiversity, and the promotion of environmental education.[14]

Guideline articles 134, 135, 136, 138, and 139 (see Appendix) also develop this subject, but only within that section of the Guidelines. In the rest of the policies, the environmental dimension remains insufficiently treated.

Guidelines 256, 260, 262, 263, 264, and 265 (see Appendix) propose to stimulate the tourist sector by means of diversification; however, some of these propositions—such as marinas, golf courses, cruise ship terminals, and real estate development—will require reconsideration in the future because they will have unfavorable consequences for environmental sustainability.

The noted Cuban sociologist Mayra Espina points out aspects of this area of Cuban social policy that have not received sufficient attention. These include the country's housing situation and expansion of marginal neighborhoods around the major cities (both of which produce environmental ills) and the impact of industrial and tourist facilities owned by the state.[15]

The new model of economic and social updating requires deeper examination of the concepts and dimensions of development under today's conditions, as has been argued by the Center for Local Development, which identifies four such dimensions: economic, productive, environmental, and institutional.[16] Likewise, the model should take into account social and geographic dimensions and active participation by the community. In this context, the role of science in describing social interactions with the environment and use of resources must be strengthened. In this chapter, I focus on a particular resource—water—bearing in mind that it is one of the priorities reflected in the National Environmental Strategy.

Management of Water Resources

Water as a natural resource for the population and the economy began to show signs of local crises and disruption in the 1990s and early 2000s. These problems stemmed from human activities, and they have sharpened due to new consumption variables.[17] Equally, in the opinion of some experts,[18] water constitutes the major environmental challenge for Cuba's sustainable development.

Cuba has few natural water resources because of its geologic and morphologic characteristics that determine the prevalence and disposition of this resource. As a long, narrow island, Cuba has no lengthy or high-volume rivers, and its basins do not exceed 200 square kilometers (Figure 8.2), which means that the river network depends on physico-geographic features such as rainfall, geologic and geomorphic conditions, plant cover, and the hydro-physical properties of the soils.

Figure 8.2: Hydrographic Basins of National Interest

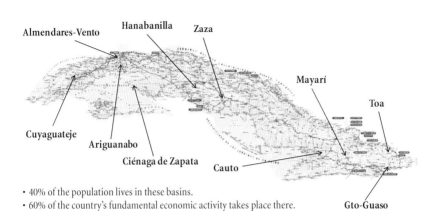

- 40% of the population lives in these basins.
- 60% of the country's fundamental economic activity takes place there.

Source: Fuente: Díaz Duque (2015)

The hydrologic potential of Cuba totals 38.1 cubic kilometers, of which 31.6 km³ (82.9 percent) are surface water and 6.5 km³ (17.1 percent) are underground. Of this potential, only 24 km³ are exploitable, and only 13.6 km³ of those are available, of which surface water totals 67 percent[19] (Figure 8.1).

Cuban hydraulic development has enabled utilization of 13.7 billion cubic meters annually, equal to 57 percent of potentially usable water resources. This was made possible by the creation of technical infrastructure that multiplied the country's reservoir capacity two hundred times and made potable water available to 96 percent of the population and sanitation to 95 percent[20] (Figure 8.3).

The National Environmental Strategy 2007–2010 (Spanish initials EAN) was the first to identify scarcity of water as one of Cuba's main environmental problems, even though hydraulic development had elevated the reservoir capacity to more than 9.6 billion cubic meters since 1959. In that sense, the EAN says, ". . . the scarcity of water for meeting economic, social, and environmental needs on the island persists, aggravated by natural disasters (prolonged droughts and changes in seasonal patterns), as well as man-made impacts (including saline intrusion, overexploitation, pollution, etc.)."[21]

Both natural and human-generated causes affect water scarcity in Cuba, including:

Figure 8.3: Utilization of Water Resources (%)

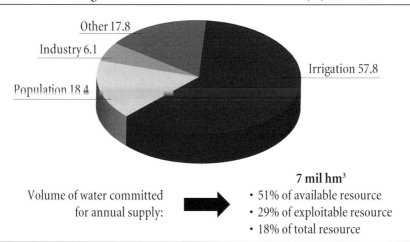

Other 17.8

Industry 6.1

Population 18.4

Irrigation 57.8

7 mil hm³

Volume of water committed for annual supply:
- 51% of available resource
- 29% of exploitable resource
- 18% of total resource

Source: Fuente: Díaz Duque (2015)

- Cuba's being a long, narrow island with many islets and keys.
- The country's topography, in which a central divide spans the length of the main island, with two slopes, northern and southern, along which almost all the rivers flow at right angles to the divide, with relatively short courses and variable, precipitation-dependent flows.[22]
- Almost 70 percent of the areas occupied by aquifers being of karstic origin.[23]
- The predominance of rivers whose courses measure less than 40 kilometers, with hydrologic basins smaller than 200 square kilometers in surface area.[24]
- The location of major aquifers in coastal areas, placing their waters in direct contact with seawater.
- The low natural availability of water, amounting to only 1,221.5 cubic meters per inhabitant for all uses.[25]
- A downward historical trend in mean annual precipitation, dropping by 133 millimeters for the 1961–2000 period as compared to the previous period of 1931–1960, resulting in a new reference mean of 1,335 mm. Rainfall has decreased in all three regions of the country, particularly in the eastern region with a 260 mm decline, with special impact on the Cauto basin with a 367 mm drop and in the Guantánamo-Guaso one with a 155 mm one.[26]

The major phenomena affecting the process of water scarcity brought on by human activity in Cuba are:

- Intrusion of salt water, producing a gradual deterioration of water quality in coastal areas.
- Over-exploitation of some hydrographic basins, both surface and subterranean. More water is extracted than is replaced.
- Contamination of bodies of water by dumping wastes from human settlements, pig farms, sugar mills, and other industry.

At the same time, the Cuban Meteorological Institute has signaled the impact of climate change on the water system and water availability given Cuba's condition as an archipelago. Salinization of coastal aquifers will increase as a result of saline intrusion resulting from a drop in the volume of accessible fresh water. Droughts will be more intense, frequent, and geographically widespread, affecting reserves of both surface and subterranean fresh water. The frequency of years with drought events will also increase; there will be a daily deficit in water supply of approximately 500,000 cubic meters, and a progressive drop in rainfall totals between 2021 and 2100 estimated at ten to twenty percent.[27]

Management of water resources in Cuban society is coordinated by the National Institute of Hydraulic Resources (INRH), the branches of CITMA, the instruments of environmental management, and especially the National Water Policy, a guiding instrument that regulates use of the resource. This policy establishes four priorities: rational and productive use of water; efficient use of the hydraulic infrastructure; management of risks associated with water quality; and management of risks associated with extreme climate events. The main instrument for implementing the policy is, in turn, the Water Balance,[28] an evaluative and strategic document created by the base units of INRH.

According to these directives, water consumption in the country is supposed to supply (in order of priority) the human and animal population, agricultural irrigation, industrial food production, other industries, reservoirs for aquaculture, recreational and environmental uses, and hydroelectric power generation. To provide continuity and to follow the National Water Policy and the Guidelines for Economic and Social Policy of the Party and the Revolution that refer to hydraulic development, INRH through the National Department of Hydraulic Planning is preparing a strategy which will coordinate actions in a Program of National Hydraulic Development involving thirty-two state institutions, to run through the year 2020.[29]

As far as implementation of this national instrument is concerned, some problems persist. These include, among others, wastewater treatment, material and financial recourses to support the work, and failure to completely reflect the priority given by the Guidelines to renewable sources of energy and specifically hydro power.[30] Also there is need for much more consideration of social and community dynamics, which can raise public understanding of risks and promote a culture of integrated water use and management drawing on a sense of social responsibility.

Some Best Practices

Some local efforts deserve special mention for their pursuit of participatory management of water, illuminating and responding to the structural conditions underlying conflicts. For example, in the communities of El Granizo and Yaguanabo in the municipality of Cumanayagua in Cienfuegos, a project called "Support for active citizen participation for environmental rehabilitation" has been implemented under the aegis of the Centro Félix Varela. This project's goal is to support citizen and institutional participation in concerted planning and implementation of strategic actions for environmental rehabilitation and response to climate change. Its actions in this regard include digging a well for improved water service, partial repair of the system of wastewater treatment, installation of motorized pumps, supply pipes, and accessories in the water system, continued repairs throughout the waste system, and training in maintenance and sustainability of the wastewater system for both communities.

The provinces of Artemisa and Guantánamo are implementing a project called "Capacity building for coordination of information and monitoring systems/MST in areas with problems of water resource management," led by the Environmental Agency of CITMA. This initiative is the second phase of the United Nations Development Program Country Partner Program, "Support for the implementation of the National Action Program for Combatting of Desertification and Drought" (known as OP-15), which, with financing from the Global Environment Facility, promotes sustainable land management (Spanish initials MST) as a strategy for the use of natural resources in agriculture.

At the national level, this project seeks to define the necessary information for decision-making about MST in Cuba; supplying the equipment, materials (hardware, software, imaging, data bases, monitoring stations, etc.), and training needed to assure the availability of that information; and providing support for setting up a system for managing the information for the institutions involved in activities related to MST in a way that allows for the making of inter- and multisectoral decisions.

Within this framework, a diagnostic communication study identified the symbolic elements that mediate the issue of water use in the intervention sites. It found the following principal problems:[31]

- Low levels of information about the state of hydraulic resources and about MST as an alternative among the people involved in agricultural production in the demonstration sites.
- Weak role of the communications media, especially local ones, in the treatment of subjects related to MST and the dissemination of best practices in the integrated management of water resources.
- Producers' and planners' lack of awareness and knowledge about alternative practices in the management of water resources.

Other successful projects include the Program for Saving and Rational Use of Water (PAURA), whose objectives included increased publicity directed toward all audiences, designed to broaden and deepen the culture of rational water use. Among other things, it prioritized the creation and transmission of public service messages, distribution of the magazine *Voluntad Hidráulica*, creation and support of interest circles, a PAURA contest, and the national Trazaguas contest.

These best-practice experiences have some things in common, such as their attention to national Cuban environmental policies and priorities for resource management as these are adapted to local and regional particularities and contexts. Other common factors are an important role for communities in participation, design, and implementation of strategies; support from the social structure of Cuban localities; integration of the structures of macro- and micro-society; education and training practices for local actors as central and fundamental aspects, set up in a way that responds to general and particular interests of the local area and the whole society; integration and coordination of actors; and contributions to the current Cuban context through knowledge management.

Principal Challenges of Cuban Environmental Policy

I agree with sociologist Mayra Espina that environmental sustainability in Cuba requires the following: greater participation by the actors in the solution of their main environmental problems; increased public consultation; understanding environmental and climate-related variables as factors capable of producing social disadvantage; more progress in reducing vulnerabilities through compensation for historical damage and fighting conditions that reproduce inequality; orienting the new cooperative and private entrepreneurs toward social and environmental responsibility; and encouraging agendas of regional and international integration.[32] Hence the various actions that will unfold need to focus on these issues.

University of Havana Social Communications Professor Willy Pedroso stresses the importance of considering economic valuation of environmental services in policy design at the regional or local level. Economic valuation is an instrument of environmental management that assigns monetary values to the goods and services obtained from interaction with the ecosystem which, together with qualitative valuation, offers rational data for decision-making about investments and plans. This element should be integrated into the system of economic accounting, and it should include environmental inventory (identification of the components of the environment that meet social needs, understood as natural goods, with special attention to those in danger), evaluation of environmental impacts (determination of how a given socioeconomic activity affects the environment), and such forms of analysis as cost-benefit, cost-efficiency, risk-benefit, multi-criteria and decision analysis. Also, economic valuation allows for balancing social policies and adaptation measures.[33]

To these elements we may add:

- The need to overcome the high degree of state centralization.
- The need to move away from bad practices that limit solutions to the most pressing needs.
- The need to deepen the concepts and dimensions of development, so as to consider and apply effective integration of social, economic, environmental, and cultural aspects.
- The need to address the country's housing situation and the expansion of marginal neighborhoods around the major cities (both of which express environmental ills) and the impact of industrial and tourist facilities owned by the state. The need to take the social dimension of regional planning into account so as to encourage participation.
- The need for greater participation by actors in the solution of their main environmental problems.
- The need for administrative and financial self-management and local participatory practices.

In addition, there is a need to educate and train local decision-making actors, because they generally deal with short-term problems, and so environmental issues may be relegated behind priorities that seem more pressing. The challenge is to change this mentality toward commitment to local and regional integrated development, as well as offering these people the knowledge and skills they need to address the issues mentioned here. One effective tactic can be to highlight positive results as they are achieved.

Conclusions

Some factors account for success in Cuban environmental policy: political will on the part of the people and the institutional structure; links among all the management agencies down to the regional and local levels; and employment of the country's scientific and research potential. Cuban environmental policy is an important part of social policy, which has not yet found effective paths for implementation in synergy with the other dimensions of social development.

The future of an integrated environmental policy in our country will depend on overcoming the push for economic growth and expanding the regulatory and strategic instruments so that they are shared by the actors responsible for implementation on the local level. Cuba finds itself at a moment of change, marked by an opening to new forms of management that could generate deep social transformations. In this context, the development of a true environmental culture among the population will be essential, and will determine the degree of communities' activity and involvement in the solution of their environmental problems.

Management of water resources is implemented through the National Water Policy, and one of its greatest challenges is to stimulate a truly local response, which includes heightening awareness, sensitivity, and capacity-building for administrative actors and the citizenry. In water resource management, it is possible to identify and replicate best practices at the local level, putting national priorities in dialogue with the demands of local and regional populations so as to shape a joint response.

On the theoretical level, it is necessary to systematize the information and referents that allow for understanding the environmental issue as a trans-disciplinary object in dialogue with the rest of the issues and dynamics of sustainable development.

Notes

1. Mateo, José Manuel. 2012. *La dimensión espacial del desarrollo sostenible: una visión desde América Latina*. Havana: Editorial UH / Editorial Científico Técnica.
2. Multiple authors. 2004. *Política social: El mundo contemporáneo y las experiencias de Cuba y Suecia*. Montevideo: Prontográfica.
3. Cited by Darío Muriel, Rafael. 2006. "La Gestión Ambiental." In *Ide@ Sostenible. Espacio de Reflexión y Comunicación sobre Desarrollo Sostenible*. Number 13 (Year 2006).
4. Ibid.
5. Zabala, M.A. 2015. "Desafíos para la equidad social en Cuba." In M.A. Zabala, D. Echevarría, M.R. Muñoz, and G.E. Fundora, eds., *Retos para la equidad social en el proceso de actualización del modelo económico cubano*, pp. 1–14. Havana: Editorial de Ciencias Sociales.

6. Ley 81: del Medio Ambiente

7. Pedroso Aguiar, Willy. 2015. "Podemos más con el MST: Estrategia participativa de comunicación ambiental para el manejo sostenible de tierras." Undergraduate thesis, Facultad de Comunicación de la Universidad de La Habana.

8. Pedroso Aguiar. 2016. "Recuperar los ecosistemas en Cuba para adaptarnos al cambio climático: ¿una buena idea?" Forthcoming in Inter-Press Service, IPS-Cuba.

9. Ministerio de Ciencia, Tecnología y Medio Ambiente. 2011. "Estrategia Ambiental Nacional 2011–2015."

10. Peña, Angela. 2013. "Vulnerabilidad ambiental y reproducción de la pobreza urbana. Algunas reflexiones sobre su relación en territorios periféricos de Ciudad de La Habana." In Centro Félix Varela, *Algunas claves para pensar la pobreza en Cuba desde la mirada de jóvenes investigadores.* Havana: Publicaciones Acuario.

11. Ibid.

12. For the Guidelines, see Partido Comunista de Cuba, Comité Central. 2011. "Lineamientos de la Política Económica y Social del Partido." Havana. Consulted at www.cubadebate.cu/lineamientos, 18 February 2016. [Official English translation from: "Sixth Congress of the Communist Party of Cuba, Resolution on the Guidelines of the Economic and Social Policy of the Party and the Revolution," consulted 23 August 2016 at http://www.cuba.cu/gobierno/documentos/2011/ing/l160711i.html.]

13. Mateo, 2012. *La dimension*, p. 220.

14. Partido Comunista de Cuba. 2011. Official English translation, see note 12.

15. Espina, Mayra. 2013. "Justicia climática: un enfoque alternativo para las políticas de equidad." In *Revista Temas*, Number 73: 66.

16. Louro, A. 2014. "La gestión administrativa y financiera local, una necesidad para el desarrollo." In Omar E. Pérez and Ricardo Torres, eds., *Miradas a la economía cubana desde una perspectiva territorial*, p. 60. Havana: Editorial Caminos.

17. Soriano, Armando. 2006. "El Derecho Humano al agua en Cuba." In Fundación Heinrich Boll, *La Gota de la Vida: Hacia una Gestión Sustentable y Democrática del Agua.* Mexico: Oficina Regional para C.A., México y Cuba.

18. Ibid., and *Cuba: Objetivos de Desarrollo del Milenio. Segundo Informe de Cuba.* 2005. Cited in José Antonio Díaz Duque, "Hacia el uso sostenible del agua en Cuba." Presentation at Cuarta Convención Cubana de Ciencias de la Tierra, GEOCIENCIAS 2011, Havana 4–8 April, 2011.

19. Ibid.

20. Ministerio de Ciencia, Tecnología y Medio Ambiente. 2007. "Estrategia Ambiental Nacional 2007–2010."

21. Ibid. [Official English translation by Rebecca Crocker et al., pp. 22–23, consulted at https://www.edf.org/sites/default/files/9623_Cuba_Enviro_Strategy_2007-2010.pdf, 23 August 2016.]

22. Núñez Jiménez, A. 1965. *Geografía de Cuba*, p. 526. Havana.

23. Núñez Jiménez, A., V. Panos and O. Stelci. 1968. *Carsos de Cuba. Serie Espeleológica y Carsológica, No. 2.* Havana: Academia de Ciencias de Cuba, Instituto de Geografía, Departamento de Espeleología.

24. García Fernández, J. M. 2006. "Experiencias cubanas en la institucionalización del manejo integrado de cuencas." In *Revista Voluntad Hidráulica.* No. 98: 15–28.

25. Oficina Nacional de Estadísticas e Información. 2008. *Panorama Medioambiental CUBA 2007.* Havana.

26. Servicio Hidrológico Nacional. 2008. "Nuevos logros en el estudio de la pluviosidad en Cuba: Mapa Isoyética para el período 1961–2000." In *Revista Voluntad Hidráulica*, No. 98, 2–14.

27. Planos, E, R. Vega, and A. Guevara. 2013. *Impactos del cambio climático y medidas de adaptación en Cuba.* Havana: Instituto de Meteorología, Agencia de Medio Ambiente, Ministerio de Ciencia, Tecnología y Medio Ambiente.

28. Contraloría General de la República. 2014. "Informe de Auditoría Coordinada a los Recursos Hídricos." Havana, February, 2014.

29. Núñez Jiménez, et al. 1968.

30. Ibid.

31. Pedroso Aguiar, "Podemos más."

32. Espina. 2013.

33. Pedroso Aguiar. 2016.

PART

IV

The Latin American
Social Policy Context

9

The Impact of Remittances on Poverty and Inequality for Cuba: Lessons from Latin America

Lorena G. Barberia

Introduction

Researchers have long sought to estimate how the monetary sums sent by migrants influence poverty and inequality trends in Latin America (Fajnzylber and López, 2008). Large numbers of low-income families live in Latin America and their conditions spur many citizens to migrate in search of improved livelihoods, in turn sending money back home. This chapter briefly reviews the theories and literature on the impact of international and domestic remittances on poverty and inequality in Latin America and the Caribbean. Several research findings suggest that remittances have reduced poverty in many countries in the region; at the same time, scholars point out significant differences across countries and across time in the region due in part to particular migration rates and economic conditions in the sending country. Yet research to date is less conclusive on how monetary flows affect inequality dynamics in Latin America.

Studies on how migrant funds influenced development trajectories in Latin America may contribute to understanding the impact of remittances on Cuban society. Starting in the 1990s, Cuba experienced an unprecedented surge in remittances. Remittances quickly became the largest type of international financial inflow and came at a rapid and increasing pace into Cuba. Three decades after the collapse of the Soviet bloc and Cuba's insertion into the world economy, they remain larger than either capital inflows or official development assistance.

Concomitantly, the share of Cuban families struggling under economic duress has persisted, and income differentials between those who earn income in foreign currency (including remittances) and those families primarily tied to the state peso economy have widened. Based on a review of the limited research on remittances to Cuba, I argue, evidence suggests that remittances have reduced the severity of poverty in Cuba, while also increasing inequality. Yet scholarship on how these flows impact poverty and inequality has been limited and suffers from various methodological challenges.

How the research has been carried out to date reveals trends that underscore how the Cuban case is the same and different from the others. In comparison with Latin America, Cuban families receiving remittances are also the beneficiaries of a comprehensive social safety net provided by the Cuban state. Welfare provision remained a policy priority throughout Cuba's transition and in periods of greatest duress. Families are entitled to a minimum consumption food basket through a ration card. Universal health care and education are provided to Cubans regardless of household income levels. The elderly receive pension income, even if meager. Thus, remittances in the Cuban context may not necessarily be directed at meeting the types of basic needs so often found to be sustained by migrant flows in Latin American countries. At the same time, growing numbers of Cuban families struggle to secure sufficient income to meet basic needs. How do remittances help these families? How much have remittances exacerbated inequality? In the context of this book, I explore whether remittances make it easier or more difficult for Cuban social policy to address the challenges of poverty and inequality, pondering whether remittances co-fund or substitute for current social policies or instead aggravate Cuba's burden of poverty and widen inequalities. Insights from the comparative literature on remittances in Latin America may help to guide the research design of studies aiming to understand these important questions.

In the chapter's final section, I underscore the lacunae that remain in the study of remittances in Cuba. To date, the methods and data that have been employed are limited; they suffer from serious methodological problems that produce biases in research regarding the link between remittances and poverty in Cuba. To advance understanding of the impact of remittances on Cuba, I argue that more robust testing with more suitable research designs must be undertaken. In the interest of advancing future studies of remittances and poverty dynamics in Cuba, I emphasize the methodological challenges and solutions that must be adopted to advance this field of research in Cuba. There are data and sample measurement challenges in measuring private and often informal transactions within families; there are also research design challenges in studying and in making inferences of the relationship between remittances and poverty.

Remittances, Poverty, and Inequality in Latin America

Latin American and Caribbean countries have experienced net emigration since the early 1960s and 1970s with nearly all of outflows to the United States (Economic Commission for Latin America and the Caribbean (ECLAC), 2002). During this period, Latin Americans in growing numbers headed north, propelled by the severe economic crises, military coups and civil wars striking the region. Countries closer to the United States in North and Central America and the Caribbean have sent larger shares of immigrants there relative to South America.

Figure 9.1 presents the total number of Latin American immigrants in the United States in 2010 and the share of this emigrant population relative to population in the country of origin. In the figure, countries were ranked by the largest number of immigrants residing in the United States. Official data on migration are recognized as incomplete; statistics do not include the fraction of Latin American residents who migrate and work as part of the undocumented workforce. Nevertheless, the information that is available shows that Mexico, El Salvador, Cuba, the Dominican Republic and Guatemala were the countries with the largest numbers of immigrants living in the United States in absolute terms. Mexico stands out, as nearly two out of every three Latin American immigrants living in the United

Figure 9.1: Stock of Latin American Immigrants in the United States, and as a Share of the Population in the Country of Origin, 2010

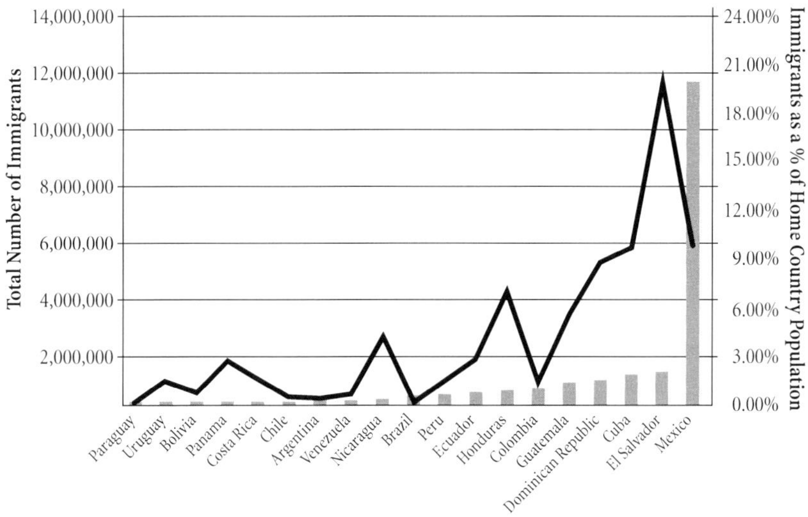

Source: Migration Policy Institute (2016) and World Bank (2016)

States were Mexican by 2010. More than twenty percent of El Salvador's domestic population was living in the United States, making it the country with highest proportional share of its population outside its borders in the region. Relative to their country of origin, Mexico, the Dominican Republic, Guatemala, Honduras, Cuba and Nicaragua also each had 3 percent or more of their citizens living in the United States.

Although there is considerable discrepancy regarding the measurement of remittances, as the concepts, definitions, and methods to measure and report them vary across countries and organizations, there is consensus that the cross-border financial flows to home countries from Latin American immigrants working primarily in the United States have risen dramatically (World Bank, 2007). Measures based on the components of balance of payments data indicate that migrants sent a total US$64.4 billion to the 19 Spanish and Portuguese-speaking countries in the region by 2012 (Maldonado and Hayem, 2015; World Bank, 2007).[1] Although data based on the receipt of remittances in household surveys suggest that cross-border flows are overestimated in BOP statistics, there is strong correlation showing that irrespective of measurement source, the countries with the largest stock of migrants living in the United States are also the largest recipients of remittances. In addition, among these countries, Mexico, El Salvador, the Dominican Republic, Guatemala and Cuba are the highest-ranked.

Yet remittances vary as GDP percentages in Latin American countries in Latin America (Maldonado and Hayem, 2015). On average, remittances represented 4.3% of gross domestic product (GDP) in 2014. Mexicans migrants sent 40% of total remittances, but these resources represented less than 2% of GDP in 2014. In contrast, remittances were equivalent to 16.8 and 17.4% of GDP in El Salvador and Guatemala respectively. They are also unequally distributed within countries. As discussed below, there are differences between geographic regions and income groups.

The Impact of Migration and Remittances on Poverty and Inequality

Poverty

Whether migration reduces poverty or not depends on the original income status in the country of origin. Since the seminal models developed by Harris and Todaro (1970), scholars have sought to show why populations migrate from low-income, rural regions to relatively high-income, urban or foreign economies in search of higher earnings even when significant rates of unemployment exist in destination economies (Massey et al., 1993; Stark, 1985). However, studies have also shown that the poor are disproportionately less likely to embark on these ventures, as high costs and barriers exist to cross international borders (De Blij, 2009; Stahl, 1982). Furthermore, the poor may be particularly risk averse and have limited social insurance options, both factors making them less likely to migrate (Morduch, 1999).

Formal micro-economic models have also developed frameworks to explore the motives that may fuel remittance sending (Rapoport and Docquier, 2006). One set of motivations, such as altruism or exchange, is likely to drive migrants to send goods and money to their families and social networks back home (Coleman, 1990); these motivations may be particularly high during periods of economic crisis and natural disasters (Stark and Lucas, 1988; Yang, 2008). Migrants, including those who seek to eventually return their country of origin, may also be guided by the desire to make investments and acquire insurance to guard against risks. Rapoport and Docquier (2006) show that models based on different motives share many common predictions.

Figure 9.2 provides evidence to suggest a relationship between the flow of cross-border remittances and poverty rates in Latin America. As remittances have increased, the proportion of the poor declined from 1986 to 2014.[2] There are several reasons, however, why it is much more difficult to make causal inferences that link higher remittances with lower poverty rates based on macro-level, cross-country studies (McKenzie and Sasin, 2007). A number of factors drive poverty and remittance patterns in Latin America, and these dynamics have changed across time and countries. Furthermore, an endogenous relationship exists between remittances and poverty. Remittances may help reduce poverty, but poverty may also influence the amount of monies received by a particular country. For these reasons, it is difficult to isolate and identify a causal relation. Recognizing these methodological challenges and the limitations of many earlier studies, social scientists are struggling to implement research designs that diminish bias. Below, I discuss some studies on the subject, highlighting factors that are particularly important as they pertain to Cuba.

At the macro-level, models based on time series cross-country data have been used to test whether higher levels of remittances reduce poverty levels. To address the estimation difficulties posed by the endogenous relationship between poverty and remittances, these studies have typically adopted an instrumental variable approach in which an explanatory variable highly correlated with remittances and uncorrelated with poverty is used to identify how remittances contribute to changes in poverty. Acosta et al. (2006) find that cross-border transfers reduce poverty more in Latin America than in other regions of the world. Using balance of payment statistics for fourteen countries, the authors report that on average every one per cent increase in the ratio of remittances to GDP causes a reduction in poverty headcounts of between 0.35 and 0.40 per cent. Based on a sample of 71 developing countries, however, Adams and Page (2005) find no statistically significant differences reported in the majority of regressions testing for the impact of international migration and remittances on poverty for the Latin American region. Thus, prevailing macro-level studies remain inconclusive on the impact of remittances on poverty.

Figure 9.2: Remittances and Poverty in Select Latin American Countries, 1986–2014

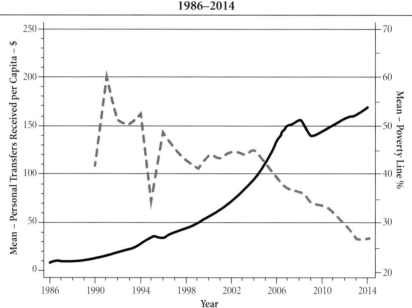

Source: Poverty: ECLAC. Remittance: World Development Indicators (WDI)

Notes:

1. Remittances do not include Chile and Uruguay due to long periods with missing observations, nor Cuba due to differences in measurement. Nicaragua is included after 1992.

2. Poverty is the national poverty rate according to ECLAC. When national data is not available, the urban poverty rate was used. The following poverty data were imputed using an average of the previous and the future observations: Bolivia (1998, 2003 and 2010), Brazil (1991, 1994, 2000 and 2010) and Mexico (1993, 1995, 1997, 1999, 2001, 2003, 2007, 2009 and 2011). There is no data for Argentina (2014), Bolivia (2012, 2013 and 2014), Colombia (2014), Honduras (2014), Mexico (2013 and 2014), Peru (2014), Uruguay (2014) and Venezuela (2014). The poverty line does not include Chile, Guatemala and Nicaragua.

Micro-level studies have sought to remedy the causal-inference challenges of macro-level studies. The majority of these studies analyze how remittances influence poverty based on data collected from nationally representative household survey data. Table 9.3 presents a summary of these empirical studies. In Latin America, case studies delve into the impact of Mexican, Salvadoran, Guatemalan and Nicaraguan remittances on poverty.

As Table 9.1 shows, the first set of seminal studies using Latin American household data examined how domestic inter-household transfers]reduced income inequality (Cox and Jimenez, 1990; Kaufmann and Lindauer, 1986). The most insightful studies examine the impact of in-country transfers while also considering the cross-border monetary resources received by Latin American households. Generally, these studies show that more migrants move internally than internationally, but the level of domestic remittances is less, as the potential to earn higher incomes in urban areas is not as high as it is for those who migrate abroad. Nevertheless, Adams (2004) argues that internal remittances might be more beneficial to the poor than international remittances because the poor may only have the resources to migrate internally.

Micro-level studies based on household survey data have helped to identify how remittances affect poverty at a specific point in time. Adams (2004) compares the poverty headcount, the poverty gap, and the squared poverty gap of 1,656 urban and rural Guatemalan families that received remittances from international and/or internal migrants, with 5,665 households that did not receive remittance income. Almost 15% of recipients received help from family members working within Guatemala, whereas 8.1% received international remittances, mostly from the United States. To address the methodological challenges of the endogenous effect of remittances on household income, the author compares the observed outcome with a counterfactual scenario in which household incomes include the earnings migrants would have received had they remained in their home country. Based on differences in the amount of pre- and post-migration household expenditures, Adams reports that both internal and international remittances reduced poverty, which was measured as the level of per capita expenditures needed to meet the costs of attaining minimum food requirements of 2,172 kilocalories/person/day in 2000.

Like most analysts of the effect of remittances on poverty, Adams (2004) also measures poverty based on minimum consumption or income levels. He recognizes that the magnitude of the reduction in poverty depends on the metric used for evaluation. Total remittances from domestic and international sources reduced the severity of poverty (the "poverty gap") by between 19 and 21%; inter-household domestic transfers caused a greater drop in this rate. On the other hand, the decline in the poverty rate (headcount) was less; internal remittances decreased the level of poverty by 0.6% and international remittances produced a 1.1% decrease.

Table 9.1: Remittances, Poverty, and Inequality in Selected Countries in Latin America and the Caribbean

Country and Segment of the Population	Year	Household Sample Size	Households with international migrants (%)	Households that received international remittances (%)	Households with internal migrants (%)	Households that received internal remittances (%)	International remittances as a share of total household income for recipients (%)	Internal remittances as a share of total household income for recipients (%)	Source
Mexico; Two Rural Villages in Michoacan	1982	61	Village 1 (26%); Village 2 (70%)	NA	Village 1 (71%); Village 2 (47%)	NA	Village 1 (9%); Village 2 (27%); Overall (43%)	Village 1 (22%); Village 2 (11%)	Stark, et al. (1986)
Mexico; Two Rural Villages in Michoacan	1988	55	NA	NA	NA	NA	24.9%	NA	Taylor (1992)
Nicaragua; Managua	1989	1525 (Coyuntura Survey); 801 (Ortega Survey)	21.7% (Coyuntura Survey); 25.8% (Ortega Survey)	36% (Coyuntura Survey); 53.9% (Ortega Survey)	NA	NA	NA	NA	Funkhouser (1992)
Bluefields, Nicaragua; 3 neighborhoods	1991	152	57.2%	33.3%	NA	NA	36.7%	NA	Barham and Boucher (1998)
El Salvador, Santa Elena	1999	199	31% (Town); (22%) Canton	NA	NA	NA	36.0%	3.30%	Taylor et al. (1999)
Guatemala, Urban and Rural	2000	7,276	NA	8.1%	NA	14.6%	24.3%	18.0%	Adams (2004)
Mexico, Rural Households in 14 states	2003	1,782	16.2%	NA	25.8%	NA	11.0%	5.0%	Taylor, et al. (2005)

The study on Guatemalan inter-household transfers carried out by Adams also seeks to understand why these flows have had such a dramatic impact on the reduction in the severity of poverty and a more limited decrease in the overall number of poor in urban and rural areas. The author concludes that higher-income households account for the largest share of remittance recipients in Guatemala. For El Salvador, Cox-Edwards and Ureta (2003) report similar findings. Greater shares of urban households in the highest income decile report receiving remittances. However, among rural households, the poorest deciles receive higher shares of remittances.

Using data from a nationally representative sample of 1,782 rural households in fourteen Mexican states in 2003, Taylor et al. (2005) report similar improvements in poverty reduction and the equalizing of income across households. This study also advances our understanding of how the variation in migration patterns within countries affects development (Taylor et al., 2005).[3] By dividing the state sample into five regions, the authors show significant variations in the impact of remittances on poverty in Mexico. The overall magnitudes of these improvements, however, are rather small. Other things being equal, a 10% increase in international remittances reduces poverty by 1.64% in the high migration, West-Center region compared with only 0.11% in the low migration, South-Southwest region of Mexico. The authors also argue that the marginal effect of international remittances on reductions in poverty and inequality is positively correlated with the increase in the prevalence rates of international migration in rural areas. In other words, higher migration today will lead to future higher remittance earnings. Though a similar relationship holds in the case of internal migration, Taylor et al. conclude that this correlation is weaker.

Inequality

Theoretical models on how remittances influence inequality dynamics underscore that patterns depend on the initial wealth level of migrants in their country of origin (McKenzie and Rapoport, 2007). When migrants are from households at the upper-middle of income distribution, as is the case in Cuba, inequality will initially increase as such households get even richer from income earned abroad. Empirically, several studies show that the impact of migration can either increase or decrease inequality for Latin American households (Barham and Boucher, 1998; Taylor et al., 2005). Together, these studies are conclusive in showing that that the impact of migration differs by whether individuals move within the country or outside its borders, the distance of the sending region to international borders, and the magnitude of these patterns across time. Unfortunately, most of the studies directed at this problem are not generalizable to the country level. Instead, their results are limited to small rural communities, often in high-migration regions. They are also cross-sectional, providing a snapshot of inequality at a specific time.

Stark, Taylor and Yitzhaki (1986) studied 61 households from two Mexican villages in the state of Michoacán, with differing shares of migration across the 2,000 kilometers north of the Mexico-Arizona border in 1982. They find that income inequalities decreased overall in both villages when remittance income from both internal and international migrants was incorporated into the analysis. However, the authors also show that remittances from Mexican migrants in the United States had a favorable effect on income distribution in the village with considerable experience of such migration, whereas transnational transfers produced an increase in inequality in the village with less international migration.

In a follow-up study, Taylor returned and interviewed households in these same villages in 1989. Seven years later, he found that migrant remittances had decreased as a proportion of total household income while the share of non-remittance farm incomes had risen significantly. In addition, remittances had also produced a small equalizing long-run effect on the household-farm income distribution through their influence on the accumulation of income-producing assets for the 55 households who had remained in the rural villages. Based on the 1982 data for two villages in Michoacán, Stark, Taylor and Yitzhaki (1988) refine their earlier findings, showing that the impact on inequality is sensitive to the weight given to the lowest-income households in Gini calculations that measure the degree of income dispersion between families. The authors also stress that the highest-paying migrant jobs are more available to middle-income households than to households at the bottom of village income distribution.[4]

By comparing income distributions with and without remittances based on surveys conducted with 152 Nicaraguan households randomly selected in three neighborhoods of Bluefields in 1991, Barham and Boucher (1998) found that overall transfers from family members working abroad were equivalent to 37% of total household income in these communities. The authors show that differences in the impact of remittances result from whether these flows are assumed to be exogenous transfers or a substitute for home earnings. Viewed as exogenous transfers, earnings differences would be 10% more unequal. The alternative assumption in which remittances replace home earnings produces an increase in inequality with the variation in the Gini coefficient rising in equivalent percentages in both exercises.

In an innovative study gathering historical data from earlier migrations patterns to the United States to be used as instruments to avoid endogeneity, Mckenzie and Rappaport (2007) explore the impact of remittances on inequality in 271 Mexican rural communities. Across the cross-section of rural communities, they find suggestive evidence that there is a nonlinear, inverted-U-shaped (Kuznets) relationship; at lower levels, migration increases inequality and as migration increases, inequality falls. This study provides a snapshot of inequality at a given point in time (circa 1990).

Longer-Term Effects

Considering poverty and unmet needs, several important advances in research methods show how remittances influence employment, education and health outcomes of recipient families in Latin America.[5] In these studies, researchers weigh the short-term versus long-terms benefits and costs of migration as compared to remittances. The example of education is particularly illustrative and has received significant attention in Latin America (Borraz, 2005; Calero et al., 2009; Cox Edwards and Ureta, 2003; Ilahi, 2001).

When migrants leave their households, the local family must adjust. If the migrant is the eldest child, siblings may have to enter the labor market (often informal), drop out of school, or take on more responsibilities at home in the short term to make up for the loss of the elder sibling. On the other hand, once remittances are sent back home, families may be able to reduce demands on younger siblings, providing them with opportunities to seek higher levels of training. Thus, the challenge for researchers is to figure out if there are longer-term contributions of remittances to reducing poverty and inequality and if these are outweighed by the costs of migration.

In the case of the Dominican Republic, Amuedo-Dorantes (2010) compares the educational outcomes in remittance-receiving households with a migrant currently abroad (migrant households) to the outcomes in households that receive remittances and have no migrant currently abroad (non-migrant households). There are more migrant households that receive remittances (60%) as compared to non-migrant households (13%). For non-migrant households, she shows that remittances promote children's school attendance in the Dominican Republic, particularly among secondary school-age children and older birth siblings. When she repeats the exercise with migrant-households receiving remittances, migration has a negative impact on the school attendance of children and the positive effect of remittance receipt effectively disappears.

However, one weakness of the Amuedo-Dorantes study is her focus on the link between remittance receipt and contemporaneous educational outcomes. Instead, it is more relevant to measure completion rates for children who received remittances at age 18. To address this problem, McKenzie and Rapoport (2011) use historical data to show that living in a migrant household lowers the chances of boys completing junior high school and of boys and girls completing high school. This occurs because children living in migrant households are more likely to migrate themselves than are children living in non-migrant households.

Summary

As this brief review has summarized, social scientists have advanced our understanding of how remittances influence poverty. Using macro- and micro-level data, researchers have been attentive to the problem of endogeneity and attempted to avoid making inferences based on spurious multivariate models by employing counterfactuals and instrumental variables to avoid bias. Overall, these studies suggest that there are statistically and substantively significant reductions in poverty resulting from remittance income. Unfortunately, we have less understanding of the relationship between remittances and inequality; the little we know is based on studies in rural villages in Latin America. We know less about how remittances and inequality evolve in time and even less about that relationship in more complex areas, such as large urban cities.

Poverty, Inequality, and Remittances in Cuba

Migration and Remittances

In 2000, Cuba ranked fifth among the nineteen economies in the region with the largest share of immigrants living in the United States (see Figure 9.1). The share of Cubans admitted to the United States relative to other Latin American countries has declined from the peak period of emigration in the 1960s and 1970s, when Cubans were second only to Mexicans by the numbers admitted, according to U.S. statistics. Nevertheless, by the last decade of the twentieth century and the first five years of the twenty-first century, Table 9.2 demonstrates that Cuban émigrés were the fourth largest Latin American population admitted into the United States, surpassed only by migrants from Mexico, the Dominican Republic and El Salvador.

Since the onset of the economic crisis sparked by the collapse of trade with the Soviet bloc in 1989, and despite significant regulations by both U.S. and Cuban governments on cross-border inter-household transfers, international remittances to Cuba, mostly from the United States where

Table 9.2: Latin American Immigrants Admitted to the United States, 1961–2005 (Thousands)

Country	1961–70	1971–80	1981–90	1991–2000	2001–2009	2010–2014
Argentina	49.4	30.3	23.4	30.1	48.0	20.8
Bolivia	6.2	5.6	9.8	18.1	21.9	9.9
Brazil	29.2	18.6	22.9	50.7	82.1	46.0
Chile	12.4	15.0	19.7	18.2	19.8	8.8
Colombia	68.4	71.3	105.5	138.0	236.6	102.5
Costa Rica	18.0	12.4	25.0	17.1	21.6	10.9
Cuba	202.0	256.5	132.6	159.0	271.7	180.0
Dominican Republic	83.6	139.2	221.6	359.8	291.5	227.5
Ecuador	34.1	47.5	48.0	81.4	108.0	53.2
El Salvador	14.4	29.4	137.4	273.0	251.2	89.9
Guatemala	14.4	23.8	58.8	126.0	157.0	50.6
Honduras	15.1	15.7	39.1	72.9	63.5	36.0
Mexico	441.8	621.2	1,009.6	2,757.4	1,704.2	694.2
Nicaragua	10.4	10.9	31.1	80.4	70.0	15.4
Panama	22.2	21.4	33.0	28.1	18.1	6.9
Paraguay	1.2	1.5	3.5	6.1	4.6	2.2
Peru	19.8	25.3	50.0	110.1	137.6	63.1
Uruguay	4.1	8.4	7.2	6.1	9.8	6.6
Venezuela	20.8	11.0	22.4	35.2	115.4	56.0
Latin America	**1,067.4**	**1,365.1**	**2,000.7**	**4,367.8**	**3,632.6**	**1,680.6**
All Countries	**3,213.7**	**4,248.2**	**6,244.4**	**9,755.4**	**10,299.4**	**5,143.4**

Source: U.S. Department of Homeland Security

the majority of émigrés reside, dramatically surged within a relatively short time span (Barberia, 2004). From virtually no remittances in the three prior decades, ECLAC estimated that roughly US$3 billion in remittances entered Cuba between 1989 and 1996 (1997).[6] Ten years after the legalization of the U.S. dollar and the opening of channels to receive remittances in Cuba, these remittances totaled approximately US$839 million in 2003, which was equivalent to 50% of export earnings and 46% of international tourism receipts and surpassed foreign direct investment (FDI), private non-FDI flows, and official development assistance to Cuba. With remittance flows to Latin America and the Caribbean totaling US$32.7 billion in 2003, Cuba ranked tenth among the nineteen countries in the region in terms of total remittance volume and seventh in terms of remittance receipts per capita.

The withdrawal of the U.S. dollar from circulation in November 2004 and the 10% surcharge on the conversion of U.S. dollars into convertible Cuban pesos, combined with tightened U.S. regulations on the sending of remittances, decreased the rapid rate of increase in remittance volumes in the 2000s (see Figure 9.3). Given the large volume of remittances sent through informal channels and Cuba's decision not to publish official remittance receipt statistics, the most accurate estimates of flows to Cuba are based on calculations derived from sales in Cuba's hard-currency retail stores, the remittance amounts sent to the island through official channels, and the resources carried by visitors to Cuba. Based on this methodology, Morales (2007) estimates total remittance volumes reached US$2.6 billion by 2012.[7]

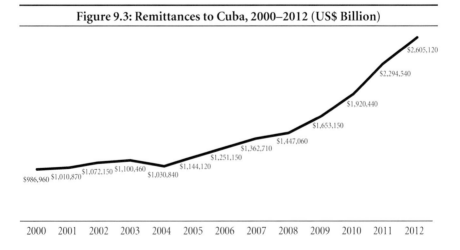

Figure 9.3: Remittances to Cuba, 2000–2012 (US$ Billion)

$986,960 $1,010,870 $1,072,150 $1,100,460 $1,030,840 $1,144,120 $1,251,150 $1,362,710 $1,447,060 $1,653,150 $1,920,440 $2,294,540 $2,605,120

2000 2001 2002 2003 2004 2005 2006 2007 2008 2009 2010 2011 2012

Source: Morales (2013)

Poverty and Inequality

Concomitant to the marked rise in remittances, there has been a marked increase in Cuban families living in conditions of economic duress and in the wealth gaps among Cubans (Espina Prieto, 2004). Table 9.3 presents data on the proportion of the urban population characterized as being "at-risk of not meeting basic needs," a concept developed by Angela Ferriol from the National Institute of Economic Research (INIE) (1999)[8] and the Gini coefficient. The data, based on nationally representative samples of surveys of households, are available for the late 1980s through 1999; they help to understand Cuban society prior to the fall of the Soviet bloc. Similar to poverty measures normally employed to gauge unmet needs, Ferriol (1999) calculates the "at risk population" based on the percentage of the population that is unable to meet a minimum level of consumption. Almost three-fourths of Cuba´s population was considered to be urban in that period, according to Cuban population statistics (Oficina Nacional de Estadística e Información (ONEI), 2016). Relative to the pre-crisis period, the table also shows that the measure of inequality of income distribution nearly doubled in ten years, reaching 0.39 by 1996. The share of the "at-risk population" more than doubled in eight years, so that by 1996 approximately 15% of Cuban households living in urban areas could be considered at risk of not being able to meet their basic needs. Three years later, in 1999, the at-risk of poverty share of the population increased by a further 33%, and the Gini coefficient also worsened though by only a magnitude of 5%.

Year	Gini Coefficient	Percentage of population "at-risk" in all urban areas	Percentage of population "at-risk" in City of Havana (*only peso earnings*)	Percentage of population "at-risk" in City of Havana (*peso and US$ earnings*)
\multicolumn{5}{c}{**Table 9.3: Cuba: Estimates of Poverty Risk and Inequality, 1986–1999**}
1986	0.22			
1988		6.80%		4.30%
1995			20.3%	20.10%
1996	0.39	14.70%	15.80%	11.50%
1999	0.407	20.00%		

Sources: Gini coefficient data for 1986, 1996 and 1999 reported by Brundenius (2002). Data on at-risk population for 1988, 1996 and 1999 reported by Ferriol (1999 and 2003).

The only nationally representative studies that have been carried out on mapping unmet needs in Cuba confirm that remittances have reduced the proportion of families in this group. For 1996 and 1995, Ferriol (1999) presents data on the percentage of the "at-risk population" based on only peso incomes and peso and foreign currency earnings for the City of Havana. Foreign currency earnings are defined as including remittances and other possible sources of income such as tips from tourism; they were converted into pesos based on currency conversion rates in the informal market. Ferriol argues that foreign currency earnings decrease poverty. The data about the City of Havana, where 26% of urban Cubans lived then, is presented in columns 3 and 4 of Table 9.3. After dollar earnings are included, the at-risk population in the City of Havana fell from 15.8 to 11.5%. Assuming that most of these earnings come from remittances, which is likely given the low number of tourism receipts during that year, this household survey data provides evidence that remittances reach the poorer segments of the Cuban population.

Unfortunately, further studies based on nationally representative household surveys are not publicly available for Cuba. There is no further data for additional years on poverty and consumption, nor is information on the percentage of the population receiving international remittances based on reliable statistical samples. To supplement this gap, social scientists have conducted research based on small non-probability samples. The most common sampling method in subsequent studies that have provided insights into remittances and poverty in Cuba have been based on snowball sampling, which has the major drawback of sampling bias, as it is highly unlikely that the sample is representative of the larger population from which the sample was drawn.

Table 9.4 summarizes the studies that have reported findings on remittances based on snowball sampling methods. Rather than comparing consumption measures with pre-defined minimum levels to assess if migrant resources ameliorate poverty, such studies have emphasized the relative importance of remittances relative to other income sources. In a 2000 study seeking to examine rising geographic inequalities within the metropolis, Iñiguez Rojas, Ravenet Ramírez and Pérez Villanueva (2003) report that remittances are unevenly distributed among income groups, with the wealthier strata benefiting most from remittance receipt. In their sample, 35% of the sample of 77 families in the Province of the City of Havana received international remittances. The division of the sample into four social strata by total household income from state, non-state, social security and remittance sources revealed that remittances were highly correlated with higher non-remittance income. The highest income strata reported receiving 63 % of the remittances, and 13% of families in this echelon rely on these inflows as their primary income source. In the lowest income strata, only 5% of households reported receiving transfers from outside Cuba and the same share declared that this was the leading income source.

The Iñiguez Rojas, Ravenet Ramírez and Pérez Villanueva study is unique among Cuban studies on the subject because data were collected for both intra-household transfers from abroad (remittances) and domestic intra-household flows. Contrary to international remittance flows, which are disproportionately received by higher-income households in the sample and albeit lower in terms of the contribution to total income, domestic income flows account for more than sixty percent of households in all four social strata, though a higher proportion of households in the highest of the four income strata (26%) identify this survival strategy as their primary earning source relative to those in the lower strata (15%). This extent of intra-household domestic transfers echoes findings found in the rest of Latin America; larger shares of resident nationals receive help from kin and non-kin networks on the island, yet these resources are comparatively less significant as compared to international transfers. In the case of Cuba, this pattern is particularly strong due to the purchasing power of the U.S. dollar.

Based on a sample of 74 families receiving remittances interviewed in the late 2010s, Delgado Vásquez (2016) explores whether international émigré dollars are channeled towards consumption or investment-related activities by recipient families in Havana. She concludes that 55.4% of recipients use remittances for consumption, and of these 46.5% state that this income is channeled primarily for subsistence, or guaranteeing minimum consumption.[9] The consumption expenditures range from buying food, toiletries, clothing and footwear to savings and investments including housing improvements, purchasing household appliances and transportation; lower-income households whose heads are females and relatively younger are more likely to spend resources on basic necessities. The remaining 44.6% of remittance recipients primarily use these resources to finance small-scale private businesses (the so-called *cuentapropistas*). These recipients are relatively older and more educated.

Welfare provision remained a policy priority throughout Cuba's transition and in periods of greatest duress. Families receive a minimum consumption food basket through a ration card. Universal health care and education are provided to Cubans regardless of household income levels. The elderly receive pension income, even if meager. For these reasons, social scientists often claim that remittances in the Cuban context may not

Table 9.4: Remittances, Poverty, and Inequality in Cuba

Locality and Segment of the Population	Year	Household Sample Size (Non-Probabilistic Selection)	Households with international migrants (%)	Households that received international remittances (%)	Households with internal migrants (%)	Households that received inter-household transfers (%)	International remittances as a share of total household income for recipients (%)	Internal remittances as a share of total household income for recipients (%)	Source
Havana, Santa Clara and Santiago de Cuba	1996–2002	>500	NA	25%	NA	NA	NA	NA	Espina Prieto and Rodríguez Ruiz (2003)
City of Havana	2000	334	51%	34%	NA	NA	59%	NA	Blue (2004;2007)
City of Havana	2000	77	NA	35%	NA	63.6%	NA	NA	Iñiguez Rojas, Ravenet Ramírez and Pérez Villanueva (2003)
City of Havana	2010	74	NA	100%	NA	NA	NA	NA	Delgado Vásquez (2016)

necessarily be directed at meeting the types of basic needs so often found to be sustained by migrant flows in Latin American countries. On this point, Delgado Vásquez (2016) provides evidence suggesting that a growing numbers of recipients rely on remittances as a complement or substitute to the resources once solely provided by the Cuban state. Nearly a third of recipients confirm that they spend a portion of remittance income on education for their children; in some cases, children pursue complementary activities (sports, tutoring or language instruction), while other parents enroll their children in private kindergarten schools. Remittance recipients attest that a share of international remittances is received in-kind, including in the form of medicines and other health care items.

Scholars have also called attention to the links between remittance flows and inequality, with heightened attention to growing racial and spatial disparities. This claim is often backed by the assumption that since the majority of Cubans in the diaspora tend to be white, white Cuban families benefit most from remittances (de la Fuente, 2001; Sawyer, 2006). Most assessments are based on conclusions drawn from examining U.S. census data on Cuban émigrés living in the United States. According to the 2004 American Community Survey, a nationwide survey conducted monthly by the U.S. Census Bureau, 86% of all Cuban émigrés identified themselves as white (Pew Hispanic Center, 2006). Authors cite the small proportion of black Cubans in the United States relative to the black or mulatto domestic population in Cuba to argue that foreign remittances must be targeted disproportionately to white Cubans.

Significant differences in the proportion of recipients by ethnicity detected in the six-year period are reported by Espina Prieto and Rodríguez Ruiz at the Centro de Antropología in a study initiated in 1996, based on more than 500 interviews with residents in the cities of Havana, Santa Clara and Santiago de Cuba from 1996 to 2002 (2004). Though information on remittance-receipt patterns across time and on the sample size in each city is not provided, the study reports that whereas 25% of the sample received remittances, approximately 35% of whites receive international remittances but only 15% of *mestizos* and 10% of blacks did so.

In this same study, the correlation between ethnicity and receipt of remittances is also controlled by employment categories that measure whether Cubans are employed in the so-called emerging economy, which is linked to tourism and joint-venture operations, or work in traditional occupations in state-run firms. Whites are more likely than blacks to be employed in the emerging economy. Working-class laborers in the state sector are less likely to receive international remittances as compared to professionals in the emerging economy. Similar findings appear in research on Havana-only samples in 2000 and 2015 (Blue, 2004, 2007; Vásquez, 2016).[10]

Recommendations for Further Research

Despite theoretical advances in our knowledge on the impact of migration on poverty, Taylor et al. (2005) conclude that "interactions between migration and poverty—both at migrant origins and destinations—are among the least researched and understood topics in economics." As this chapter has stressed, a similar conclusion can be reached with respect to the impact of remittances on poverty and inequality for Latin America, and this is even more true with respect to Cuba. The research produced to date has yielded findings that are far from conclusive; instead, they generate additional questions and demands for further, more in-depth research. This concluding section focuses on recommendations for the Cuban case, as it is one of the most dynamic and little understood cases in the region. I argue that more should be done to improve both data collection and research methodologies on the impact of remittances on the well-being of Cuban households.

With respect to the accounting of remittances, data reported in both Cuba's balance of payments statistics and in household survey instruments need to be significantly strengthened. It should be emphasized that efforts to improve data collection and measurement on remittances are not problems unique to Cuba. Indeed, the magnitude of remittance flows in Latin America has long been considered to be imprecise, and steadfast efforts are being directed in other countries to address these problems.

Across countries, problems appear when remittance flows are measured with aggregate data compiled as part of the balance of payments accounts. International Monetary Fund (IMF) authorities report that "remittances are subject to the variations of compilation on a national basis. Concepts and methodologies are not applied uniformly across all countries" (Reinke and Patterson, 2006). Cross-border flows sent through informal channels, such as monies hand-carried by friends or family members, or in-kind remittances are not included.

When remittances are studied based on samples of households responding to surveys in the sending country, measurement problems persist. Household surveys are unable to capture the seasonal volatility in flows, for example. There may also be sampling problems. Household surveys are designed to obtain income and consumption patterns for a nationally representative sample of citizens, but this sample design may not be a representative sample of remittance-recipient families. Moreover, there are major discrepancies when estimates obtained from nationally representative household samples are compared with balance of payments (BOP) statistics. For a sample of 10 Latin American countries, Acosta et al. (2006) find that BOP-based remittance statistics tend to be on average about 70% higher than the corresponding figures calculated from household survey data.

Cuban balance of payments statistics do not disclose remittances as a line item; remittances are reported as net transfers, but official data on inflows are not reported. This lack of transparency reveals the heightened sensitivity to the issue by political actors. But, as in other countries in Latin America, it is likely that official balance of payment statistics will be insufficient and imprecise at capturing total flows. Since their onset, the Cuban and U.S. governments have attempted to control the flow and use of remittances, and most such resources are therefore channeled informally (Barberia, 2004). For this reason, just as in other countries in Latin America, data based on nationally representative, micro-samples provide a more complete and accurate picture.

Across the region and in Cuba, measurement instruments need to be more carefully designed in alignment with best research practices. Thus far, studies in Cuba of remittance receipt rarely specify the kinship of the donor to the recipient. Some studies in other Latin American countries only consider immigrants who are parents, children or siblings of the household head, and who would have thus lived in the household had they not emigrated. However, others do not control for the relationship between the recipient and the donor. The literature suggests that control for family kinship is significant. For example, in a study of Nicaraguan households in Managua in 1989, Funkhouser reports that survey data indicated that roughly one-third of the sample reported receiving remittances from a relative abroad, but depending on the survey instrument, the figure is closer to between 21.7% and 25.8% of households with an emigrant member who is an immediate relative (1992).

Household survey data will help to delve into some of the difficult issues related to understanding how remittance flows ameliorate poverty in Cuba, but the insights from these data can be even more helpful if researchers will be able to work with data collected for repeated time periods. A common hypothesis in the migration literature on Cuba argues that recent émigrés, though poorer, not only often emigrated with the intent of helping family back home, but their transnational family ties also are stronger (Eckstein and Barberia, 2002). Taylor (1992) shows that in the short term, pioneer migrants tend to come from households at the upper-middle or top of the sending area's income distribution, and the income remittances they send home are therefore likely to widen income inequalities in migrant-source areas. Over time, however, access to migrant labor markets becomes diffused across sending-area households through the growth and elaboration of migrant networks. If households at the middle or bottom of the income distribution gain access to migrant labor markets, the authors argue, the initially unequalizing effect of remittances may be dampened or reversed. Such theories can only be tested for Cuba with micro-samples across time.

In survey instruments, considerable attention also needs to be directed at in-country remittances. In Latin America and in Cuba, with the sole exception of the study by Iñiguez Rojas, Ravenet Ramírez and Pérez Villanueva (2003), limited attention has been directed at examining differences between international and internal migration and international and internal remittances. Studies should examine how these two different types of migration and remittances impact poverty and inequality. Such data could help in understanding whether certain types of remittances more favorably affect the distribution of income via a filtering-down effect; e.g., if they result in an increased demand for the products and services of the poorest households.

In this chapter, I have highlighted research on remittances and poverty in Latin America that employs more sophisticated research designs to avoid bias and spurious inferences. In this respect, the research to date carried out for Cuba is vastly behind. Yet it is clear that the endogeneity issues identified in other countries are extremely relevant for Cuba. For example, remittances have been recognized to be unevenly distributed within regions inside a country. In Mexico, López-Córdova reports that just 5 states receive 45% of all remittances (2006). For Cuba, Espina Prieto and Rodríguez Ruiz (2004) report that a greater proportion of residents in the City of Havana received remittances relative to Cubans living in Santiago de Cuba. For research on remittances, poverty and inequality, the strong correlation between wealthier regions and higher international remittance receipts represents a challenge which should be considered carefully in the research designs and methodologies being implemented to study Cuba. Given that researchers rely on non-probabilistic sampling, discussion of this issue has been avoided. Nevertheless, even if researchers are not able to use household surveys gathered by the Cuban government's statistical agency, research designs can still be improved with greater efforts to reduce bias in the context of endogeneity.

Notes

1. With the exception of Cuba, the data used in this paper come from the World Bank's *World Development Indicators* database World Bank, 2016. World Development Indicators. World Bank, Washington, D.C., which reports remittances using the data published by the International Monetary Fund (IMF). In the case of Cuba, remittances were calculated based on a slightly different methodology. Official Cuban government statistics report remittances as a part of "net current transfers"; this follows standard practices followed by the IMF in which international balance of payments statistics include remittances under this same line item. The source of the data on international migrants' remittances for Cuba from 1994–1999 were computed as the difference between net current transfers and official development assistance from data reported in the World Bank's *World Development Indicators (WDI)*. For the period between 2000 and 2003, the data for net current transfers were not available from the WDI database; the data were reported by ECLAC and INIE Economic Commission for Latin America and the Caribbean (ECLAC) and National Institute of Economic Research (INIE), 2004. Política Social y Reformas Estructurales: Cuba a principios del Siglo XXI (Anexo Estadístico). ECLAC and INIE. The data for 2003–2012 are the data reported by Morales (2013) as data were were not available from either of these sources.

2. The poverty line includes the percentage of the population living in destitution. ECLAC calculates poverty line based on the number of households unable to access a consumption basket of basic necessities on a per capita basis. Destitution is defined as the percentage of households who cannot afford the consumption of even only the food items in the minimum consumption basket Economic Commission for Latin America and the Caribbean, 2007. Social Indicators and Statistics Database (BADEINSO).

3. There are 32 states in Mexico including the Federal District. The sample was representative of eighty percent of the Mexican population considered to be rural; communities with fewer than 500 residents were not included in the survey.

4. Taylor et al. Taylor, J.E., Zabin, C., Eckhoff, K., 1999. Migration and rural development in El Salvador: a micro economywide perspective North American Journal of Economics and Finance 10(1), 91–114. undertake a similar exercise for El Salvador.

5. There are additional issues beyond this brief review that merit discussion as they also are important for thinking about the interactions between social policy and remittances. In Managua, Funkhouser Funkhouser, E., 1992. Migration from Nicaragua: Some recent evidence. World Development 20(8), 1209–1218. reports that remittances have a negative effect on labor force participation and a positive effect on self-employment of non-migrants.

6. Cuba does not publish data on the inflow of current transfers or remittances in its Balance of Payments statistics. For a discussion of the difficulties in measuring remittances to Cuba, see Barberia (2004).

7. The data are estimates and are considered reliable, as Morales is a former senior executive in Cimex, one of the primary state enterprises that own and control dollar and/or convertible Cuban peso (CUC) sales. However, the author is not precise in explaining his model or data sources.
8. Ferriol underscores that this concept is purposefully used instead of classifying the population living below the poverty line to denote the difference of being below a certain threshold of basic needs in Cuba as compared to countries in Latin America. For further discussion of this viewpoint, see Ferriol Ferriol Muruaga, A., 2003. Acercamientos al estudio de la pobreza en Cuba, Poverty and Social Policy in Cuba: Addressing the Challenges of Social and Economic Change: A Two-part Policy and Research Roundtable. David Rockefeller Center for Latin American Studies, Harvard University, Cambridge. For further discussion on the measurement of poverty and inequality in Cuba, see Barberia, Briggs and Uriarte Barberia, L.G., Briggs, X.d.S., Uriarte, M., 2004. The End of Egalitarianism?: Economic Inequality and the Future of Social Policy in Cuba in: Domínguez, J.I., Pérez Villanueva, O.E., Barberia, L. (Eds.), The Cuban Economy at the Start of the Twenty-First Century. Harvard University David Rockefeller Center for Latin American Studies ; Distributed by Harvard University Press, Cambridge, Mass., pp. 319–353. and references therein.
9. The author does not detail if families were coded as remittance consumers or investors based on self-assessments or the author's selection criteria.
10. The classification of race is a complex undertaking. Both Espina and Rodriguez (2004) and Blue (2004, 2007) rely on a classification of racial groups as made by the research subjects.

References

Acosta, P., Calderón, C., Fajnzylber, P., López, H., 2006. Remittances and Development in Latin America. World Economy 29(7), 957–987.

Adams Jr., R.H., 2004. Remitances and Poverty in Guatemala, World Bank Policy Research Working Paper 3418. World Bank, Washington, D.C.

Adams, J.R.H., Page, J., 2005. Do international migration and remittances reduce poverty in developing countries? World Development 33(10), 1645–1669.

Amuedo-Dorantes, C., 2010. Accounting for Remittance and Migration Effects on Children's Schooling. World Development 38(12), 1747.

Barberia, L.G., 2004. Remittances to Cuba: An Evaluation of Cuban and U.S. Government Policy Measures, in: Domínguez, J.I., Villanueva, O.E.P., Barberia, L.G. (Eds.), The Cuban Economy at the Start of the Twenty-First Century. Harvard University Press, David Rockefeller Center for Latin American Studies, Cambridge, MA.

Barberia, L.G., Briggs, X.d.S., Uriarte, M., 2004. The End of Egalitarianism?: Economic Inequality and the Future of Social Policy in Cuba in: Domínguez, J.I., Pérez Villanueva, O.E., Barberia, L. (Eds.), The Cuban Economy at the Start of the Twenty-First Century. Harvard University David Rockefeller Center for Latin American Studies ; Distributed by Harvard University Press, Cambridge, Mass., pp. 319–353.

Barham, B., Boucher, S., 1998. Migration, remittances, and inequality: estimating the net effects of migration on income distribution. Journal of Development Economics 55(2), 307–331.

Blue, S.A., 2004. State Policy, Economic Crisis, Gender, and Family Ties: Determinants of Family Remittances to Cuba. Economic Geography 80(1), 63–82.

Blue, S.A., 2007. The Erosion of Racial Equality in the Context of Cuba's Dual Economy. Latin American Politics & Society 49(3), 35–68.

Borraz, F., 2005. Assessing the Impact of Remittances on Schooling: the Mexican Experience. Global Economy Journal, 5(1).

Calero, C., Bedi, A.S., Sparrow, R., 2009. Remittances, Liquidity Constraints and Human Capital Investments in Ecuador. World Development 37(6), 1143–1154.

Coleman, J.S., 1990. Foundations of social theory. Harvard University Press, Cambridge, Mass.

Cox, D., Jimenez, E., 1990. Acheiving Social Objectives Through Private Transfers: A Review. World Bank Res Obs 5(2), 205–218.

Cox Edwards, A., Ureta, M., 2003. International migration, remittances, and schooling: evidence from El Salvador. Journal of Development Economics 72(2), 429–461.

De Blij, H.J., 2009. The power of place : geography, destiny, and globalization's rough landscape. Oxford University Press, Oxford.

de la Fuente, A., 2001. A Nation for All: Race, Inequality, and Politics in Twentieth-Century Cuba. The University of North Carolina Press, Chapel Hill, NC.

Eckstein, S., Barberia, L., 2002. Grounding Immigrant Generations in History: Cuban Americans and Their Transnational Ties. International Migration Review 36(3), 799–837.

Economic Commission for Latin America and the Caribbean, 1997. La Economía Cubana: Reformas Estructurales y Desempeño en los '90. Fondo de Cultura Económica, Mexico City.

Economic Commission for Latin America and the Caribbean, 2007. Social Indicators and Statistics Database (BADEINSO).

Economic Commission for Latin America and the Caribbean (ECLAC), 2002. Globalización y Desarrollo. ECLAC, Santiago, Chile.

Economic Commission for Latin America and the Caribbean (ECLAC) and National Institute of Economic Research (INIE), 2004. Política Social y Reformas Estructurales: Cuba a principios del Siglo XXI (Anexo Estadístico). ECLAC and INIE.

Edwards, A.C., Ureta, M., 2003. International migration, remittances, and schooling: evidence from El Salvador. Journal of Development Economics 72(2), 429–461.

Espina Prieto, M.P., 2004. Social Effects of Economic Adjustment: Equality, Inequality and Trends towards Greater Complexity in Cuban Society, in: Jorge I. Domínguez, O.E.P.V., Mayra Espina Prieto and Lorena G. Barberia (Ed.), The Cuban Economy at the Start of the Twenty First Century. David Rockefeller Center, Harvard University Press, Cambridge: MA, pp. 209–244.

Espina Prieto, R., Rodríguez Ruiz, P., 2004. Raza y Desigualdad en la Cuba actual, Poverty and Social Policy in Cuba: Addressing the Challenges of Social and Economic Change: A Two-part Policy and Research Roundtable. David Rockefeller Center for Latin American Studies, Harvard University, La Habana.

Fajnzylber, P., López, J.H., 2008. Remittances and development : Lessons from Latin America. World Bank, Washington, D.C.

Ferriol Muruaga, A., 1999. Pobreza en Condición de Reforma Económica: El reto a la equidad en Cuba, Paper presented at the XXI Latin American Studies Association (LASA) Congress, XXI Latin American Studies Association Congress, LASA: Chicago.

Ferriol Muruaga, A., 2003. Acercamientos al estudio de la pobreza en Cuba, Poverty and Social Policy in Cuba: Addressing the Challenges of Social and Economic Change: A Two-part Policy and Research Roundtable. David Rockefeller Center for Latin American Studies, Harvard University, Cambridge.

Funkhouser, E., 1992. Migration from Nicaragua: Some recent evidence. World Development 20(8), 1209–1218.

Harris, J.R., Todaro, M.P., 1970. Migration, Unemployment & Development: A Two-Sector Analysis. American Economic Review 60(1), 126–142.

Ilahi, N., 2001. Children's work and schooling does gender matter? Evidence from the Peru LSMS panel data, Working Paper. World Bank, Washington, D.C.

Iñiguez Rojas, L., Ravenet Ramírez, M., Pérez Villanueva, O.E., 2003. Una Aproximación a las Desigualdades Espacios-Familias en La Provincia Ciudad de La Habana, in: Rojas, L.I., et.al. (Ed.), Desigualdades espaciales del Bienestar y la salud en la provincia Ciudad Habana. Resultado del Programa Territorial de Ciudad de la Habana. Efecto de las medidas de ajuste sobre la ciudad. 2001–2003. Centro de Estudios de Salud y Bienestar Humanos de la Universidad de La Habana, Cuba, La Habana.

Kaufmann, D., Lindauer, D.L., 1986. A model of income transfers for the urban poor. Journal of Development Economics 22(2), 337–350.

López-Córdova, E., 2006. Globalization, Migration and Development: The Role of Mexican Migrant Remittances, INTAL-IDB Working Paper 20. IDB, Washington, D.C.

Maldonado, R., Hayem, M.L., 2015. Remittances to Latin America and the Caribbean Set a New Record High in 2014. Multilateral Investment Fund, Inter-American Development Bank, Washington, D.C.

Massey, D.S., Arango, J., Hugo, G., Kouaouci, A., Pellegrino, A., Taylor, J.E., 1993. Theories of international migration: a review and appraisal. Population and Development Review 19(3), 431.

McKenzie, D., Rapoport, H., 2007. Network effects and the dynamics of migration and inequality: Theory and evidence from Mexico. Journal of Development Economics 84(1), 1–24.

McKenzie, D., Rapoport, H., 2011. Can migration reduce educational attainment? Evidence from Mexico. J Popul Econ 24(4), 1331–1358.

McKenzie, D., Sasin, M.J., 2007. Migration, Remittances, Poverty, and Human Capital : Conceptual and Empirical Challenges, Policy Research Working Paper No. 4272.

Morduch, J., 1999. Between the State and the Market. World Bank Research Observer 14(2), 187–207.

Oficina Nacional de Estadística e Información (ONEI), 2016. Anuario Estadístico de Cuba 2014. ONEI, Havana.

Pew Hispanic Center, 2006. Fact Sheet: Cubans in the United States. Pew Hispanic Center, Washington, DC.

Rapoport, H., Docquier, F., 2006. Chapter 17 The Economics of Migrants' Remittances. Handbook of the Economics of Giving, Reciprocity and Altruism 2, 1135–1198.

Reinke, J., Patterson, N., 2006. Remittances in the Balance of Payments Framework: Current Problems and Forthcoming Improvements. International Monetary Fund (IMF), Washington, D.C.

Sawyer, M.Q., 2006. Racial Politics in Post-revolutionary Cuba. Cambridge University Press, New York.

Stahl, C.W., 1982. Labor Emigration and Economic Development. International Migration Review 16(4), 869–899.

Stark, O., 1985. The new economics of labor migration. The American economic review 75(2), 173–178.

Stark, O., Lucas, R., 1988. Migration, Remittances, and the Family. Economic Development and Cultural Change 36(3), 465–481.

Stark, O., Taylor, J.E., Yitzhaki, S., 1986. Remittances and Inequality. Economic Journal 96(383), 722–740.

Stark, O., Taylor, J.E., Yitzhaki, S., 1988. Migration, remittances and inequality : A sensitivity analysis using the extended Gini index. Journal of Development Economics 28(3), 309–322.

Taylor, J.E., 1992. Remittances and inequality reconsidered: Direct, indirect, and intertemporal effects. Journal of Policy Modeling 14(2), 187–208.

Taylor, J.E., Mora, J., Adams, R., Lopez-Feldman, A., 2005. Remittances, Inequality and Poverty: Evidence from Rural Mexico, Working Paper No. 05-003 Department of Agricultural and Resource Economics, University of California, Davis, Davis, CA.

Taylor, J.E., Zabin, C., Eckhoff, K., 1999. Migration and rural development in El Salvador: a micro economywide perspective North American Journal of Economics and Finance 10(1), 91–114.

Vásquez, D.D., 2016. Efectos del uso diferenciado de las remesas en la desigualdad social: Un estudio en la capital cubana, Informe CLACSO. CLACSO, Buenos Aires.

World Bank, 2007. Final Report of the International Working Group on Improving Data on Remittances. World Bank, Washington, D.C.

World Bank, 2016. World Development Indicators. World Bank, Washington, D.C.

Yang, D., 2008. Coping with Disaster: The Impact of Hurricanes on International Financial Flows, 1970–2002. The B.E. Journal of Economic Analysis & Policy 8(1).

10

The Micro-Foundations of Non-Contributory Social Policy in Latin America

Soledad Artiz Prillaman

Before the late 1990s, social policy in most Latin American countries was dominated by social protection programs targeted exclusively at workers employed within the formal economy. When categorizing cross-national systems of social protection and welfare, Latin America is generally seen as having a system of its own, most notably differentiated from other systems of social protection due to highly segmented labor forces (Schneider, 2013). With generally 30–40% of the labor force employed by the informal sector, this allocation scheme created a highly stratified system of social benefits, with important consequences different from the traditional social welfare systems of Western Europe (Portes and Hoffman, 2013). The provision of social protection has been an important responsibility of the state in Latin America for some time, with social insurance spending on average making up between 15 and 20% of total expenditures (Wibbels and Ahlquist, 2013). Yet because of how these policies are targeted, over 20% of the labor force within Latin America remained uncovered by social insurance programs (Schneider and Karcher, 2010).

However, social policy in many Latin American nations has undergone marked changes since the late 1990s, with benefits extended to previously uncovered workers and citizens. Table 10.1 documents the adoption of non-contributory pension policies, universal health care, and conditional cash transfer programs (CCTs) across Latin America since 1990. The adoption of more inclusive social policies has been widespread in Latin America over the recent decades and demonstrates a clear shift and expansion in the targeting of social expenditures. Where traditional social insurance exclusively benefited the formally employed, these three policy areas offer benefits to former "outsiders." Within the realm of pension reform there are two major categories: those that have reformed pensions to target the poor, and those that have reformed pensions with the aim of universality (Rofman, Apella and Vezza, 2015). As seen in the second column of Table 10.1, several Latin American nations have reformed pension policies, extending benefits to informal and rural workers and instituting systems of non-contributory pension programs which guarantee a minimum level of income in old age, regardless of past contributions (Schwarzer and Querino, 2002). Non-contributory pension policies provide old-age insurance that is not tied to former employment status and is financed by general tax revenues (Carnes and Mares, 2013). These policies redistribute resources to the generally low-income and informally employed individuals, depending on the type of reform. Universal pension reform is therefore the clearest extension of benefits to those outside the formal workforce that were traditionally reserved only for the formally employed. Thirteen Latin American countries have now some form of non-contributory pension plans and seven introducing universal non-contributory pensions. This marks an important shift in the structure of social policy across Latin America.

In addition to the implementation of non-contributory pension programs, since the debt crisis and the wave of democratization in the 1980s, nine Latin American countries have undertaken major health care reforms with many developing systems of universal health coverage. As Arretche (2004) notes in the case of Brazil, until the creation of the new Brazilian Constitution in 1988 the health care system was tied to the Social Security system, and therefore only benefited formal sector employees. The new constitution stated that health care was a right of all citizens and since 1988, with the implementation of the Unified Health System (SUS), Brazil, like many other Latin American nations, has worked towards universal health coverage.

Additionally, conditional cash transfer programs aim to redistribute income to the poorest families, most of whom are employed outside of the formal labor force. In 1997, Mexican President Ernesto Zedillo enacted the conditional cash transfer program *Progresa*, which extended social assistance for the first time to many of the nation's most impoverished. Since 1997, fifteen Latin American countries have instituted conditional cash transfer programs aimed specifically at improving the welfare of the poor. Generally, these programs provide direct cash assistance to poor mothers, contingent upon their children's attendance in school and regular medical check-ups, and are supplemented by scholarships for education and health care for the family. Unlike former policies targeted at those with formal employment, these social policies are targeted at the poor regardless of employment status. Overall, the creation of cash-assistance programs for the poor and the reforms to existing social insurance policies have marked a sharp transition from a social protection system benefiting almost exclusively those within the formal employment sector to more inclusive social protection coverage with less stratification by employment status.

Table 10.1: Adoption of Expansionary Social Policies in Latin America since 1985

Pension Reform		Universal Health Care Adoption	Conditional Cash Transfer Program
Means-Tested	**Universal**		
Colombia (2004)	Argentina (2003)	Argentina (2002)	Argentina (2004)
Costa Rica (200)	Bolivia (2008)	Brazil (1988)	Bolivia (2006)
Ecuador (2006)	Brazil (2006)	Chile (2005)	Brazil (2001)
El Salvador (2009)	Chile (2008)	Costa Rica	Chile (2002)
Paraguay (2010)	Mexico (2003)	Uruguay (1997)	Colombia (2001)
Peru (2010)	Panama (2009)		Costa Rica (2006)
	Trinidad & Tobago (2010)		Dominican Republic (2005)
			Ecuador (2003)
			El Salvador (2005)
			Guatemala (2008)
			Honduras (1998)
			Jamaica (2002)
			Mexico (1997)
			Panama (2006)
			Paraguay (2005)
			Peru (2005)

Sources: Rofman, Apella and Vezza (2015), Carnes and Mares (2013), World Bank, ILO Social Security Department, Barrientos, Nio-Zarazúa and Maitrot (2010)

A considerable amount of research has proposed macro-level explanations for this expansion of non-contributory benefits. This chapter instead focuses on the micro-level demand for these policies by evaluating public opinion data from across Latin America. I first review existing explanations for the adoption of non-contributory social programs in Latin America. I then present theoretical arguments linking macro-level economic structures to micro-level political demands. This theory provides a different look at the root causes of the shift towards non-contributory policies by focusing on the changing demands of workers. Finally, using both public opinion data and national political data, this chapter provides empirical support for these theoretical propositions. This evidence is then used to draw implications for Cuba.

The case of Cuba provides a unique lens for understanding the importance of the micro-foundations of non-contributory policies. Cuba has had programs of universal coverage for pensions and health care long before these were adopted in other Latin American countries. But the contemporary Latin American experience, examined in this chapter, is pertinent for Cuba in three important ways. First, given the changing Cuban economy, what is and what should be the balance between contributory and non-contributory social policies in contemporary Cuba and what lessons may Cuba draw from its Latin American neighbors? Second, with a rise in Cuba's poverty rate since the economic crisis of the early 1990s, there is concern that the nation should refocus its social policies of assistance to the poor. What may Cuba learn, therefore, from the Latin American experiences of special support for the poor through conditional cash transfer programs and means-tested pension programs? Third, by examining the experience of other Latin American countries, can we better understand what might drive Cuba's government to enact changes in its social policies?

Previous Explanations of Social Policy Expansion

Globalization and De-industrialization

One type of research has focused on the role of trade policy and international economic structures in explaining the formation of social protection schemes. The emergence of formal-sector social insurance programs in Latin America has been explained by the level of trade openness and the nature of factor endowments, the amount of land, labor, capital, and entrepreneurship that a country possesses and can exploit for manufacturing.

Given that most Latin American countries industrialized late and were more dependent on and integrated into the world economy, international relations had important consequences for social policy formation. Huber, Mustillo, and Stephens (2008) explain that in the 1970s, many Latin American countries were pursuing strategies of import-substitution industrialization (ISI), focusing on inward growth and the protection of domestic markets. To meet the demands of employers and encourage investment in skills, targeted and stratified programs of social insurance were developed. In the 1980s, however, the region faced a major debt crisis, requiring many Latin American countries to become more open economically and retrench their extensive social programs. Finally, in the 1990s, as credit stabilized and economic growth resurged, some redevelopment of social programs occurred (Huber, Mustillo, and Stephens, 2008).

Explaining the relationship between globalization and welfare state development broadly, Katzenstein (1985) reported that greater economic openness leads to larger welfare states in order to compensate for the increased risk of job losses because of outsourcing in international markets (Cameron, 1978; Carnes and Mares, 2007). Drawing from the observed pattern in Latin America, however, Kaufman and Segura-Ubiergo (2001) argue that as trade openness increases, social spending declines. They hypothesize that this inverse relationship is the result of states wanting to increase their global competitiveness, which, from an efficiency stand-point, can only be done with low levels of social spending. Countering this argument, Wibbels and Ahlquist (2013) suggest that this relationship only holds for "early industrializers." Given that Latin American nations were "late industrializers," Wibbels and Ahlquist argue that the structure of factor endowments determines whether countries pursue more protectionist trade policies, which incentivize social spending aimed at protecting workers in the formal economy. In particular, where capital and labor were scarce, Wibbels and Ahlquist demonstrate that developing countries pursued protectionist growth policies coupled with large social protection programs targeted at members of the formal economy. Carnes and Mares (2009) second this argument, suggesting that countries might implement high levels of social insurance spending in order to encourage a highly skilled labor force; this, they argue, is most likely in large domestic markets with scarce labor and high inequality.

Iversen (2001) finds that the underlying mechanism driving the relationship found by Katzenstein (1985) in developed economies is driven by de-industrialization, or the decline in employment in agriculture and industry rather than trade openness. The risk associated with a shift towards service industries because of low transferability of skills increased demand for social protection. In fact, Iversen (2001) argues that "where people in the most risky labor market positions are more prone to vote in elections, and where left parties dominate government power, welfare state expansion has entailed a heavy dose of low-priced public services, as well as more egalitarian social transfer programs and wage policies."

Carnes and Mares (2013) agree that de-industrialization was the critical factor driving welfare state expansion to "outsiders" in Latin America in recent decades, but they contend that the rise in "vulnerable" employment was also key. Their theoretical approach is the closest to mine and provides the foundation for studying the role of labor market forces in social policy change in Latin America. In particular, they argue that in Latin America, de-industrialization led to the rise of low-skilled service sector jobs, which increased informality and vulnerability within the formal labor force. As a result, low skill transferability was not a concern. Increased vulnerability, Carnes and Mares (2013) argue, shifted political coalitions and ultimately increased demand for universal social insurance.

Overall, this research suggests that the widespread adoption of non-contributory social policies was the result of macro-economic and even global forces. From this, we must consider that domestic market size, relative abundance or scarcity of labor, asset inequality, the openness of the international economy, and the form of de-industrialization may all have been driving forces in Latin American social policy expansion (Carnes and Mares, 2009).

Democratization and the Shift to the Left

Focusing less on the role of the international economy, alternative accounts of social policy development in Latin America document the domestic political institutions and structures which have conditioned and led to changes in the inclusiveness of social policy. Three key explanations have been proposed for the universalization and decreased stratification in social policy in some Latin American countries: electoral competition, democratization and civil society mobilization, and political leadership and financial crisis.

First, Pribble (2013) argues that increased party competition led to more centrist and universalistic policies rather than segmented policies (see also Melo (2008)). She highlights two mechanisms underlying this effect. First, when parties face high levels of electoral competition, they must appeal to a broader set of constituents. This incentivizes party officials to offer more broad-based and universal party platforms. Second, when electoral competition derives from parties at opposite ends of the political spectrum, these parties must moderate their platforms and adopt more centrist appeals. This also encourages the support for broad-based policies.

Second, democratization, which for most of Latin America occurred in the 1980s and early 1990s, allowed for citizen demands to be heard and responded to. Coupling this with the mobilization of civil society by the Catholic Church and rural unions arguably created the political space for the extension of benefits to those outside of the formal sector (Garay, 2010; McGuire, 2010; Weyland, 1996). Garay (2010) argues that social policy expansion was triggered by both high electoral competition for outsiders' votes and mobilization from below. Huber, Mustillo, and Stephens (2008) and Stephens and Huber (2013) hypothesize that democracies will spend more on broader, more inclusive social protection programs, and their panel analysis suggests that democracy matters in the long run both for social security, welfare, health, and education spending; whereas, unlike in OECD countries, partisanship does not matter. Yet, despite these claims, Carnes and Mares (2009) argue that regime type does not account for differences in the origins of social policies, and many programs of social protection were instituted under authoritarian rule.

However, democratization alone does not appear to sufficiently explain non-contributory policy adoptions. In 1980, Latin America contained 11 democracies and by 1990, 10 additional countries had democratized. However, when comparing the list of countries which were democracies to the list of countries which have implemented expansionary policies (see Table 10.1), the relationship is unclear. In fact, most of the countries that have implemented some form of non-contributory policy were amongst the group of countries that democratized in the 1980s.[1] These democracies didn't begin to implement these expansionary policies for over a decade. As a result, democratization appears to be a necessary but not sufficient explanation for policy expansion and adoption.

Finally, research on the emergence of conditional cash transfer and means-tested cash assistance policies has focused on changes to political structures as the result of fiscal crises. For example, De La O (2013) argues that the Mexican peso crisis of 1995 left over 16 million people in poverty and unable to access the social protection guaranteed only to insiders within the labor force. This outcome, De La O argues, provided the political capacity for the enactment of *Progresa*. Separately, De La O (2010) argues that the emergence of conditional cash transfer programs generally is related to the institutional power and the electoral strength of the president. (Haggard and Kaufman, 2008, pp. 262) note that "difficult economic times posed major policy dilemmas. Governments were pressed to address the inequities in the distribution of social insurance and services, while at the same time facing demands from stakeholders seeking to defend entitlements." Weyland (1996) contends that reforms towards less stratified social policies came from above, with strong technocratic leaders acting within contexts of economic emergency.

While this line of research focuses on the political determinants of social policy expansion, the focus remains on macro-level institutions. Missing from this story are the underlying factors that shaped the behavior and demands of citizens in newly democratized nations. For this, we need additional research.

Labor Market Segmentation

For a more micro-level understanding of individual behavior and preferences, we turn to a vast literature that draws from the European experience. Moene and Wallerstein (2001) extend the traditional Meltzer and Richard (1981) model, which argues that the level of redistribution is set by the shape and skew of the income distribution, by incorporating the role of labor market segmentation and risk, and differentiating between social insurance and redistribution. They show that employees with higher levels of labor market risk are more supportive of social insurance spending and as risk aversion increases, the optimal tax rate, and therefore the optimal benefit level in their model, also increases. Although developed in the context of Western European welfare states, this model suggests that the position of an employee in the labor market strongly affects his or her preferences and demands for social insurance and redistribution. Rehm (2011) confirms this by demonstrating that preferences for social insurance are driven by income and risk of unemployment. As an individual's risk of unemployment increases, she prefers more redistribution to compensate for this risk. As workers' income increases, however, they prefer less social insurance because they are better able to protect themselves from risk. At the macro-level, Rehm (2011) argues that demand for redistribution is determined by the homogeneity of the risk pool: if most individuals share the same level of unemployment risk (highly homogeneous risk pool) then all will demand more redistribution, and the level of redistribution will be higher.

In addition, Estevez-Abe, Iversen, and Soskice (2001) differentiate among skill types and show that the system of social insurance expenditures is tied to them. Where education systems and mode of capitalism (see Hall and Soskice, 2001) encourage the attainment of firm- or industry-specific skills, such regimes must have high levels of protection and coverage of workers to incentivize this skill investment. Their primary argument is that exposure to risk is inversely related to the portability of skills, and those with very specific skills will be more inclined to support social protection, as they will have high levels of labor market risk, whereas those with general skills will find social insurance more costly (Iversen and Soskice, 2001) Similarly, Rueda (2005) argues that the interests and preferences of labor are divided, and labor cannot be viewed as a solitary unit. Instead, he claims that the labor market is composed of insiders, those with secure employment, and outsiders, those without secure employment. He explains the rise in unemployment in Western Europe by demonstrating that social democratic countries have protected the interests of insiders but not of outsiders, because insiders are more politically active and therefore a more important political base.

Overall, these studies suggest that the risk of unemployment and the structure of the labor force are important mechanisms in determining preferences for redistribution and ultimately the type of social protection system. The theory proposed here builds on this framework by arguing that in the case of Latin American countries, it is not just the risk of unemployment which drives preferences for social protection, but also the risk of informal employment (loss of formal employment). Additionally, in Latin America, labor markets are primarily segmented along the lines of formal versus informal employment rather than on the basis of skill level or pure unemployment risk. Although this reality is completely different from Western European labor markets and welfare states, the key theoretical premise, that labor market segmentation and risk shape preferences over social policy, provides an important basis for study in the context of Latin America.

A Rational Choice Explanation of Non-Contributory Policy Expansion

Latin American labor markets have traditionally consisted of those with formal employment and those without formal employment. Traditionally, formal employment has come with a myriad of benefits, such as social security and health care. Prior to economic liberalization, this division was stable, with little movement of individuals between the formal and informal work forces.

Economic liberalization has been accompanied by a shift in the structure of the economy and has resulted in more flexible labor market boundaries. Specifically, a decline in manufacturing has left many lower-skill formal sector workers without their traditionally secure employment. The low transferability of manufacturing skills and the scarcity of still secure high-skill and public sector jobs has led many former "insiders" (Rueda, 2005) to consider work in the informal sector. Furthermore, the rise of the service sector has led to an overall increase in the size of the informal labor market and has lowered the barriers to entry for low-skill, formal-sector, service positions.

As a result of these structural changes, the entrenched interests of economic insiders saw a marked change in the 1990s. As employees began to face greater risk of unemployment and movement out of the formal labor force, this politically salient population shifted its preferences towards less corporatist social policies and towards more universal and redistributive social policies. Whereas previously these employees faced little risk of unemployment and therefore demanded social insurance that protected only those within the formal sector, this increased movement between formal and informal sectors led these vulnerable workers to demand policies which would protect them and continue to insure them even if they fell outside of the formal sector. This pressure may have contributed to the political support for universal health care policies, as many formal workers feared loss of health coverage if they temporarily fell out of the formal sector. Overall, the greater risk of unemployment or informalization faced by previously protected workers and a breakdown of the barrier between the formal and informal sectors altered the incentives of now more vulnerable insiders to demand policies that would benefit the outsiders. This alignment of interests created the political coalition necessary to demand more inclusive social policy reforms.

Importantly, traditional economic insiders were also political insiders and therefore had greater access to political information and networks. Through previous engagement with the system, traditional insiders knew how to both make demands on politicians and to engage with the institutions of social protection. Politicians were more responsive to insiders as these workers traditionally made up the bases of political support and power prior to democratization. This political knowledge and saliency, I argue, carries over even after changes to the structure of the labor market.

Coupling this with the extension of democracy to many Latin American countries in the 1980s and the extension of political rights and opportunity to those on the periphery (rural and informal workers) provided the additional coalition necessary for the expansion of social policy to those outside of the formal workforce. Some scholars have argued that the extension of democracy and the mobilization of the poor through a strong civil society help to explain the rise of pro-poor social policies in Latin America (Garay, 2010). I argue that this mobilization was *necessary but not sufficient* to create a political coalition with the strength to demand the implementation of these social policies. Support by many of the traditionally formal sector workers provided the remaining and pivotal political support to drive the introduction and expansion of these policies. In particular, structural economic changes that resulted from economic liberalization created an alignment of interests between labor market outsiders and low-skill labor market insiders facing greater labor market vulnerability. Additionally, the increased movement across labor force lines increased contact between previous insiders and outsiders and increased the informational flows to those in the protected sector regarding inequities within society and potential efficiency gains achievable through relatively cheap pro-poor policies (Haggard and Kaufman, 2008).

Ultimately, this perspective suggests that non-contributory social policy implementation may have been the result of a shift in *preferences* of a politically pivotal group, namely at-risk formal sector workers. I argue that this group reacted to structural economic changes in a rational and economically self-interested way by aligning with informal workers and demanding non-contributory social insurance. The increase in the political *power* of traditional labor market outsiders provided the political capacity and breadth behind the implementation of non-contributory social policies. Contrary to some theories of welfare state expansion, this argument suggests that the lynchpin of universalistic policy formation was not a shift in power towards the lower classes and informal workers due to democratization alone but a shift in the preferences of the existing ruling class.

Preferences for Non-Contributory Policies across Latin America

This chapter differentiates itself from past research by focusing on individual demands and preferences. Few studies on the extension of non-contributory policies deal with mass public preferences, and even fewer link the prevailing macro-factors with micro-behaviors. A deeper analysis of individual preferences will shed light on the micro-level mechanisms driving demand for non-contributory social policies and help to parse out how economically self-interested behavior contributes to rising support for more universalistic policies. To do so, I use data provided by the Latinobarometro survey, which surveys individuals from 18 Latin America countries from 1995 to 2010. Given that most non-contributory social policies emerged in the late 1990s and early 2000s (see Table 10.1), this study explores the determinants of preference formation over the past 20 years.

Employment Vulnerability following De-industrialization

Did de-industrialization make workers less secure? Using Latinobarometro data on unemployment concern,[2] Figure 10.1 plots trends in aggregate unemployment concern *for those who were formally employed* over time. Of the entire sample, 31.4% of respondents reported that they were very concerned with future unemployment. As Figure 10.1 portrays, corresponding with the period of trade liberalization, unemployment concern was at its highest during the late 1990s, peaking at more than 50% of formally employed respondents reporting great concern of unemployment in 1996. The line for Bolivia denotes the first adoption of non-contributory pensions in Latin America. Unemployment concern has declined since 2000, dropping to only 20% of respondents reporting concern in 2010. This suggests that the period of de-industrialization which led to structural economic changes placed many people in vulnerable economic positions. Additionally, this vulnerability was experienced most by those with low levels of education and skills. In 1996, 54% of respondents with low education reported that they were very concerned with unemployment, while only 44% of highly educated respondents were similarly concerned. By 2006, however, respondents with both low and high levels of education reported similar rates of extreme concern, around roughly 22%.

Figure 10.1: Percent Concerned with Future Unemployment

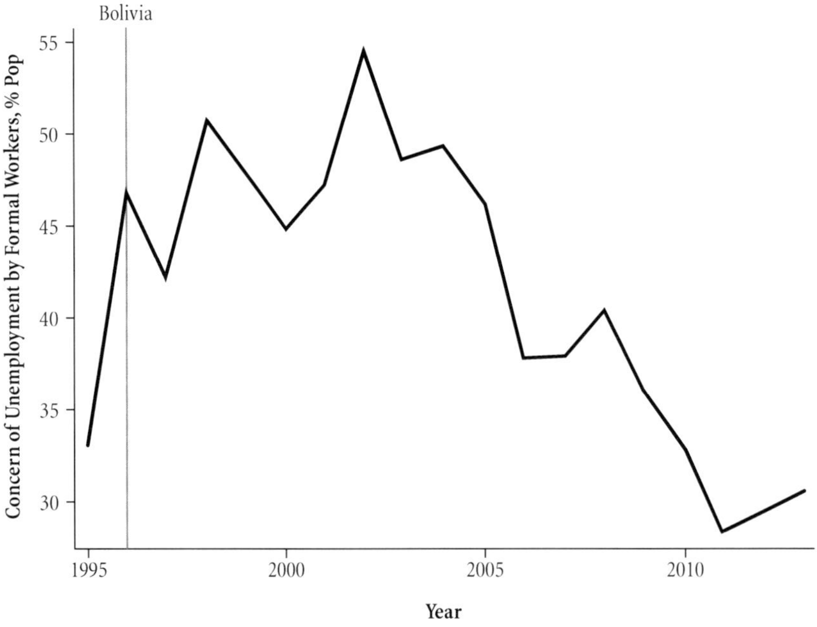

Source: Latinobarometer, 1995–2013
Note: Bolivian adoption is depicted to highlight the first introduction of these programs.

Additionally, Figure 10.2 plots the aggregate proportion of those in the labor force who are informally employed.[3] As with employment vulnerability, starting in the late 1990s there is a sharp rise in the number of workers reporting that they are informally employed. Taken together, this provides support for the claim that the period following de-industrialization was a time of changing labor markets. The growing informal labor force suggests a new exodus out of the formal labor force and greater uncertainty around secure employment, which occurred alongside the shift towards de-industrialization.

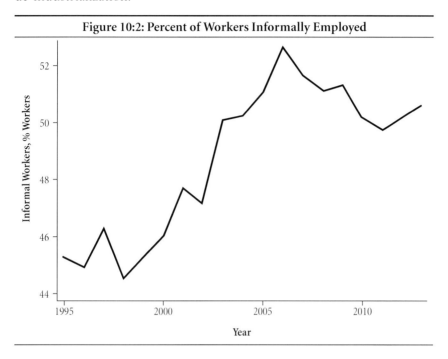

Figure 10:2: Percent of Workers Informally Employed

Demand for Non-Contributory Social Programs

The theoretical propositions above lead to one primary hypothesis: individual preferences regarding universal social policies depend on the workers' status in the labor market. Specifically, the preferences of formally employed workers with job insecurity will be different from the preferences of formally employed workers with job security, *and* the preferences of the first group will be closer to those of informally employed workers. Figure 10.3 and Tables 10.2 and 10.3 descriptively show these differences in preferences. In all of these, the total labor force is divided into five categories: formally employed with secure employment; the same with insecure employment; informally employed with secure employment; the same with insecure employment; and the unemployed—and all are the percentage of those in the *labor force.*

Figure 10.3 plots respondents who state that low salaries, health, unemployment, poverty, or instability in employment are the most important problem facing their nation, disaggregated by labor market status. In comparing total averages across the formally and informally employed, it would appear that there is little difference in beliefs over which problems

Table 10.2: Of Course the Government's Responsibility Should Be to ...

	Formal:		Informal:		
	Secure	Insecure	Secure	Insecure	Unemployed
Give work to all those who want to work	82.85	86.7	83.78	87.87	85.01
Give health care to the sick	83.75	88.63	85.72	89.21	87.03
Provide a decent standard of living for the elderly	58.82	69.61	63.69	72.78	69.84
Provide a decent standard of living for the unemployed	65.34	76.58	68.08	79.85	74.15
Reduce the differences between the rich and the poor	68.12	76.38	67.34	77.05	75.12
N	2,422	2,136	2,414	2,193	1,084

Source: Latinobarometer 1996

Table 10.3: In Your Country, It Would Be Better to Spend More on ...

	Formal:		Informal:		
	Secure	Insecure	Secure	Insecure	Unemployed
Pensions	87.19	88.21	86.32	87.59	90.44
Health	94.26	94.46	94.33	93.3	95.38
Insurance against Unemployment	79.38	83.01	80.11	84.19	86.13
N	2,545	2,613	2,285	2,540	852

Source: Latinobarometer 1998

are the most important. However, when we account for labor market insecurity, a more varied picture emerges. In relation to unemployment, secure informal workers more frequently stated that unemployment was the most important problem than secure formal workers. And insecure formal workers were even more likely than secure informal workers to state that unemployment was the most important problem, signaling this concern at a rate similar to that of insecure informal workers. In fact, preferences of insecure formal and informal workers aligned more closely regarding health, unemployment, and instability in employment.

Figure 10.3: Most Important Problem Cited by Labor Market Status

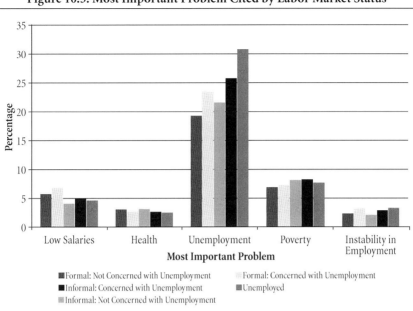

Source: Latinobarometer, 1996–2013

This alignment of preferences among insecure workers is reaffirmed when evaluating preferences over social policy provision. Table 10.2 surveys a different set of preferences: whether it is the government's responsibility to provide work, health care, pensions, unemployment insurance, and redistribution of wealth. Across the board, a majority of the population believes that it is the government's responsibility to provide all of these services. More than 80% of respondents believe that the government should provide work and health care irrespective of labor market status. However, insecure workers are statistically significantly more likely than secure workers to believe that it is the government's responsibility to provide all of these services.[4] Yet simple t-tests comparing the reported preferences of insecure formal workers and those of insecure informal workers are not statistically significant for three of the five policy areas.[5] This further suggests that the preferences of insecure formal workers are more closely aligned with the preferences of insecure informal workers than they are with secure formal workers.

Table 10.3 provides another descriptive test of these claims by comparing preferences over government spending on pensions, health care, and unemployment insurance by labor market status. As before, insecure workers are more likely to report that the government should spend more on all three of these policies—especially unemployment insurance—than secure workers, whether they are in the formal or informal labor force.

In total, these tables suggest that despite the traditionally targeted nature of government spending and social policies, labor market insecurity may matter more for social policy preferences than labor market status.

Adoption of Non-Contributory Policies across Latin America

At the macro-level, the theoretical arguments proposed here suggest that the rise of non-contributory policies in Latin America is the result of a complex relationship between national economic structures, individual employment vulnerability, and partisan politics.

Data

Social Policy. To explore trends in Latin American social policy, Table 10.1 was used to construct dichotomous variables for each type of policy adoption (Carnes and Mares, 2013). For example, for CCT adoption, the data for Argentina would be coded as 1 for all years following 2004 (the year of adoption), including the year of adoption. For pension policy adoption I include two key measures: a two-part measure of any pension reform and a two-part measure of universal, non-contributory pension reform. Although this allows for coverage of all non-contributory policies, this measure does not provide a sense of the scale or size of these programs. Additionally, I include an analysis of pension coverage rates, with data collected from Rofman and Oliveri (2012). The pension coverage rate data provide a measure of the percent of the aged 65+ population receiving benefits from state pension schemes, both contributory and non-contributory. I also include a measure of the non-contributory pension coverage rate, which is the percentage of the economically active population's contribution to state pensions subtracted from the total pension coverage rate. This is the most direct measure of the universalization of pension policy, as it directly reflects the proportion of the population covered by pension policies without contributing directly to the policy itself.

Domestic Politics. According to the above hypothesis, the root of expansionary social policy in Latin America lies in a change in the structure of political coalitions. To examine this hypothesis, an analysis of the support for the left is included, as well as its political representation. Support for the left is measured by the proportion of the population for each country-year, aggregated from the Latinobarometro data used previously. The representation of the left is measured using the legislative seat share of left parties.

Data on the seat share of the left and center-left parties in lower houses are provided by Huber et al. (2008) during periods of democratic rule.

Additionally, the theory proposed suggests that the role of democratization in shaping social policy development was to stimulate political participation and electoral competition, particularly for those who had been previously excluded. I include a dichotomous measure of democracy, where a country is scored as a democracy if it has a Polity score of 6 or greater.

The Labor Market. To test the hypothesized mechanism regarding changes in the structure of the labor force, the subsequent analyses include five measures of the labor market. First, using aggregated Latinobarometro data, I include a measure of the size of the informal labor force as a percentage of all in the labor force. An individual is considered informally employed if they are self-employed or informally salaried. Second, I include a measure of employment insecurity using aggregated Latinobarometro data on the percentage of the population reporting that they were concerned with unemployment. Third, to capture the sectoral shifts following economic liberalization that left many formal sector employees at a greater risk of unemployment and informalization, I include a measure of trade openness, which is from the World Bank Development Indicator. Last, I include measures of the unemployment rate and the average duration of unemployment to more directly capture risk and occurrence of unemployment, separate from risk of informalization and benefit loss. Data on the unemployment rate are provided by the World Development Indicator, and data on the average duration of unemployment were calculated from domestic surveys and come from the Socio-Economic Database for Latin America and the Caribbean.

Control Variables. Given small sample sizes, the controls are limited. All of the variables were collected either through the World Development Indicator database or from Huber et al. (2008). The results do not change with the inclusion of these control variables; however, the sample size does reduce the results because of missing data. Additionally, the models of policy adoption include measures of policy diffusion, which represent the number of countries that have implemented a given policy at a certain point in time.

Economic Liberalization and Employment Vulnerability

Figures 10.4 and 10.5 depict the overall economic changes that took place in Latin America throughout the 1990s as well as the resulting trends in the labor market. The 1990s was a period of trade liberalization and economic opening, with the end of import substitution industrialization (ISI). The increase in imports that occurred during this period held significant consequences for the overall structure of the economy. Figure 10.4 demonstrates that during the period of economic liberalization, agricultural employment plummeted and industrial employment declined while the share of employment in the service industry rose to roughly 65%. In economies that had traditionally been clearly divided between the formally and informally employed, this structural change began to disrupt this barrier, creating greater employment insecurity.

A noticeable increase in unemployment occurred in the late 1990s and early 2000s (see Figure 10.5). Importantly, the rise of unemployment in the late 1990s, following the changes in the structure of the economy, was felt mostly by those with low and middling levels of education. From roughly 1995 until 2000, those with no more than a high school degree faced unemployment rates over 2% higher than those with higher levels of education. The effect of economic liberalization on the labor market was not only to increase the risk of unemployment, but as importantly to increase the risk of informal employment. In a policy environment where only those formally employed had any claim to social benefits, these structural changes to the economy carried important consequences for the welfare of workers, and particularly low-skill workers.

Non-Contributory Social Policy Adoption. Table 10.4 evaluates the link between labor market status, employment insecurity, trade liberalization, and social policy adoption and coverage. It includes both labor market and political variables as predictors of policy adoption. The three models of policy adoption are estimated using a linear probability model, and the coverage models utilize linear regression. All models include country-fixed effects, i.e., what precipitated changes within a country.

There is a positive correlation between labor market insecurity and *pension* reform. As evidenced in Table 10.4, high levels of employment insecurity are associated with a higher probability of adoption of pension reform in general, as well as a specifically universalistic, non-contributory pension reform.[6] Accounting for economic insecurity, trade openness is not a significant predictor of pension reform. Modeling a more direct measure of the expansion in coverage of social benefits, the second and third columns of Table 10.4 evaluate the link between the labor force and (1) the proportion of people over age 65 who are beneficiaries of pensions; and (2) the difference between this total coverage rate and the percentage of people

Figure 10.4: Sectoral Employment Shares

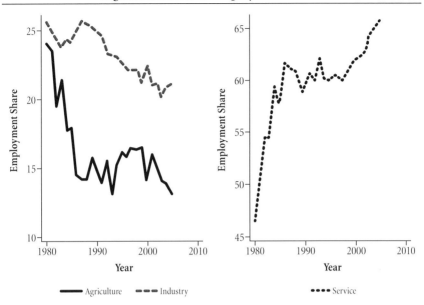

Figure 10.5: Unemployment Rate, by Education

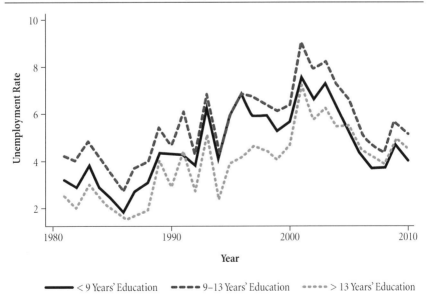

Table 10.4: Modeling Non-Contributory Policy Adoption and Pension Coverage

	Pension Reform	Universal Pension Reform	Pension Coverage Rate	Pension Coverage Non-Contributors	Universal Health Care Adoption	CCT Program Adoption
% Informal	0.232	−0.044	25.597	33.732**	−0.942**	0.494
	(0.303)	(0.165)	(16.149)	(16.737)	(0.374)	(0.552)
Employment Insecurity	0.307*	0.342***	−6.994	−4.844	−0.028	0.148
	(0.162)	(0.088)	(7.789)	(7.785)	(0.212)	(0.316)
Trade Openness	0.002	0.001	0.126	0.110	0.0001	0.004
	(0.002)	(0.001)	(0.086)	(0.091)	(0.002)	(0.003)
Unemployment	0.001	0.001	0.232	0.789**	−0.018*	−0.017
	(0.008)	(0.004)	(0.406)	(0.385)	(0.010)	(0.015)
Duration of Unemployment	−0.018*	0.006	1.274**	2.223***	0.029**	0.031
	(0.011)	(0.006)	(0.570)	(0.536)	(0.014)	(0.020)
Support for Left	−0.026	0.033	−6.213	−1.016	0.195	−1.193***
	(0.238)	(0.129)	(12.071)	(13.194)	(0.295)	(0.429)
Democracy Indicator	−0.083	−0.014	−6.111	−11.118	−0.055	0.209
	(0.118)	(0.064)	(5.842)	(7.373)	(0.149)	(0.218)
Universal Pension Reform			−0.108	−3.503		
			(8.198)	(7.250)		
Pension Diffusion	0.037***	0.022***				
	(0.011)	(0.006)				
Universal Health Diffusion					0.092***	
					(0.023)	
CCT Diffusion						0.054***
						(0.006)
N	135	135	125	106	135	135
R-squared	0.904	0.968	0.937	0.919	0.825	0.664

***p < .01; **p < .05; *p < .1

Note: Standard errors in parentheses. All models include a constant term and country-specific fixed effects and are modeled using linear regression (linear probability models for policy adoption).

who are contributing to pensions, measuring the percentage of the population that receives pensions without contributing. While labor market dynamics do not correlate with the total coverage rate of pensions, there is a positive correlation between informal employment and the coverage of non-contributors. When taken in coordination with models of universal pension reform, this suggests that policies may be enacted because of employment insecurity amongst workers and then bear direct benefits for informal workers.

Unemployment does not appear to bear significantly on pension reform; however, the average duration of unemployment is an important predictor of both pension and health care reform, although in opposite directions. An increase in the average duration of unemployment is associated with higher probabilities of adoption of pension reform. Surprisingly, higher levels of informal employment are actually associated with a lower probability of universal health care adoption. Ultimately, the dynamics underlying health care reform stand in contrast to those for pension reform, suggesting more work is needed to disentangle these policy determinants.

CCT program adoption is not correlated with labor market dynamics, suggesting that economic insecurity and labor market fluctuations affect social insurance but not redistribution.

Conclusion

The major economic and political changes that occurred in Latin America in the 1980s and 1990s unsurprisingly bore substantial consequences for the welfare of citizens. The end of protectionist policy reshaped the structure of industry within many countries, resulting in an overall de-industrialization and decline in the manufacturing and agriculture sectors. Despite the unique form of capitalism that had evolved in Latin America, particularly the highly segmented labor markets that had developed, this economic transition eroded existing boundaries and reshaped the interests of the previous economic "insiders."

Unlike what would be traditionally expected, this de-industrialization did not lead to a race to the bottom when it came to social policy, but actually stimulated an expansion of social benefits to those outside of the formal labor force. This chapter documents this expanded coverage of benefits and provides an explanation rooted in individual behavior and economic interests.

What happened is that the end of protectionist economic policy led to a restructuring of industry and employment that broke down the barrier between the formal and the informal labor markets. As a result of increased employment vulnerability and uncertainty, the entrenched interests of the low-skilled "insiders" aligned with the economic interests of "outsiders," creating a new political coalition with a shared interest in universalizing social protections. Increased political participation of outsiders as a result of democratization and the realignment of low-skill insiders provided the base of support necessary for fundamental social policy change.

For Cuba, at present in a time of economic transition, there is a clear lesson from the analysis in this chapter. Cuba's state employment has been declining systematically; many more Cubans now are self-employed or work in new small private businesses. Alongside this movement, employment vulnerability and uncertainty have increased, and low-skilled public sector workers may now be even more insistent that the state should afford them a greater social protection than the extent to which they have previously been entitled. The results from this chapter suggest that structural economic changes, like those we are seeing in Cuba, can have major consequences for policy demand and potentially also for policy implementation. For Cuba, this might signal a change in the priority of social programs: targeted benefits to the public sector rather than to the poor. Is that the future for social policy in Cuba, to protect the formerly secure but not the currently poor?

Notes

1. This includes Argentina, Belize, Bolivia, Brazil, Chile, El Salvador, Haiti, Honduras, Nicaragua, Panama, and Uruguay.

2. I use a question asked in every year of the Latinobarometro survey regarding concern about unemployment. Specifically, the question asks "How concerned would you say you are that you will be left without work or unemployed during the next 12 months? Very concerned, concerned, a little concerned, or not at all concerned?" To simplify this measure, I create a dichotomous variable which takes a value of 1 if the respondent reported that they are very concerned about future unemployment.

3. Informal employment is denoted as 1 if the respondent reported his or her occupation as being self-employed or informally salaried. This follows the common definition described in Bosch and Maloney (2008).

4. A simple t-test comparing the preferences of secure formal workers and insecure formal workers results in a statistically significant difference at the .05 level for each of the five preference variables. The same is true in a simple t-test comparing secure informal workers and insecure informal workers.

5. A simple t-test comparing the preferences of insecure formal workers and insecure informal workers results in a statistically significant difference at the .05 level for provision for the elderly and unemployed but not for provision of work, health care, or redistribution.

6. According to Rofman, Apella, and Vezza (2015), Argentina, Bolivia, Brazil, Chile, Mexico, Panama, and Uruguay have all implemented pension reforms that strive towards universality rather than targeted means-tested benefits.

Bibliography

Arretche, Marta. 2004. "Toward a Unified and More Equitable System: Health Reform in Brazil." in *Crucial Needs, Weak Incentives: The Politics of Health and Education Reform in Latin America.* Washington DC: Woodrow Wilson Center Press/Johns Hopkins University Press.

Barrientos, Armando, Miguel Nio-Zarazúa and Mathilde Maitrot. 2010. "Social Assistance in Developing Countries Database." *Brooks World Poverty Institute.*

Bosch, Mariano and William Maloney. 2008. "Cyclical Movements in Unemployment and Informality in Developing Countries." World Bank.

Cameron, David R. 1978. "The Expansion of the Public Economy: A Comparative Analysis." *The American Political Science Review* 72(4): 1243–1261.

Carnes, Matthew E. and Isabela Mares. 2007. "The Welfare State in Global Perspective." *Unpublished manuscript.*

———. 2009. "Social Policy in Developing Countries." *Annual Review of Political Science* 12: 93–112.

———. 2013. "Coalitional Realignment and the Adoption of Non-contributory Social Insurance Programmes in Latin America." *Socio-Economic Review* 12(4): 695–722.

De La O, Ana. 2010. "The Politics of Conditional Cash Transfers." *Unpublished manuscript.*

———. 2013. "Do Conditional Cash Transfers Affect Electoral Behavior? Evidence from a Randomized Experiment in Mexico." *American Journal of Political Science* 57(1): 1–14.

Estevez-Abe, Margarita, Torben Iversen and David Soskice. 2001. "Social Protection and the Formation of Skills: A Reinterpretation of the Welfare State." in *Varieties of Capitalism: The Institutional Foundations of Comparative Advantage.* Oxford: Oxford University Press.

Garay, Candelaria. 2010. *Including Outsiders: Social Policy Expansion in Latin America.* Dissertation manuscript.

Haggard, Stephan and Robert R. Kaufman. 2008. *Development, Democracy, and Welfare States: Latin America, East Asia, and Eastern Europe.* Princeton, NJ: Princeton University Press.

Hall, Peter A. and David W. Soskice. 2001. *Varieties of Capitalism: The Institutional Foundations of Comparative Advantage.* Oxford: Oxford University Press.

Huber, Evelyn, Thomas Mustillo and John D. Stephens. 2008. "Politics and Social Spending in Latin America." *The Journal of Politics* 70(2): 420–436.

Huber, Evelyn, John D. Stephens, Thomas Mustillo and Jennifer Pribble. 2008. *Social Policy in Latin American and the Caribbean Dataset. 1960–2006.* University of North Carolina.

Iversen, Torben. 2001. "The Dynamics of Welfare State Expansion: Trade Openness, De-Industrialization and Partisan Politics." in *The New Politics of the Welfare State.* Oxford: Oxford University Press.

Iversen, Torben and David Soskice. 2001. "An Asset Theory of Social Policy Preferences." *American Political Science Review* 95(4): 875–894.

Katzenstein, Peter J. 1985. *Small States in World Markets: Industrial Policy in Europe.* Ithaca, NY: Cornell University Press.

Kaufman, Robert R. and Alex Segura-Ubiergo. 2001. "Globalization, Domestic Politics, and Social Spending in Latin America." *World Politics* 53(4): 553–87.

McGuire, James W. 2010. *Wealth, Health, and Democracy in East Asia and Latin America.* Cambridge: Cambridge University Press.

Melo, Marcus André. 2008. "Unexpected Success, Unanticipated Failures: Social Policy from Cardoso to Lula." in *Democratic Brazil Revisited*. Pittsburgh, PA: University of Pittsburgh Press.

Meltzer, Allan H. and Scott F. Richard. 1981. "A Rational Theory of the Size of Government." *The Journal of Political Economy* 89(5); 914–927.

Moene, Karl Ove and Michael Wallerstein. 2001. "Inequality, Social Insurance, and Redistribution." *American Political Science Review* 95(4): 859–874.

Portes, Alejandro and Kelly Hoffman. 2013. "Latin American Class Structures: Their Composition and Change during the Neoliberal Era." *Latin American Research Review* 38(1): 41–82.

Pribble, Jennifer. 2013. *Welfare and Party Politics in Latin America*. Cambridge: Cambridge University Press.

Rehm, Philipp. 2011. "Social Policy by Popular Demand." *World Politics* 63(2): 271–299.

Rofman, Rafael, Ignacio Apella and Evelyn Vezza. 2015. *Beyond Contributory Pensions: Fourteen Experiences with Coverage Expansion in Latin America.* World Bank Group.

Rofman, Rafael and Maria Laura Oliveri. 2012. "Pension Coverage in Latin America." *The World Bank.*

Rueda, David. 2005. "Insider-outsider Politics in Industrialized Democracies: The Challenge to Social Democratic Parties." *American Political Science Review* 99(1): 61–74.

Schneider, Ben Ross. 2013. *Hierarchical Capitalism in Latin America.* Cambridge: Cambridge University Press.

Schneider, Ben Ross and Sebastian Karcher. 2010. "Complementarities and Continuities in the Political Economy of Labour Markets in Latin America." *Socio-Economic Review* 8(4): 623–651.

Schwarzer, Helmut and Ana Carolina Querino. 2002. "Non-contributory Pensions in Brazil: The Impact on Poverty *Reduction*." *International Labour Organization* (ESS Paper No. 11).

Stephens, John and Evelyn Huber. 2013. *Democracy and the Left: Social Policy and Inequality in Latin America.* Chicago, IL: University of Chicago Press.

Weyland, Kurt. 1996. *Democracy without Equity: Failures of Reform in Brazil.* Pittsburgh, PA: University of Pittsburgh Press.

Wibbels, Erik and John Alquist. 2011. "Development, Trade, and Social Insurance." *International Studies Quarterly* 55(1): 125–149.